OXFORD STUDIES IN
SOCIAL AND CULTURAL ANTHROPOLOGY

THE ARABESK DEBATE

OXFORD STUDIES IN SOCIAL AND CULTURAL ANTHROPOLOGY

Oxford Studies in Social and Cultural Anthropology represents the work of authors, new and established, which will set the criteria of excellence in ethnographic description and innovation in analysis. The series serves as an essential source of information about the world and the discipline.

OTHER TITLES IN THIS SERIES

Organizing Jainism in India and England
Marcus Banks

Society and Exchange in Nias
Andrew Beatty

The Female Bridegroom: A Comparative Study of Life-Crisis Rituals in South India and Sri Lanka
Anthony Good

Of Mixed Blood: Kinship and History in Peruvian Amazonia
Peter Gow

Exchange in Oceania: A Graph Theoretic Analysis
Per Hage and Frank Harary

THE ARABESK DEBATE

Music and Musicians in Modern Turkey

MARTIN STOKES

CLARENDON PRESS · OXFORD
1992

Oxford University Press, Walton Street, Oxford OX2 6DP
Oxford New York Toronto
Delhi Bombay Calcutta Madras Karachi
Petaling Jaya Singapore Hong Kong Tokyo
Nairobi Dar es Salaam Cape Town
Melbourne Auckland
and associated companies in
Berlin Ibadan

Oxford is a trade mark of Oxford University Press

Published in the United States
by Oxford University Press, New York

British Library Cataloguing in Publication Data
Data available

Library of Congress Cataloging in Publication Data
Stokes, Martin.
The Arabesk debate : music and musicians in modern Turkey
Martin Stokes.
(Oxford studies in social and cultural anthropology)
Includes bibliographical references and index
1. Music—Turkey—History and criticism. I. Title. II. Series.
ML345.T8S8 1992 780′.94961′8—dc20 91-39946
ISBN 0-19-827367-3

Typeset by BP Integraphics Ltd, Bath, Avon
Printed in Great Britain by Bookcraft Ltd, Midsomer Norton, Avon

ACKNOWLEDGEMENTS

The research for this book was funded principally by an Economic and Social Science Research Council grant between 1985 and 1988. Additional financial assistance was provided by the Peter Lienhardt Memorial Fund.

Without the help and guidance of a number of people, the research upon which this book is based would not have happened. Harry Johnstone nurtured my interest in ethnomusicology in the context of the undergraduate music degree course at Oxford. Geoffrey Lewis introduced me to the Turkish language. I began to attend his Turkish classes as a fugitive from the rigours of renaissance and baroque counterpoint. The hours spent learning Turkish certainly appeared to have a beneficial effect upon my formal music studies, no doubt as a result of his calm insistence on clarity and logic, but they also provided me with an excellent preparation for field-work in Turkey. More than anyone else, this book owes its present form to my supervisor Michael Gilsenan. His particular blend of criticism, encouragement, and good company have ensured for me that writing continues to be a pleasure and an exploration.

I should also like to record an intellectual debt to my two previous supervisors, the late Edwin Ardener, who was the first to see, and impress upon me, the possibility of change from musicology to social anthropology, and Peter Lienhardt. The two examiners of my thesis were Nick Allen and Paul Stirling. Their comments in the course of my viva have shaped the research that I have done in Turkey since then, and I am grateful to them for their advice and help on this and subsequent occasions.

Colleagues and students at the Department of Social Anthropology at The Queen's University of Belfast have challenged, bluntly refuted, and sometimes supported my ideas in seminars and classes which have been argumentative and intensely sociable. I could not have hoped for more stimulating conditions in which to write this book. I am particularly indebted to Hastings Donnan, Peter Parkes, and Suzel Ana Reily for their comments on drafts of this text.

I gratefully acknowledge the assistance, advice, criticism and patience of the following people: Irene Markoff, Andrew Finkel,

Rosemary Josephs, Gerd Baumann, Martin van Bruinessen, Lale Yalçın-Heckmann, John Baily, Colin Irwin, Neil May, Ian King, and Chris Wortley. Emine Gürsoy-Naşkali and Saliha Paker have provided invaluable help in the perplexing task of rendering arabesk lyrics intelligible to the English-speaking reader. I also thank my wife, Lucy Baxandall, for her comments on the text and assistance with the German texts mentioned in the bibliography. Any mistakes which remain are of course my own.

In Turkey I thank İbrahim Tosun, Levent Taşkın, Osman and Mehmet Can, Tunçay and Cumhur Gülersoy, Tahir Bakal, Volkan Konak, Ersin Baykal, Yavuz Top, Sümer Ezgü, Soner Özbilen, Süleyman Şenel, Cihangir Terzi, Tunçer İnan, Esat Kabaklı, Saim Koşar, Coşkun Gülâ, Necat Birdoğan, Abdüsselam Kayacı, Necmi Çınar, Ali Çömezoğlu, Mehmet Bayraktar, Ünal Özel, Ahmet Özdemir, Timur Zeren, Metin Eke, Reyhan Dinlettir, Mehmet Koç, Temel Çavdar, Ali Osman Erbaşı, Fethi Demir, Mustafa Keser, İbrahim Dulkadıroğlu, Murat Belge, their families and friends, and particularly İbrahim Can, whose generous hospitality and indefatigable good humour remain a constant inspiration. Over the last ten years, these people have taught me all I know about Turkish music, and a great deal more besides.

CONTENTS

TECHNICAL NOTES

Spelling and the choice of synonyms in Turkish are contentious issues, and an integral part of the themes explored in this book. The range of words and spellings available for 'music' is a case in point. The choice of the 'pure Turkish' *küğ*, the Arabic *musiki* (or, to represent its Arabic orthography more accurately, *mûsikî*), or the French *müzik* says much about the writer's or speaker's idea of what music is, or should be. Orthography in this book favours the simplest recognizable version (i.e. *sema* rather than *semâ'*), and where synonymns are contested, I indicate what the issues are, and choose the most widely used term for the sake of consistency (*müzik* rather than *musiki* or *küğ*). The Turkish orthography of Arabic musical terms is used (e.g. *makam*, *şedd*), but Arabic and Turkish words which have common European equivalents (e.g. 'Koran', 'Hadith') follow the spellings which are familiar in English.

For those not familiar with Turkish orthography, the following will serve as a rough guide to the pronunciation of Turkish words:

a as in English 'apple'
c 'j' in English 'jam'
ç 'ch' in English 'church'
ğ unpronounced, lengthening the previous vowel.
i 'ee' in English 'speech'
ı back 'i', close to the second 'i' in English 'original', or the 'er' in 'singer'
j French 'j'
o 'o' in English 'operate'
ö German 'ö'
s 's' in English 'sin'
ş 'sh' in English 'shark'
u 'oo' in English 'school'
ü German 'ü'

The Turkish *izafet* construction, linking nouns, adds an i/ı to a word. If this word ends in a vowel an 's' is interposed, and if a word ends in a 'k', as in *ayak*, the final 'k' is changed to a 'ğ', e.g. Kerem *ayağı*.

Musical notations should be regarded as being supplementary to the text, and can be ignored without impairing the general direction of the textual argument. Staff notation is not an infallible or objective method of representing musical performance in its totality. Notations in this text draw attention in a highly selective way to specific aspects of the music. I have tried to indicate what these are in as clear a manner as possible, so that readers with no knowledge of musical notation will be able to follow the general argument in detail. Ideally, the reader will refer the transcriptions to recordings of the music. A cassette including this material is available from the author. At the time of writing, all of the music discussed in this book can be purchased easily from Turkish shops in Hackney and Stoke Newington in London. Whilst the cassettes do not have a long shelf-life, at the time of writing the Turkish recording industry has just begun to produce its first arabesk compact discs, which will greatly facilitate the documentation of this music.

In notating art and folk music, the notational conventions of Turkish musicians are observed. The microtonal intervals of art music are notated according to the more widely used Ezgi-Arel, rather than the Töre system. The accidentals, with their comma values, are represented in the table.

	sharp (*diyez*)	flat (*bemol*)
1	𝄲	𝄳
4	♯	𝄬
5	𝄰	♭
8	𝄱	𝄭
9	×	𝄫

In the notation of folk music, I observe the most widely established convention according to which the number of commas by which a note is sharpened or flattened is written above the accidental. A note flattened by two commas would therefore be indicated by the sign $\flat^2$.

FIGURES

MAP

1
Introduction

Arabesk is a music of the city and for the city. It portrays a world of complex and turbulent emotions peopled by lovers doomed to solitude and a violent end. It describes a decaying city in which poverty-stricken migrant workers are exploited and abused, and calls on its listeners to pour another glass of *rakı*, light another cigarette, and curse fate and the world. In any predominantly Muslim society this music would be highly contentious. In the context of a secularizing state such as Turkey in which policy towards culture is explicitly formulated and implemented, the existence of this music has provoked bitter debate at every level. Its existence flaunts the failure of a process of reform whose icons and symbols dominate every aspect of Turkish public life. For Turks, the arabesk debate embraces perceptions of themselves as individual human beings, their urban environment, their state and government. As well as a musical form, arabesk is an entire anti-culture, a way of life whose influence, it is often said, can be detected as an aura of chaos and confusion surrounding every aspect of urban existence, from traffic to language, from politics to kitsch.

Music is an omnipresent, almost atmospheric, property of public space in the city, in cafés, night-clubs, baths, brothels, shops, buses, taxis, and *dolmuş* (shared taxis), providing a continual counterpoint to the rhythms of everyday life. This study of arabesk is a study of issues relating to the experience of urban existence in Turkey. It examines representations of urban existence, and looks at the way in which these representations are used and manipulated by musicians and non-musicians alike. At the same time, it is implicitly an investigation of our own understanding of Middle Eastern societies and their music. Turkish and Western representations of Turkish music have a closely interlinked history, although the perception that 'Turkish music' is focused essentially upon loss, separation, and ecstatic abandonment is maintained from a variety of ideological and political perspectives in Turkey and elsewhere. Critics of 'the

Eastern' in Turkish culture have been obliged to draw upon the language of Western orientalism to support the programmes of reform that they have advocated. Western scholars of Turkish music have similarly been obliged to define their research projects in terms of officially sanctioned distinctions between rural and urban culture, distinctions which have been vital in maintaining the momentum of state reform projects, and the positions of power that these projects legitimize.

My own position, as an enthusiast and only later as a social anthropologist studying Turkish music, has been far from aloof. For a young traveller with an undergraduate's arrogant distaste for the music of the Anglican church and the rigours of Renaissance counterpoint, this gravely precise music with its naked emotional intensity provided a glimpse of distant horizons. This enthusiasm emerged from a search for what I believed to be the missing heart and soul of my formative musical training, a quest for the authentic experience which motivates a turn towards 'other cultures' in many academic disciplines. This misplaced romanticism has its problems. Not only does it lead people to abrogate responsibility in their own society for the belief and commitment that alone invests any experience with meaning, but it immediately involves the researcher as an often unwitting pawn in the cultural politics of the society that they are studying. The fact that I had initially come to discover 'the real' music of Turkey was used on a more or less daily basis in highly public arenas to advance a claim, to provide weight for an argument about what 'real' Turkish music was, and who should have the responsibility for its preservation. My general state of nervousness and shaky control of the Turkish language meant that in radio and television interviews I stuck to what I knew I could say clearly, and knew would exclude any awkward cross examination in official media circles. Official discourses were thus boosted around their tight circuit by the highly publicized opinion of a foreign 'expert'.

Any field-worker is prone to absorb and replicate the dominant ideologies of the society they study in this way. One is obliged to seek the advice and guidance of people who have most successfully absorbed these discourses: media experts, highly published academics, and so on. Legitimate academic language is controlled by these people to such an extent that it is difficult to think in any other way, or at least, difficult to maintain a sensitivity to the 'muted voices' of a society, whose viewpoint often has most to express to the social anthropologist.[1] It was only on my return from a year's field-work in 1988 that I realized that every bit of data that I had gathered related directly or indirectly to arabesk, a subject that I had refused to put right at the centre of my research project simply because it was a subject for which ethnomusicology and social anthropology provided no obvious models.[2] At every level, official language about music implied and invoked that image of disorder with which it was apparently obsessed, arabesk.

This book looks at language about music and the ways in which it is used. Whilst this approach is not new,[3] its implications in any ethnographic study of urban music-making needs to be elucidated. Firstly it implies that any study of a popular musical genre has to situate the analysis of the material in a total cultural field. As Middleton and others have stressed, it is not possible to deal with any musical form or genre in a society in which everybody has either active or passive access to the channels of the mass media, as if it existed in a hermetically sealed cultural environment.[4] Nothing is heard in isolation. Individual listening habits all over Turkey invariably embrace a variety of musical genres. A corollary of this is that no popular, mass-produced music can be considered simply as the sole cultural property of any social group or class. As Adorno has emphasized, every genre bears the mark of the contradictions and tensions which exist in the society as a whole: 'Instead of searching for the musical expression of class relationships one will do better so to conceive the relation of music to classes that any music will present the picture of an antagonistic society as a whole.[5]

The necessity of seeing popular genres in terms of an entire social, historical, and cultural field was also suggested by the career paths of

[1] Ardener 1972.

[2] In spite of Kunst's seminal definition of ethnomusicology as the study of 'the music of all cultural strata of mankind' (Kunst 1959, 1), ethnomusicologists have been reluctant to consider urban popular musics, particularly in the Middle East. Nettl's definition of Oriental, Folk and Primitive music as the only legitimate objects of ethnomusicological enquiry (1956, 1–2) left significant gaps which have been hard to fill. Kiel's pioneering foray into the ethnography of urban blues (Kiel 1966) had few successors outside Europe and North America. Waterman's study of Juju (1990) and Pena's study of the Mexican Conjunto (1985) are recent developments of an ethnographic approach to popular urban music-making outside Europe.

[3] Charles Seeger's writing stresses from an early date the importance of studying music as a concept existing in the universe of 'speech communication' (Seeger 1961, 77), as well as being a means of logical communication in its own right. See also Blacking 1982.

[4] See Middleton 1990 and Frith 1983.

[5] Adorno 1976, 69.

urban Turkish musicians. Even those employed by the official media perform different kinds of music as professional musicians in the *piyasa*, the commercial market. Those who play, sing, or compose arabesk may be motivated by a desire to maximize the career strategies available to them, or may reflect a belief that the divisions maintained by official policy, and the exclusion of arabesk from the radio and television airwaves, peripheralize the kinds of music that they want to play, and 'the people' want to hear. Their unofficial musical training with individual teachers or in urban music clubs often provides them with a broad musical education, embracing Turkish classical (sanat) music and Turkish folk (halk) music. The most popular stars, who no longer need the security of jobs in the official media, move from one genre to another with great rapidity and freedom. Recording companies do not specialize to a high degree, but produce a range of material. The studio producers, technicians, and session musicians that they employ find themselves involved in the production of a wide range of musical genres. As far as the commercial market is concerned, the conditions of studio production do not differ markedly from one genre to another, and the end products, as far as the listener is concerned, resemble one another greatly. For two reasons it clearly makes little sense to look at a particular musical genre in isolation: the first is that this would imply an acceptance of divisions which have an ideological function, and that these divisions have to be seen in terms of the institutions and individuals who maintain them; secondly, it makes little sense in terms of the professional activities of musicians in the city.

1.1. Centres and Peripheries

Urban music-making involves individuals, groups, networks, clubs, and institutions of learning, to which the basic anthropological techniques of participation and observation can be applied.[6] This kind of local-level analysis provides a very different perspective to the claims of mass-culture theorists for whom popular music and culture is instrumental in the socialization of passive workers and consumers in advanced capitalist societies.[7] In Turkey, arabesk is also used by

[6] Finnegan's study of music in Milton Keynes (1989) is perhaps the most systematic application of ethnographic techniques to urban music-making.

[7] See Adorno 1941.

Turkish sociologists and journalists to argue political and ideological points with very little reference to the general social field of urban music-making and the activities of musicians in the city. In particular, arabesk is often seen in terms of reaction to a powerful central reformist tradition by a disenchanted periphery, who have been excluded from cultural and economic participation in the state project. This dualism, which owes much to a reading of the Weberian concept of patrimonialism by a number of influential Turkish sociologists,[8] has been maintained from a variety of political perspectives. For the Ataturkian centre-left, arabesk is the result of a reaction to values of state reform which alone have the power to transform Turkey into a modern and European society. The present government, the Motherland Party of Turgut Özal, which took over from the military in the elections of 1983, advocates *laissez-faire* economics and the relaxation of state control over religious and cultural expression. For its critics, arabesk and Islamic 'reaction' (*irtica*), both actively encouraged at the highest levels, provide evidence for the 'hegemony of the periphery' and the collapse of the reform tradition. Academic research in Turkey, as anywhere, is politically implicated. Sociologists in Turkey such as Güngör and Eğribel have argued that arabesk is the inevitable and undesirable result of reaction to ideologically sound, but misapplied and heavy-handed processes of reform.[9] These processes, as Berkes, Mardin, and others have pointed out, dispossessed people of the Ottoman cultural heritage but provided nothing coherent in its place.[10] For the right, arabesk is an aspect of the democratic freedoms in which the economic and cultural participation of the periphery must be developed if the country is to gain eventual acceptance by the European family of nations.

Anthropologists have criticized this dualism in a variety of ways. The Tappers have looked at the ways in which Ataturkian secularism and Sunni religious practice interpenetrate and support one another for the small town bourgeoisie of Eğridir in western Turkey.[11] Ataturkian secularism has become sacralized through its public images, iconography, and historiology, whilst religious practice has been secularized and rationalized. Fasting in Ramadan is

[8] See Mardin 1980 and Heper 1985.

[9] See Güngör 1990 and Eğribel 1984. At the time of writing these are the only book-length studies devoted entirely to arabesk.

[10] Berkes 1964, Mardin 1989.

[11] Tapper and Tapper 1987.

advocated not just in conformity to religious practice but for its known scientific benefits to health. In conditions of comfortable prosperity, the ideologies associated with centre and periphery support and maintain one another. Hann's study of tea cultivation in the Eastern Black Sea region has provided another critique.[12] He focuses on the social and economic organization of 'the periphery' between 1950 and the present day, pointing out the long existence of mediating power structures which have made the Hegelian distinction between transcendent state and civil society impossible to uphold. Anthropological studies from Stirling's classic account of Sakaltutan and Elbaşı onwards have stressed this local-level identification with the state project.[13] This leads Hann to describe the process as 'the domestication of the state', and not as a situation in which state and civil society are operating in constant mutual antagonism.[14]

The extent to which Hann's 'intensifying fusion'[15] of Atatürkian values and local-level domestic and religious experience is always the case remains open to question. In Istanbul in the 1980s, the decade of arabesk, the language of democratic popular opposition to imposed reform maintained its ability to mobilize demonstrations and violence against the Hat Law and other key symbols of Atatürkian secularism. But, at the same time, the music associated with these same traditions of reform, the Anatolian halk music propagated by the Turkish Radio and Television (TRT) and State Conservatories has been appropriated at a mass level in Turkish cities. Whilst this music bears many of the characteristics of a 'reinvented tradition,'[16] musicians such as Belkis Akkale, whose style was developed in the context of TRT ensembles and performance practice, rank amongst the most popular musicians in Turkey today. Private clubs and teaching centres known as *dernek* and *dershane* run by prominent *bağlama* players once associated with the TRT, such as Yavuz Top and Arif Sağ, enjoy substantial support from a class which might be identified as the most peripheral social group in Istanbul: first- and second-generation migrants from the south-east of Turkey inhabiting the *gecekondu* squatter town on the edges of the city. The second chapter of this book looks at the role of the *dershane* in the context of the process of reform, and argues that reformed music

12 Hann 1990. 13 Stirling 1965. 14 Hann 1990, 60.
15 Ibid. 67.
16 See Hobsbawm and Ranger 1982.

must be seen not just as an élite activity which has little to do with the 'real' musical tastes of the people, but as a genre which enjoys widespread support and participation at a local level of music-making. The rural *bağlama*, an instrument which has become a key symbol in an official construction of Turkish identity, and is consequently the focus of continuing attempts to reform and systematize Turkish music, is now a widely popular and cheap instrument mass produced in Istanbul.

Conversely, the activities of musicians at 'the centre', associated with the sanat- and halk-music sections of the Istanbul TRT radio centre at Harbiye, involve them closely with 'the periphery'. Musicians release cassettes of, or including, arabesk music on the commercial market, and include popular numbers in their live performances in the *piyasa*. Their commercial cassettes use electric instruments, strong percussion, and sometimes string orchestras, so that songs which might belong to the sanat- or halk-music repertoire conform closely to the musical aesthetic of arabesk. Since these cassettes function as an advertisement for their skills as live performers, musicians can move in and out of arabesk and maintain their posts at the TRT and a marketable identity as halk- or sanat-music singers. Whilst the concept of centre and periphery, of a transcendent state tradition and an authentic cultural level associated with civil society, is maintained at certain levels of discourse, its use as a tool in the analysis of the activities of musicians in Istanbul is extremely limited. For professional musicians I would argue that musical reform has provided them with a language in which their professional activities can be positively and legitimately represented in a society in which music always treads the outer boundaries of permissible behaviour.

The first part of this book looks at the process of reform, and argues that the disputed results of this official reform today must be seen in terms of local-level urban musical practice and the strategies of urban professional musicians. The systematization and self-conscious rationalization of music theory and instrument construction in modernizing states in Asia and the Middle East has been examined in detail by a number of ethnomusicologists.[17] This process has used a Western language of systematicity and rationality precisely in order to determine a unitary national culture distinct from that of Western 'internationalism'. The extent to which these

[17] See Slobin 1969, Signell 1974, Marcus 1989, and Farhat 1990.

reforms have been absorbed, 'domesticated', and attained a degree of autonomy at local level is however an issue which has remained relatively unexplored. This subject is a matter of lingering distaste for ethnomusicologists and social anthropologists, since it is assumed perhaps that these statist discourses have no separate and autonomous existence on the ground. A number of musicians associated with the reformed tradition of Anatolian folk music use this very music today as an overt symbol of social and political protest.

1.2. Cities and Migrants

The second part of the book deals more directly with arabesk. Chapter 3 looks at representations of arabesk and its association with rural–urban migration. In common with a number of states on the fringes of Europe, Turkey exists on the periphery of world economic systems, into which it has been absorbed from the mid-nineteenth century onwards.[18] Integration into these systems has involved industrialization, urbanization, and large-scale demographic movements, necessitated by the uneven distribution of wealth, development, and employment opportunities that have been an inescapable part of these processes. In the context of rapid and radical social changes of this nature, the language of disorder and disintegration focuses on the problems of labour migration and 'migrant culture'. In Turkey, arabesk is considered to be the music of labour migrants from the south-east of the country, a backward and exotic orient existing as a revealing anomaly in a Westernized and secular state.

Invariably, migrant culture is portrayed in indigenous discourses as a negative and self-destructive force whose effects spread out of their cultural locus, the squatter towns that surrounded all Third World cities, and pollute the entire body politic. In these discourses, the city bears the mark of successive transformations.[19] The focus of this perception of pollution is an inner 'otherness' which confronts and refutes official cultural identities espoused by the state. Herzfeld points to the dualism in which the Hellenic is opposed to the Romaic

[18] Keyder 1987.

[19] Gilsenan's discussion of the symbolic aspects of urban space in the North African city (1983) is of significance here in a city which has been transformed through capitalism and, less directly, colonialism in quite different ways.

in modern Greece.[20] The former stands for the progressive heritage of the ancient Greeks as prototype Europeans. The latter stands for a barbarized oriental culture, perverted and undermined by centuries of Ottoman domination. These two cultures are perceived by modern Greeks to oppose one another in a state of constant tension and antagonism, and correspond to two distinct registers of discourse, *Ellenismos* and *Romiossimi*. Rebetika is an essential element of this oriental and barbarized past, and is closely identified with refugees from Western Anatolia after the destruction of the predominantly Greek city of İzmir by Turkish troops in 1923. As Petropoulos and others have pointed out,[21] Rebetika is associated with the 'rebetis' or 'mangas' ('wide-boy') culture of Athens and Piraeus from the early 1820s on. The image of Rebetika as the music of the Smyrnaic refugees, bearers of an orientalized Greek musical culture, has persisted. Through such symbolic associations, the idealized order of the city is perceived to have been violated and polluted by a class of indigenous outsiders settling on its fringes, confronting the ideal with an image of its perverted *alter ego*.

In very different situations in states on the periphery of world economic systems, popular music, perceptions of a pernicious interior otherness, and migrant cultures on the fringes of cities in these states are closely interconnected. In repressive political conditions these are likely to be early victims of state censorship, or simply excluded from representation in the official media. Chicha music in Peru is associated with rapid urbanization and an exoticism imported by Andean migrants in Lima. Country and western music in Ireland is often interpreted as the consequence of a society which has been culturally crippled by emigration to the United States. Rock mizrahi has provided a focus for the problems of integrating Western and Eastern Jewish experience in the Israeli state.[22] Rai in Algeria has a history of identification with emigration to France and the problems of Algerian youth in coming to terms with life as Muslims and North Africans in post-colonial Western Europe. Like arabesk, Rai is considered in Algeria to be a social problem in its own right which can be controlled by being contained and denied the right to expression on official media channels.

Popular music throughout most of the Third World is a mass-

[20] Herzfeld 1987, 64.
[21] Petropoulos 1986, Pitharas 1988.
[22] Shiloah and Cohen 1983.

produced music marketed and sold in the form of cheap and disposable cassettes. This mass production adapts pre-existing popular genres to the tastes and demands of the new urban proletariat. The process, as Hennion and others have argued, imposes its own demands on musical style, from the combination of instruments that can be used in the recording studio to details of vocal technique.[23] The new musical styles that evolve in the recording studio are a product of the same processes of industrialization and automation which are transforming the society as a whole. If a connection is made between mass-produced music and mass demographic movements, it is because both are symptoms of more fundamental transformations. The musical sounds of arabesk and the rural–urban migrants in the *gecekondu* squatter towns, which constitute the most visible and obviously problematic aspect of this transformation, are closely linked together in Turkey at a variety of levels.

For the sociologists, journalists, and media spokespeople who constitute the most vociferous critics of arabesk, this is a transient culture of kitsch artefacts manufactured in pursuit of short-term profit and short term gratification. Like the *gecekondu* problem itself, it is a resourceful but unacceptable response to inadequate state planning for the cultural needs of the populace.[24] The association of arabesk with migration is the association of a musical style with a symptom of social change and not its cause, which is the overall transformation of an urban society from the cultural and administrative centre of the Ottoman empire to an industrialized periphery of a global economic system. This transformation has a long but inexorable history, which, as Brown points out in his study of the Moroccan city of Salé, cannot be reduced to simple turning points, or views of 'before' and 'after' change.[25] It is a process which has affected everybody in the city, whether they are migrants or not. Arabesk musicians and their audiences are not all migrants from the south-east of the country. In spite of this, the music continues to be described as *gecekondu* music, expressing a situation peculiar to this peripheralized class. This association continues to provide a focus and image for the disjunct cultural condition of the city and the state in which, to a greater or lesser extent, everyone has become marginalized.

23 Hennion 1983, Wallis and Malm 1984.

24 Eğribel 1984, 32–40.

25 Brown 1976, 7.

1.3. Discourses of Sentiment

This disjunction is expressed in an image of the political and social body. It is also explored as an image of the human body, self, and emotions. Feld's study of the aesthetics of Kaluli musical expression has demonstrated that a study of music implies a study of the social construction of selfhood and the emotions which pertain to it.[26] Kaluli concepts of music make no sense without an understanding of Kaluli concepts of selfhood and the emotions, which in turn make no sense without an understanding of the musical performance contexts in which these concepts are enacted. Arabesk is similarly a language of the emotions and the inner self (the *gönül*) which is seldom elaborated outside the performance contexts of arabesk. To ignore arabesk would be to ignore an indigenous exploration of the inner nature of selfhood and emotions. These forms of exploration are excluded, if not actually dismissed, by the official representations of selfhood delivered in the verbal, exegetic form which provide the kind of direct and unambiguous data required by social anthropologists on their field-work. The problem is that official, verbal representations often obscure the more subversive discourses of selfhood and the emotions, elaborated in the context of music, song and poetry. The techniques of field-work favour 'hard' verbal data, and there is a huge temptation for the field-worker to gravitate towards those people who are most fluent and articulate in their manner of verbal exegesis. As Ardener illustrated, control of these kinds of discourse is a symptom and reinforcement of other forms of social control and power.[27] The disciplinary divide which continues to separate musicology, ethnomusicology, and social anthropology has ensured that these areas of discourse have remained elusive for researchers.

In anthropological studies of the Mediterranean and Middle East, the grip of these discourses has been hard to evade. The 'honour and shame' complex has provided the principal paradigm for studies of Mediterranean selfhood.[28] The social modes in which these dominant and idealized representations are quietly subverted, or rendered ironic and even comic, have been discussed more recently by a

[26] Feld 1982. Blacking also insisted that music had to be understood in terms of 'a coherent set of ideas about self and other and bodily feelings' (1987, 35).

[27] Ardener 1972. From a different perspective Bourdieu (1977) also alerted anthropologists to the social control of discourse, and the need to observe the unspoken aspects of the habitus.

[28] See Peristiany 1965.

number of writers.[29] Lila Abu-Lughod's study of bedouin poetics amongst the Awlad ʿAli has focused on the discourses of sentiment which contradict and subvert the discourses of male honour.[30] Sentiment is expressed in poetry recited by women in situations occurring in the context of daily social life when the moral resources of the dominant discourses of honour are seen as hollow, inadequate, or irrelevant. Abu-Lughod suggests two quite distinct ideologies of bedouin culture providing languages which enable people to express and, in expressing, shape social experience.[31] These ideologies involve distinct notions of selfhood and emotion, which must be seen together if either is to make sense. In a similar way, arabesk must be seen as a discourse of sentiment, as a commentary upon powerlessness and the iniquity of power. This only makes sense when it is seen in a total context in which honour and power are legitimately expressed.

Perhaps the most significant difficulty for the anthropologist is the approach to material which is dismissed as 'emotion'. Arabesk is seen in Turkey as the domain of morbid emotion and sensitivity (*duygu*), a domain entirely separable from that of 'culture' (*kültür*). For most commentators in Turkey, techniques of cultural analysis have no place in understanding something which is seen as fundamentally acultural. It is perhaps the very fact that arabesk is expressed in a musical language which treads extremely close to that of the recognized 'cultural' expression of the dominant ideologies through official halk and sanat music which has made this music seem such a threat in Turkey. As Rosaldo, Lutz, and others have pointed out, emotions are 'not precultural, but pre*eminently* cultural',[32] even though most societies relegate discourses of emotion to a precultural domain, invariably associated with women, in which their implied criticism of official discourses can be confined and controlled. The powerful entrenchment of gender divisions throughout the Middle East and the Mediterranean world has ensured that the emotions remain deeply buried at the level of official discourse. Emotions are confined, like women, to an interior and inaccessible world.

These conflicting representations of self and society should be carefully distinguished from a post-modernist perspective which

29 See Herzfeld 1987, Gilsenan 1990.

30 Abu-Lughod 1986.

31 Ibid. 258.

32 Lutz 1988, 5.

emphasizes the 'polyphonic' quality of social life, in which social reality cannot be confined to any one level of discourse. This approach, which advocates the collapse of the *grands récits*[33] and the duty of anthropologists to reflect the multiple constructions of social reality in their ethnographies,[34] is apt to forget that representations are used, and that their uses reflect and maintain structures of power and domination.[35] Discourses of emotion are thus products of a particular structure of power. They are also a commentary on the nature of this power itself, and the powerlessness that it implies. In the case of the Awlad ʿAli this commentary is closely identified with gender relations. Power and powerlessness are not however confined to gender issues.

Arabesk is certainly not confined to women. The majority of people who attend the *Halk Konseri* in Gülhane Park are young men, as are the majority of musicians associated with arabesk. The dominant images associated with the genre, in films, lyrics, and the remarkable personalities of the singers, are however images of a peculiarly emasculated manhood, shorn of the power that is implied by this state. This emphasis upon powerlessness is maintained in a number of ways: the camp homosexuality of Zeki Müren, the erotic glamour of transsexual Bülent Ersoy, the impotent pathos of Ferdi Tayfur and İbrahim Tatlıses as alienated migrant workers who sink, in their films, into a state of terminal abasement, unable to protect their male honour and pride. Arabesk provides a continual commentary on the corruption of power. Its great appeal is closely related to the operations of power, and perceptions of powerlessness in urban Turkey today. As a discourse of sentiment, arabesk is constructed and shaped by musicians, but used and actively recreated in everyday situations. The transformation of the entire society has resulted in perceptions of powerlessness which are expressed at every level of discourse, from debates among friends about Turkey's national failings in an international arena of sport and competition (often focusing on Turkey's spectacular failures in the Eurovision song contest) to small domestic crises and moral conundrums. Arabesk provides a context in which these perceptions can be rendered meaningful.

[33] Lyotard 1980.

[34] All of the contributors to Clifford and Marcus 1986 stress this and other points relating to the literary techniques which evoke a privileged and objective voice in traditional ethnography.

[35] Ullin (1990) has recently argued this point in relation to the Habermas–Lyotard debate over post-modernity.

The analysis of any music must beware of imposing monolithic meanings upon cultural forms. A musical event can encapsulate a plurality of meanings generated by the musicians, their audiences at the event, and the socially constructed acts of listening involved when a cassette is put into a tape recorder or a record is put on to a turntable. The texts and musical messages themselves contain inner voices, contradicting or subverting the overt messages. The study of arabesk poses particularly complex questions of what an analysis of popular music should encapsulate. Whilst any anthropological or ethnomusicological account would stress the importance of context, what constitutes 'the context' in the case of arabesk is far from clear. The performance of arabesk includes appearances of arabesk stars in the Gazino of Taksim or Bağdat Caddesi for a clientele who pay the equivalent of the average monthly wage for an evening's entertainment, evenings in the run-down *pavyon* of Beyoğlu, Tarlabaşı, and Sulukule, and the more modest and respectable entertainment in the crowded *aile* ('family') *gazino* at Yakacık or Kumkapı. The context also includes the informal situations of musical 'sessions', those evening *muhabbet* in which a few drinks, some chat, and music are shared amongst friends. It also includes any occasion in which a cassette is put into a cassette recorder, in a shop, at home, or in a *dolmuş*. In its widest sense it must also include talk about music, conversations in which images of arabesk are invoked and discussed.

The 'performance' of arabesk thus embraces the areas traditionally seen in terms of the diametrically opposed processes of production and consumption. Whilst recording companies have undoubtedly constructed and defined the musical syntax of arabesk, and an analysis of the music must certainly reflect this fact, their influence in shaping and manipulating the act of listening must not be overrated. Conversely, 'consumption' in its most general sense is an intensely performative and creative event. As an analysis of popular music this book attempts to define and delineate these processes. It also looks beyond them to the role of the discourses of sentiment in the context of a perception of powerlessness peculiar to urban Turkish society in the 1980s.

1.4. Field-work

I went to Istanbul with only the vaguest ideas about what I wanted to study, entertaining the idea of letting my research subject grow organically out of involvement in local music-making in the city. I intended, somewhat naïvely, to go about learning music in the same way as any Turk, by buying an instrument, finding someone to teach me, and exploring the networks that these contacts opened up. This led me in three directions. Ironically, the first took me straight to the Turkish Radio and Television centre at Harbiye through a contact that I had met on a train in Bulgaria on a previous trip to Turkey. He had put a friend and me up for a week whilst we recouped the money we had had stolen on the train in Italy from our respective banks in Istanbul. As a film cameraman at Harbiye, he was able to introduce me to the professional élite of Turkey's halk-music performers within a couple of months. Renting a flat with him only a few minutes walk away from the TRT building tied me closely to TRT musicians throughout my first months in the city. As I got to know people with the aid of an insider's commentary provided by my flatmate, I was slowly able to perceive the inner circles and networks in which musicians were working within the TRT. The eventual choice of one musician, a young singer of my own age from the Black Sea region, to provide *bağlama* lessons and help me buy an instrument was bound to involve me closely with one of these cliques, which would, as I was aware, inevitably make it more difficult for me to meet people outside of this small group. But whilst this clique closed opportunities to me in the TRT, it opened others outside through the networks of *gazino* managers, accompanists, instrument makers, employees of recording companies and studios maintained and used by this musician.

The purchase of a *bağlama* was a critical step. In 1986 prices ranged from less than 10,000 TL (£10) to around 200,000 TL (£200), the sum then being spent by TRT *bağlama* players. In 1984 I had bought a *bağlama* for 6,000 TL, whose neck had warped shortly after I returned to England. There was little point in wasting time or money on something that would hardly last out the year. I was also aware that I should spend what would be seen as a significant amount of money to assert the seriousness of my intentions. In fact, the decision was made for me by my Black Sea companion, who introduced me to his own instrument maker, a certain Halil *usta* (a honorific term applied to master craftsmen and musicians) then working in Kağıthane. He quoted a price of 100,000 TL for a *bağlama* that would suit my particular purposes. It was twice what I wanted to spend, but the purchase of that *bağlama* was a success all round. İbrahim cemented his relationship with Halil, Halil had a new customer and fresh face at the musical gatherings in his workshop, and I had a new *bağlama*. This *bağlama* not only continues to play well, but rapidly increased in value as wood prices, workshop rents, and Halil *usta*'s growing prestige amongst the professional musicians of Istanbul soared upward. With this instrument I was able to demonstrate my commitment to the music and established myself among my friends, without any justification, as someone with an eye for a bargain.

Bağlama makers in Istanbul are highly respected. Since the instrument is difficult and expensive to maintain, and it is easy to lose a lot of money by buying a badly crafted instrument whose neck may warp rapidly in Istanbul's damp climate, the services of a tame *usta* are highly in demand. Their workshops are important meeting places after hours for musicians all over the city, since the act of visiting, accepting a glass of tea, and hanging around for a chat is one of the most significant ways in which prestige of this kind is conferred. The question 'Who made your *bağlama*?' was thus a particularly significant way of identifying the circles in which I was moving. The choice of a maker, a certain Halil *usta* who had a workshop Kağıthane, had significant consequences in terms of the people I met and the direction that my field-work took.

My first step out of these official circles was taken upon the advice of Halil and with the help of the bank cashier who dealt with my grant cheque, an Alevi from Sivas with a passion for the *bağlama* and its music. He introdenuced me to the first of countless private clubs, known as *dershane* or *dernek*, that I was to visit in the course of the next two years. I joined for a small monthly fee, and, thanks to an oversight by the particularly overworked secretary, was not introduced to the teachers. I was thus able to sit at the back of the classes, make friends slowly, and observe the difficulties and triumphs of my class-mates for months in a situation which would have been very different if my presence had been known and advertised. As a focus for my late afternoons and evenings at this stage of my field-work, this experience was essential in introducing me not just to the music, but to patterns of conversation and argument on the subject of music. This more than anything fuelled my interest in and awareness of the debate over arabesk which permeated every level of music-making in the city. As I progressed through this semi-formal system of education, I found myself promoted quickly to the top classes, and then, on subsequent visits in later years, pressed into service as a teacher of *solfej* (note-reading) and the instrument itself. Whilst this raised worries in my own mind about the role I was playing in changing the experience of the culture I was trying to study, a fact of life with which all field-workers have to contend, it provided me with an invaluable variety of perspectives on the system of education and pattern of sociality.

Plagued by questions and doubts about authenticity, and suitable anthropological paradigms in which to frame my research, I found that the issue of migration and migrant culture began to assume a particular importance. This provided clear anthropological models of music and identity construction in the city, and related closely to the work of Turkish sociologists and anthropologists on the *gecekondu*, identity, and social change. Two issues in which I found myself increasingly involved appeared to be diametrically opposed, but related directly to the question of migration. The first was arabesk, the shadow of every discussion of music. The second was the music of Black Sea migrants in Istanbul. I began to pursue both simultaneously. Contacts in Istanbul and the Black Sea area, through my first teacher and friends in *dernek*, provided me with a context in which to explore the relation of official regional categories of musical identity to the experience of musicians in these regions and in Istanbul. Arabesk proved evasive at every turn. Arabesk singers with whom I was able to get an audience appeared reluctant to help me, and even slightly apologetic about their art. 'Malatyalı' İbrahim (Dulkadıroğlu),[36] the first I was able to contact through his small music shop in Şehzadebaşı Caddesi, suggested bluntly that I forgot about arabesk and took myself off to Anatolia to discover some 'real' music. *Gazino* offered a range of music to a bewildering diversity of clientele, and time spent in them did not conform closely to my notions of what field-work should be. Arabesk was clearly a mass media phenomenon which was not confined to particular localities or tied to particular performance contexts. This apparent contextlessness also militated against the kind of research that I wanted to do. I was nagged by the persistent worry that what I was doing was simply 'not anthropology'.

[36] A number of arabesk singers such as 'Malatyalı' İbrahim and 'Mersinli' İsmail are known by their place of origin. Some such as 'Kıbrıslı' Mehmet are known by a place name with which they are associated for other reasons, in this case, military service in the Turkish army during the invasion of Cyprus.

A short trip to Cyprus at the end of 1986, necessitated by the ongoing process of application for a research permit, provided me with an opportunity to reflect. Whilst I felt that I needed a subject, I could also see that the search for a subject area with unambiguous boundaries was an integral aspect of what I had been observing all around me: talk and argument about music. I decided to open up another pathway for myself through the musical life of the city. Slightly frustrated by the way in which I felt I had been co-opted by cliques in the TRT, I made two provocative decisions. The first was to learn the *kanun*, a plucked zither associated with Turkish sanat music. To my teachers and advisers in the TRT halk-music department, who saw the resurgence of official funding and television air-time for sanat music to be direct evidence of the collapse of the Atatürkian reforms and ideologies that supported their own, this move was bitterly contested, but opened up whole new areas of argument and dispute. The second was simply the act of doing something on my own, without consultation. This was also rightly criticized as headstrong foolishness, involving me with total strangers whose behaviour towards me could not be guaranteed. As it turned out, my teachers and advisers need not have worried, and I met with the same helpful attitudes that I encountered at every stage of my field-work. The fact that I had made a move away from my first *bağlama* teacher established me as an independent operator, in the eyes of myself and others, and before long provided a more equitable basis on which our friendship could develop.

Through an acquaintance who taught folk dances at a club in Üsküdar and was also a keen amateur singer, I was introduced to the *kanun* player at the highly prestigious Kalamiş music society, run by Melihat Pars in Kadıköy. The usual deal was struck, in which I offered to teach English to his son in order to establish some kind of parity in our relationship. The time spent in his house in Bağlarbaşı teaching English and learning the *kanun* involved me closely with his family life, as well as the rest of his professional existence, playing popular art music and arabesk with his son in a band in the *gazino* around Yakacık, visiting his instrument maker (an army colonel), and seeing friends for music sessions and a chat. Through quite different channels I found myself in a similar musical world of domestic music-making and socializing, participation in clubs, amateur concerts and professional appearances as accompanists for popular musicians in small night-clubs throughout the city, and chains of authority linking each of us to teachers and instrument makers. My teacher was a retired officer in the Turkish army, who worked during the day in a housing co-operative for other army officers in Üsküdar. As with my experience of halk music, I was in a world which embraced all the apparent contradictions of Turkish life, in which high-ranking officers of the Turkish army, guardians of Turkey's secular cultural heritage, were deeply committed to a music which represented, in the eyes of many, that Ottoman and Islamic culture which Atatürk had spent his entire life trying to stamp out.

By the time that arabesk had come to assume a more coherent focus for my research in 1987, I was in a position to survey, from an ethnographic perspective, a range of musical activity in the city, from discussions of cultural policy at the highest levels of the State Conservatories and TRT to domestic *muhabbet* and musical sessions. This study of arabesk attempts to situate musicians, as human actors, in a total field of local-level and domestic musical practice, urban patterns of entertainment and leisure, the social organization of the music industry and the recording studio, and the wider political contexts of reform and debate. Whatever the shortcomings of this analysis, an ethnographic approach based on participation and observation does, I believe, maintain the claims of an anthropology of music to provide a distinct and relevant perspective on popular culture.

2

Discovering the Folk and their Music

Folk music in Turkey is considered by its proponents and practitioners to play a specific role in creating a culturally unified and cohesive nation-state. Its practice and performance transforms the individual, transmitting the ideology with which the music is bound up, instilling values of sociality, team-work, competition, and self-presentation. It also provides a model of logical, systematic, and rational thinking, a notion which lies at the centre of the Atatürkian philosophy of the secular regeneration of Turkey. It is a music which is both performed and performative, acting upon the individual and social body. In this it is diametrically opposed to arabesk, which is considered by its detractors to be incapable of doing anything.

Folk music is presented by many musicians and folklorists in Turkey as a timeless and self-evident fact of Turkish cultural life. However, 'the folk' and their music were discovered and redefined at particular junctures in the history of Ottoman and modern Turkey. The features of these rediscoveries and redefinitions had much in common, drawing as they did upon a fund of thought relating to European nationalisms in the nineteenth century, and to more recent movements in the newer nation-states of Eastern Europe and the Middle East. The debt that many of these movements owed to Hamann and Herder is marked, stamping them with a similar intellectual character.

The construction of folklore varies according to the political and social circumstances in which the particular nation-state comes into existence. As Herzfeld has noted, some folklore movements are associated with the birth of the new nation-state, as with the work of Zambelios in Greece, and some precede it, as in the case of Sjörgen and Poppius in Finland.[1] Within the state itself, the career of nationalist discourses and concepts of folklore are filtered through ever-changing political and social circumstances, and each is consequently understood, used, and reinterpreted in a multitude of

[1] Herzfeld 1982, 53.

ways. It is important to stress this in the Turkish context where observers are inclined to see official discourses as either accounting for Turkish social life in its entirety, or as existing in a totally fabricated and unreal world, bearing no relation to 'what is actually going on'. Discourses are above all things which are used and manipulated by people at a local level in particular situations, and their inherent ambiguities and tensions are a critical factor in their operation.[2]

In Turkey any notion of 'the folk' within the context of a modern nation-state is bound to be riddled with tensions and ambiguities. The notion of the state itself is a problem in the Muslim world, which acknowledges only the existence of the *umma*, the Muslim, as opposed to non-Muslim community. The Ottomans had a secular state tradition, often referred to as *adab*.[3] This was a notion of a hierarchical society with the sultan at its apex, dating at least from the emergence of the Turks from Central Asia. Secular notions of the state continue to run quite counter to the egalitarian and personalistic concept of *umma*. In an Islamic context, the endorsement of music and dance by official discourses is also in itself problematic.[4] This chapter therefore looks at the points at which ideology and local-level music-making meet. I argue that the present situation is to be understood not in terms of the perceived success, failure, or lack of applicability of the Turkist theory of music, but in terms of the differing applications of this discourse by the urban institutions associated with halk music, by professional and amateur musicians. Outside the narrow confines of official organizations such as the State Conservatories and the Turkish Radio and Television, the official, urban model of halk music theory and practice and the discourses which sustain it have not displaced 'Ottoman' art music or arabesk, but coexist with them. As a result, urban musicians have access to a fund of representations of themselves and their music, to legitimize their own activity, criticize others, and enable them to manage their professional existence in Istanbul. Halk music is therefore to be seen as an arena of debate and argument, in which arabesk plays an important role, and in which arabesk in turn defines itself. It is first necessary to understand the concept of 'the folk' in Turkish society, and its complex relationship with Turkish nationalism.

[2] I follow Mardin, who sees discourse as 'mobile and transformational' practice (1989, 8), but unlike Foucault, stresses social access and not exclusivity in totalitarian 'regimes of truth' (1984).

[3] Heper 1985, 25.

[4] See Ch. 7, s. 1.

2.1. Turkism

The identity of the folk pertains to the general question of Turkish ethnicity. The Treaty of Lausanne of 2 November 1922 marked the final collapse of the Ottoman empire, and the birth of the new Turkey. It was only after the 'population exchanges', the compulsory exchange of Armenian and Greek minorities between 1915 and 1924, that Turkey came to exist as a secular nation-state, inhabited predominantly by one linguistic and ethnic group.

'Turkism', the name given to the concept of Turkishness relating to this, does however have an earlier history, looking to the Turks of Central and Eastern Asia. This was generally distinguished as 'Turanism', whilst Turkism itself was taken to refer to the speakers of the Oghuz branch of the Turkic languages (Türkmence, Azeri, 'Osmanlı'—i.e. 'Turkey Turkish', and the Cypriot and Balkan dialects), or just the Turks of Turkey. Both Turkism and Turanism have two distinct strands. One is academic and the product of Western orientalism. Particularly influential was the work of Joseph de Guignes, whose *Histoire générale des huns, des turcs, des mogols et des autres tartares occidentaux, etc.* (1759) was translated into Turkish by Hüseyin Cahit Yalçın in 1825. Equally important was Lumley Davids, whose *Turkish Grammar*, presented to Sultan Selim III, also included a section on Turkish ethnography and history. These two works in particular were seen by Ziya Gökalp as seminal in the history of Western Turkism and Turanism.[5] Later in the nineteenth century, the work of the Hungarian Turkologist Arminius Vambery and the French scholar Leon Cahun were highly influential in developing the concept of the Turanian linguistic and racial family: the work of both was translated into Ottoman and became widely known in Ottoman intellectual circles. The work of Cahun in particular was known and admired by the Young Ottomans in Paris in the 1860s.[6]

The second strand is the product of indigenous scholarship. The first manifestations of Turkism in the Ottoman empire had a political character, in spite of their use and manipulation of the language and symbols of 'culture'. This was the stirring to consciousness of a centralist, Muslim, and Turkish bureaucracy embodied in the Committee of Union and Progress, against a peripheralist and largely Greek and Armenian merchant class.[7] These writings were heavily

[5] Gökalp 1923, 9. [6] Shaw 1977, 26. [7] Keyder 1988, 197–8.

influenced by the work of Davids, de Guignes, Vambery, and Cahun. The translation of the *Secere-i Türki* of Abul Gazi Bahadır Khan from Çağatay to modern Turkish by Ahmet Vefik Paşa in 1864 did a great deal to stimulate an awareness of and interest in the Turks of Central Asia. At that time Ahmet Vefik Paşa was both professor of Philosophy at the Darülfunun and an influential politician. During this period, the *Tarih-i Alem* (History of the World) of the Minister of Military Schools, Süleyman Paşa, written in 1876, was the first to make systematic use of Chinese sources, taking Turkist studies back to a pre-Islamic point of ethnic and cultural origin.[8]

There was thus a growing notion amongst the Ottoman intelligentsia of the existence of a Turkic world and Turkic culture beyond the boundaries of the Ottoman empire. For Shaw, the real founders of Turkism in Ottoman Turkey were refugee scholars from the Russian empire, many of whom settled permanently in Istanbul. A concept of Turkism had been developed in response to Russian expansionism in Central Asia throughout the nineteenth century, particularly in the Crimea and Kazan. One of the best known of these writers was İsmail Bey Gasprinski, who arrived in Istanbul in 1874. The work of many of these nationalist intellectuals was read with particular interest by the Young Turks in Paris. That of the Azerbaijani writer Ağaoğlu Ahmet, who had studied in Paris himself and had made contact with the Young Turks during this period, was particularly influential. A number of Çağatay and Uzbek Turkish writers, led by Buharalı Süleyman Efendi, established their own *tekke* in Üsküdar.[9]

With the defeat of the Ottomans and the occupation of Anatolia by British, Greek, French, and Italian forces, and the eventual formation of the Ankara resistance, these diffuse currents of Turkist philosophy were sharply focused in the figure of the leader, the *gazi*,[10] Mustafa Kemal. Pan-Islamism and pan-Turkism, ideas which had been debated and enjoyed considerable vogue among the Young Turk reformers, were rejected in favour of a focus on the

[8] Cahun had similarly stressed the importance of early Chinese sources in his *Introduction à l'histoire de l'Asie* (Paris, 1896), noting the role of the Turks in transmitting elements of Chinese culture to the Persian and Arab world.

[9] Shaw 1977, 261–2.

[10] Warrior for the faith. In spite of the secularist orientations of the Turkish armed forces since Atatürk, religious terminology continues to be used in such expressions as *gazi* and *mücahit* for soldiers who have seen active service. See also Mardin's discussion of these terms (1989, 3–5).

creation of the modern state of Turkey. Throughout the late eighteenth and early nineteenth centuries the bureaucratization and 'rationalization' of the Ottoman state structure, culminating in the Tanzimat reforms of 1839–78, were necessitated by the increasing integration of the Ottoman state into a new northern Europe-centred world commercial system. In the interests of this rational reform the *ulema*[11] found themselves marginalized from their traditional roles in the structure of government. Their official political role was finally obliterated by Mustafa Kemal. Islam came to stand for that web of localized social relations which stood between the direct relationship of state to individual. As a rival principle of organization which did not have its roots in the principles of European science, Islam could only be banished from the realm of politics. The relationship of rational state to individual citizen was defined in a largely new discourse of power, relating to the *Ata*, the father of the Turks, Mustafa Kemal himself. This was the subject of numerous studies in the West and a cultic graphomania in Turkey itself, stressing the imperative of change and renewal which could only take place through the agency of a firm and autocratic decision-maker.[12]

What survived was a modified version of Turkism. This stressed the affinity of the Turks of Anatolia with the Turks of Central and Eastern Asia and made much of the essential alienness of their Islamic cultural heritage. Its aim was not, however, the eventual unification of the Turkic world, nor did it prohibit the drive towards progress, a drive inevitably towards Westernization. Progress, to reformers from the Tanzimat period on, could never mean anything else. Atatürk himself imaged this in a historico-geographic idiom by stating on many occasions that the cultural *telos* of Turkish progress had been from East to West. They had just reached, as it were, the penultimate stop.

The intention of the reforms was to bring about a radical and thorough revolution, from macrocosmic structural change to far from insignificant details. Within a short space of time, the religious apparatus of the Ottoman state had been dismantled, and the new government had endorsed the Gregorian calendar, the employment of metric weights and measures, the compulsory adoption of surnames, reforms of dress codes, language, and every expression of cultural identity. Even though a number of critical issues were left

11 The Ottoman hierarchy of theological scholars. For a discussion of the *ulema* in this period, see Gilsenan 1983, 27–54.

12 See Kinross 1964 and Armstrong's more popular biography of Atatürk (1940).

ambiguous in ways which continue to plague Turks today, the rhetoric of the Turkish reforms allowed for no doubt that an all-embracing revolution had taken place and was continuing to sweep all before it.

The paradigm example of Atatürk's exquisite understanding of the power of the manipulation of symbols was the Hat Law, enacted in 1925. This replaced that emblem of Ottomanism, the fez, with a 'civilized' Western-style peaked or brimmed hat. The fez symbolized the perpetual readiness of the Muslim to prostrate himself in prayer; the hat allowed his head to touch the ground in the prescribed gesture of submission. But the peak of the Western hat or cap prohibited this. Geoffrey Lewis has pointed out the irony of the fact that whilst the abolition of the Caliphate attracted little attention, let alone opposition, in Turkey, the abolition of the fez, a garment that had been introduced only a century before, provoked widespread outrage.[13] But the existence of the Caliphate hardly touched the day-to-day life of the majority of Turkish citizens, whereas the networks of hierarchy established at a local level by the complex code of Ottoman headwear did. In common with many of Atatürk's reforms the symbols which he manipulated have lost none of their potency. The hat issue has recently surfaced over the question of women's headwear in universities, and the 'turban' continues to provide a focus for the aspirations of religious radicalists and secular reformers in Turkey.[14]

The picture of culture and society upon which Atatürk was acting was that of the Turkish body, from which the clothing of the pan-Islamic Ottoman cultural heritage could simply be removed, more or less at will, and replaced. This heritage represented not just a web of social relationships which had to be transformed on the road to a modern and secular nationalism, but a web of superstition, magic, backwardness, and resistance to the possibility of change that had completely immobilized the Turkish people.

2.2. Ziya Gökalp and the Turkist Theory of Culture

The most detailed theoretical justification for these reforms was heavily based on the writing of European and Ottoman Turkists.

[13] G. Lewis 1965, 94.

[14] The recent resurgence of this debate has been discussed by Olson (1985). For a Turkish perspective see *Mesele-i Türban* in *Nokta* 5 1987.

Ziya Gökalp's tract entitled *The Principles of Turkism*[15] so profoundly influenced Mustafa Kemal that it may be described as a blueprint for the entire revolution. The logic of the Hat Law can be most clearly described in terms of Gökalp's distinction between 'Culture' (*Hars*) and 'Civilization' (*Medeniyet*).[16] Gökalp pointed out that societies have both cultures and civilizations but that the two are quite different things. Culture is synonymous with language and education. It is that which binds nations together. Civilization on the other hand is what we might describe as 'high culture', the artificial product of the individual will, consisting of theology, philosophy, science, and technology. Civilization is international and freely floating, even though it tends to be shared by nations of the same continent.

This perspective owes much to the view that there was a relatively clear bifurcation of Turkish society at the time into the urban Ottoman élite and the Turkish peasantry of Anatolia. The former drew for their fund of cultural symbols upon their more recent Islamized and Middle Eastern past whilst the latter looked to their Central Asian roots. In Gökalp's view this was precisely the difference between the civilization of Turkey and the culture of Turkey. The role Gökalp saw for his concept of Turkism was in a sense psychiatric, since in his view a healthy society possessed a certain rapport between its culture and its civilization, which in this case was clearly lacking. He cites the French psychologist Ribot, who made a similar point about the relationship of mind to character. Gökalp suggests that the relationship of the individual mind to its character resembles the relationship of the national civilization to its culture, and that an imbalance is likely to lead to weakness and sterility.[17]

For Gökalp the Turks had simply outgrown the Arab civilization which had fostered them from the tenth to the early twentieth century. There were several reasons for this. Firstly the dual nature of Ottoman Turkish society had reached a state which could no longer be tolerated. Moreover, the manifestations of the high culture had reached a state of unhealthy degeneration and ugliness.[18] The only cure for this was to bring about the homogenization of national society through the reconciliation of its culture and civilization.

15 *Türkçülüğün Esasları*. A transl. has been published by Robert Devereux as *The Principles of Turkism* (Leiden, 1968). The key passages cited here are my own transl. from the Ottoman text and modern Turkish transcriptions.

16 Gökalp 1923, 27. 17 Ibid. 37. 18 Ibid. 37.

Secondly, there was the simple evolutionary fact that if the Turkish nation was to survive it would need to embrace Western civilization, which espoused rather than challenged progress. In Gökalp's view, there was no real crisis involved in changing civilization since the Turks had in effect been doing it all the time and should have been used to it. There was also the precedent of Japan, which had followed a similar path in abandoning 'Far Eastern' civilization in favour of the Western.[19]

This process was a matter of becoming a modern developed nation which had, according to his reading of Durkheim, effected the change from mechanical to organic solidarity based on the division of labour. And yet the inability of the Turks to act in a decisive enough way puzzled Gökalp, since the Japanese had been able to preserve their identity but had embraced Western civilization to the extent that they could be elected to the League of Nations.[20] His social and historical perspective was simply too wide. The notion of *haremlik*, the domestic segregation of women, was for Gökalp of recent and alien origin, having been 'invented' by the Byzantines. Nevertheless such 'recent and alien' institutions were considered by most Turks to represent the unalterable essence of Muslim Turkishness. Gökalp argued that his concern was not with Islam, which was to be relegated to the domain of individual, domestic responsibility, but with removing the outdated and inappropriate baggage of Arab civilization. Gökalp's implicit criticism of the Turkish people for footdragging, and the resultant requirement for the paternal strong hand to do what was needed provided an element of the discourse of leadership which is still very much alive in Turkey today.

The Turkish revolution might be described in a direct way as being Gökalpian–Durkheimian in inspiration. Correspondingly the course that reforms took aimed at discourses, ideologies, and the kinds of measures directed against symbols of ethnicity outlined above, rather than at socio-economic structures. These had been transformed gradually throughout the previous century as the Ottoman state was absorbed into the network of North-West European trade. There were therefore no clear grounds upon which Gökalp could define a Turkist theory of economics in opposition to his predecessors. 'Economic Turkism' remains something of an afterthought in *The Principles*, and the tension between free-market liberalism and 'etatism' enshrined by the Izmir Economic Congress

[19] Ibid. 48. [20] Ibid. 58.

of 1923 remains to a certain extent to dog Turkey today.[21] Grillo has described the creation of the nation-state as being a case of either the 'politicization of the ethnicity' or the 'ethnicization of the polity'.[22] The progress of Turkey, in terms of the Turkist ideology as it was formulated by Gökalp, was the latter: the attempt to impress upon the inhabitants of new state their essential Turkishness.

An example of the complex effect of this ideology in operation may be seen in the language reforms. These illustrate some of the particular problems involved in defining and imposing a 'Turkishness' meaningful and acceptable to the inhabitants of the Turkish state. This difficulty of replacing that which had been torn down by bureaucratic decree is a constant theme in discussions of the formation of the Turkish state,[23] emphasizing the apparently limitless power of the state to reform or dismantle what it chooses. But the dismemberment and reform of language, like music, could not simply be enacted and policed by authoritarian decree. The result of the language reforms was not the displacement of one code by another, but rather the coexistence of the reformed code with what it was intended to replace. Choice and manipulation of these codes provide their users with languages in which authoritarian or subversive discourses can be voiced.

2.3. The Language Reforms

In Ottoman Turkey, the gulf between the educated élite and the mass of Anatolian peasantry was both symbolized and maintained by that between *Osmanlı* and *Kaba* ('Crude') Turkish. The importance of this divide for the reformers lay in the obstacle to communication that it imposed between the government and the people. Furthermore, *Osmanlı* Turkish, being a complex bricolage of Arabic and Persian loosely held together by a framework of Turkish syntax, encoded not only a social division but also the pan-Islamic orientation of the Ottoman government. The importance of changing language to change modes of thought has been appreciated by all reformers; Mustafa Kemal was no exception.

The language reforms demonstrated with some clarity the conflicting forces of a rigorous puritanism and a moderate reformism. The

[21] Hale 1981, 35. [22] Grillo 1980.
[23] See Berkes 1964, Heper 1985, and Mardin 1989.

former wanted to push the reforms to their logical conclusion by removing in their entirety the vast bulk of foreign loan-words, replacing them with newly coined words of 'pure Turkish' extraction. The latter saw as its goal the restoration of a degree of intelligibility and communicability to a confused linguistic situation. This conflict can be seen clearly when we compare Gökalp's comments with the more extreme ideas of Mustafa Kemal. These came to dominate the language reforms through the agency of the *Türk Dil Kurumu* (the Turkish Language Foundation), an institution in which Atatürk maintained an active personal interest.

According to Gökalp, the role of Turkism in linguistics was nothing more than to continue a trend towards greater intelligibility in written Ottoman Turkish which had been an ongoing process since the simplification of the *Takvim-i Vakayi* newspaper in 1831 upon the decree of Mahmut II. But even though Gökalp devoted much time to the language question, his critics point out that his argument was seriously flawed by his equation of 'the people' with 'the people of Istanbul'.[24] In view of his conception of Turkism at work in other fields and the centrality of language in defining culture, this at first appears to be surprising. Considering his reformist zeal in other areas, he might have been expected to go further along the road towards a more complete Turkification of the language. However, his concern was with the maintenance of standards of intelligibility. Furthermore, in his view foreign loan-words had already become 'Turkish' through a process of phonetic moulding. This took place through the imposition of a system of vowel harmony which is entirely alien to the principal 'donor' languages of Ottoman Turkish, Arabic, Persian, and French, and also through borrowed words assuming meanings other than their original. These loan-words were an important element in Gökalp's argument, allowing him to steer a course between conservatives who wanted these 'barbarisms' (*ghalatat*) to adhere strictly to their original meanings, and radical reformers who wanted to replace them with newly coined words.

Whilst Gökalp attracted much attention to the language issue and led the way notably in his poems, *Kızıl Elma* ('Red Apple'), which made pioneering use of the isosyllabic lines of Turkish folk poetry rather than the rules of Arabic prosody known as *aruz*, his adherence in principle to the existence of certain Arabicisms and even the 'invention' of simple words using Arabic rather than Turkish deriva-

[24] Yücel 1982, 30.

tions continues to be a point of issue.[25] The difference between Gökalp's linguistic Turkism and the linguistics of the Türk Dil Kurumu was not just in the definition of the halk, but in the suitability of language as an arena for the radical reformism that had taken place in other areas of social life. Logic demanded that it should be so, but Gökalp was fully aware of the complex nature of language in society. Logic, however, prevailed and the language reforms, closely watched over by Atatürk himself went ahead as though foreign words and phrases could simply be surgically removed from the underlying language structure.

The language reforms took place in two major stages. The first was the substitution of the Roman alphabet for the Arabic. The second was the weeding out of Arabic and Persian loan-words. The first of these was officially achieved more or less overnight in 1928, Mustafa Kemal himself taking an active role in touring the countryside with blackboard and chalk and threatening his bureaucracy with the sack if they did nothing to extract themselves from their newly acquired illiteracy. As with the Hat Law, this involved the manipulation of public symbols of intense significance. The Arabic alphabet had been adopted by the Turks on their conversion to Islam in the tenth century, and was synonymous in the opinion of many with Islam itself. The Koran was conceived and revealed in Arabic, so the reform of the alphabet was in a very direct sense a violation of a sacred object. Whilst the official rationale for the change of alphabet was the unsuitability of the Arabic alphabet for the vowel sounds of Turkish, its symbolic importance lay in marking a decisive break with the Arabic- and Persian-speaking world, effectively blocking the free traffic in terminology which had existed up to that point and cutting the umbilical cord which linked Turkish Islam to the wider Islamic world.

The reform of the language made possible the more fundamental Turkicization of the language through the weeding out of Persian and Arabic loan-words. These were to be replaced by a process of recoining and substitution based on the language of the Anatolian *halk*, 'the folk'. But which folk? The complex process was explained by the Türk Dil Kurumu in the following way:

The roots selected for newly coined words are subjected to an order of preference in which the Turkish of Turkey occupies prime place. Standard

[25] Ibid. 29.

words are naturally preferred, then come the colloquial. When this resource has been exhausted, and no suitable root has been found then, in order, we fall back upon the archaic, obsolete, and dialectical words. When this search too has been unsuccessful we cross the boundaries of Turkey and go out to ancient and literary Turkish dialects, then to distant and non-literary dialects living today. In technical terms, if the search for a Turkish equivalent seems useless foreign words are tolerated.[26]

Here, as elsewhere in its more extreme manifestations, 'the Turkish' was bent wherever possible to resemble 'the Western', to enhance the impression that there was no fundamental contradiction involved in the adoption of Western civilization. Thus, in new Turkish, the shape-forming suffix *-gen* (as for example in *üçgen*, triangle), or the adjectival suffix *-sel* (that renders *tarihsel* for 'historical' in place of the Arabic *tarihî*) do have Turkish etymological explanations,[27] but are also clearly modelled on European language suffixes. An escape clause was built in by the Sun Language theory, which was officially adopted at the Third Turkish Linguistic Congress in 1936, which suggested that the Altaic languages (even then only a hazy category) conformed to the earliest stages of a model of linguistic evolution. The unilineal development of all languages being assumed, there was thus no contradiction involved in words or suffixes having this kind of joint etymology. Assisting the work of the TDK, the *Türk Ocakları* were established by Atatürk in 1931 to provide an institutional basis for research in rural Anatolia, in order to establish the linguistic and ethnographic building blocks to be used in the reconstruction of Turkish society.

The language reforms are too often judged in terms of success or failure, both in Turkey and by outside observers. Official language sees all reforms as unqualified successes, marred only by the foot-dragging of reactionaries or others who fail for various reasons to see themselves as 'Turks'. In the 1980s, the written Turkish of the 1950s could be described by students as 'old Turkish', requiring a dictionary to be understood. On the other hand, a critical viewpoint exists which perhaps overstresses the superficial and symbolic nature of Atatürk's reforms. Berkes noted the fact that the Atatürkian revolution was most eloquent in attacking the old order, and less lucid when it came to providing a substitute.[28] Heper points to the artificial and abstract quality of bureaucratic utopian thinking in this

[26] Türk Tarih Kurumu Basımevi 1951, 13.
[27] Banarlı 1972, 268–72.
[28] Berkes 1964, 502.

period.[29] Arguing from a different perspective, Keyder describes the reforms as acts of 'symbolic violence', suggesting that the revolution failed to address the 'real' (economic) roots of conflict and contradiction that were undermining the Ottoman empire, and continue to affect Turkey today.[30] Mardin suggests that the language reformers succeeded only in creating an equally incomprehensible language for the educated élite: 'The language of Turkish literature has become a parody of palace language—convoluted, arch, precious and rigid. Arabic terms, unintelligible to the lower classes, have been abandoned, but commonly accepted words have been replaced by neologisms which have meaning only for those who invented them.'[31]

It is certainly true to say that Atatürk himself delivered speeches which would not have been understood at the time, and are no less comprehensible with the benefit of decades of reformed language teaching.[32] Rather than a simple act of displacement it is perhaps more accurate to say that the language reforms created 'languages' in place of 'language'. Whilst it is not possible to take the words from somebody's mouth, particularly when these formulate relationships between God and man which had not been fundamentally changed by the reforms, it is possible to suggest alternatives. The fact that these alternatives are taught at school and used by the media invests them with the power of state authority, creating 'languages' which are symbolic and manipulable objects in their own right. The systematic application of words chosen from a Turkish lexicon, in favour of Arabic, or a word of European derivation, makes a recognizable statement about the kind of person you are. The political context changes the nature of the statements being made. In 1986, there was a widespread opposition among the Turkish left to what was perceived as the Islamist and anti-Atatürkist stance of the post-1983 government. Systematic choice of *öztürkçe* ('pure Turkish') synonyms could make this position immediately clear, as when friends of mine would express their opposition to my 'reactionary' interest in arabesk using the most reformed language they could muster. The lexicon of an individual speaker therefore shifts according to the context and the kind of statement being made.

The language reforms succeeded in creating parallel languages

[29] Heper 1985, 46. [30] Keyder 1988, 209. [31] Mardin 1969, 280.

[32] See Yücel 1982, 37, for a discussion of Atatürk's speech to the Swedish heir to the throne during the height of the language reforms. This speech was famous, amongst other things, for its total avoidance of the word 'and', the Arabic 've'.

which could be manipulated for specific purposes. In the same way, it is possible to look at the music reforms in terms not of their success or failure, but in relation to how they established a number of different, competing musical languages, each backed by varying degrees and kinds of institutional support. This is a direct result of the gaps and inconsistencies existing in the concept of the *halk* and their music.

2.4. The Construction of a National Music: from Gökalp to the TRT

In Gökalp's view, the split between culture and civilization could be illustrated by the existence of two quite distinct kinds of music, one pertaining to the Ottoman élite and the other to the rural *halk*, the folk. The former was the product of Arabo-Persian civilization, based in turn upon the civilization of the Byzantines. The latter was the true culture of the Turks. In other spheres, Turkish culture was to remain much as it was deemed always to have been, whilst the civilization only was to effect the change from oriental to occidental. Gökalp believed however that only one music could exist as the true, national music of Turkey, and this was to be achieved through a synthesis of Turkish folk music and the musical techniques of Western civilization. It was of paramount importance to Gökalp that the new Turkey should be able to produce musical genius of the calibre of the Western masters; he points out that these only occur in history when the culture and civilization of a nation are in unison.[33] Gökalp's musical philosophy is perhaps most clearly summed up in the following passage from *The Principles*:

> Today we are faced with three kinds of music . . . Which one of them is ours? Eastern music is morbid music and non-rational. Folk music represents our culture. Western music is the music of our civilization. Thus neither should be foreign to us.
>
> Our natural music, therefore, is to be born from a synthesis of our folk music and Western music. Our folk music provides us with a rich treasury of melodies. By collecting them and arranging them on the basis of Western musical techniques, we shall have both a national and modern music.[34]

[33] Gökalp 1923, 51. [34] Ibid. 131.

Gökalp was not the first to talk about the existence of a rural and Anatolian tradition of folk music, whose claim to represent the music of the Turks was superior to that of urban art music. In the decade preceding the publication of *The Principles*, articles by Rauf Yekta Bey (1911), Musa Süreyya Bey (1915), Ahmet Cevdet, and Necip Asım (1916) stessed the necessity of field expeditions to collect rural Anatolian music.[35] Furthermore, when Rıza Nur became Minister of Education in 1920 he established a Bureau of Culture (*Hars Dairesi*), which began to collect songs on organized field trips. Gökalp did not lead, but shaped and reformulated ideas already in discussion, in terms of his philosophy of *hars* and *medeniyet*. Since the passage cited above is seminal in the creation of a specific discourse of halk music, it is worth looking in detail at some of his terms.

In describing 'Eastern' music as morbid, Gökalp is clearly speaking the language of the Western orientalist. The idea of the morbidity and irrationality of the East has a history as long as that of Western orientalism, as Said points out with reference to Goethe and Hugo.[36] What is at issue is the high emotional current of oriental music, with the implicit criticism that this is not complemented by a sense of formal or structural discipline. Eastern musicians in the nineteenth century have tended to represent their own music in the same way, to a certain extent reproducing these discourses (as Said has illustrated in other contexts), but also casting their observations in the framework of their own ways of talking about emotion and its musical representation. Faris al-Shadyaq, a Lebanese Maronite convert to Presbyterianism, travelled widely in the West between 1830 and 1850, and was working in Malta when he investigated the differences between Arab and 'Frankish' music.[37] Whilst he registered due admiration for the idea of polyphony ('a poem in all the different metres of prosody') and the array of instruments he discovered, he was bored with the 'gross dissonances' and the lack of fine emotions presented whilst singing: 'they laugh whilst singing, they titter, they weep, they yawn, they sneeze, they imitate the clucking of hens, the twittering of birds and other things'.[38] He notes that 'Franks' he met in Egypt found Egyptian music saddening, and this

[35] For accounts of this early period of Turkish folk-music research see Birdoğan 1988, 7–19, and Şenel 1987.

[36] Said 1978, 168.

[37] Transl. with commentary in Cachia 1973.

[38] Ibid. 44.

he attributes to the Arab concern with 'tenderness and love', more flexibly portrayed by semi-improvised, monophonic music with its wealth of modal constructions (*maqam*). The desired quality of Arab music was in his account *tarab*, a 'lightness affecting a man as a result of either joy or sorrow'.[39] In describing 'Eastern' music as morbid therefore, Gökalp might seem to be combining two quite separate representations of the power of music to portray and move the emotions.

However, the concept of morbidity has a particular resonance in his thought, as indeed in much contemporary European sociology and psychology. Any cultural manifestation cut off from the oxygen of true national culture withers and becomes introvert, morose, ugly, and meaningless, as were the Ottoman poets of the early twentieth century that Gökalp was fond of citing in this context. This mode of talking about the high emotional current of Eastern art music runs counter to a quite separate discourse, often presented in introductory chapters to volumes of music theory, which stresses the logical and rational foundations of art music.[40] This is the *ilm-e musiqi*, with an intellectual genealogy (an integral part of the presentation of this theory) stretching back to Ancient Greek music theory and the work of the Arab systematist philosophers. And yet it was precisely this body of theory, along with the 'quarter tones' that it generated, which Gökalp found 'irrational'. Gökalp's accusation of 'irrationality' makes a certain sense in terms of his overall view of music history:

> Like Western music, Eastern music grew out of that of Ancient Greece. The Ancient Greeks, not considering adequate the tones and semitones found in folk melodies, added to them quarter, eighth, and sixteenth tones, all of which they called quarter tones. These tones were not natural, they were artificial. As a result of this they are not to be found in the folk melodies of any nation. Thus Greek music was an artificial music based on unnatural tones that involved a boring monotony, consisting of endless repetition of the same melody.[41]

It is clear from this that the irrationality of quarter tones was a direct consequence of their being unnecessary and unnatural; irrationality lay in the fact of creating them when perfectly good (folk) music did

[39] Ibid. 45.

[40] See introductory chapters in Öztuna 1986, Yılmaz 1977, Karadeniz 1965, Özkan 1974, and Yekta 1922. For an ethnomusicological perspective upon the *ilm-e musiqi* in a quite different context, see Baily 1989, 37–59.

[41] Gökalp 1920, 130.

without. What Gökalp required was a Turkish version of opera which would banish the detested quarter tones through its appeal to popular taste and in its use of harmony, and would purge Turkish music of its Byzantine excrescences. Rationality in music consisted therefore of that which was 'natural', spontaneously created and approved by the folk. Perhaps the most important element of Gökalp's conception of Western music, formulated probably by the Italian Opera which had existed in Istanbul since 1797, and the reform of the Janissary band by Mehmet III, was the idea of polyphony. Whilst this had great power as an image of the division of labour so admired by Gökalp in the West, it was also a popularizing force in Western culture, making possible the development of opera and the blasting of the 'quarter tones' of Byzantine music into historical oblivion.

Gökalp had less to say on the subject of what Turkish folk music was, than on what it was not. The existence of a folk-music culture had been determined a priori, and its role in providing melodies to serve as building blocks for Western harmonic techniques had been decided on as a matter of ideological principle. The disappearance of 'Oriental' music was left to a series of repressive measures in the 1920s, notably the abolition of the *tarikatlar* (the Sufi orders, who were active patrons of art music) and the closure of the *Doğu Müziği Şubesi* (Eastern music section) of the Dârü' l-Elhan (later the Istanbul) Conservatory in 1926. This was followed by the banning of art music, but not folk music, from the radio stations in 1934 for two years. The attempt to create a national musical culture took place through the establishment of educational and research institutions, the technical advice of European advisers, and the media. As with the language reforms, the music reforms did not simply replace the old structures but provided something new—new forms of music and new ways of representing that music—which continue to coexist with those areas of musical activity which could not effectively be touched by any amount of reformist zeal.

2.5. Reform in Action: The Institutions of Urban Halk Music

The first reaction of reformers was to establish the necessary institutions of reform, and then seek guidance from European *alim* (scholars). Necip Asım (Yazıksız) argued in 1920 for the immediate establishment of a national opera modelled on that of the Hungarians, to be directed by a Hungarian *alim*.[42] But it was only in 1935, upon the establishment of the University of Ankara, that the professor of Philology Lazlo Rasonyi was able to make the initial invitation to Béla Bartók to conduct a field-trip in Turkey.[43] This was conceived as a venture not in establishing a national opera or symphony orchestra, but in instigating the systematic and scientific collection of folk music. For Bartók it was an opportunity to pursue his interest in the connections between 'old Turkish music', collected from the Kazan and Çeremiş Turks, and an 'old layer' of Hungarian folk music. He accepted the offer with alacrity and travelled, at the subsequent invitation of the Ankara *Halkevi* (People's House) to Istanbul, Ankara and then Adana in the south of Turkey. The production of his notes and transcriptions was delayed by the return to his compositional activities, the war, his emigration, and illness, and they were only published some time after his death. Bartók's folk music collection was however considered a success in terms of the example he set, particularly in his painstaking techniques of notation and transcription. This involved recording, using an Edison phonograph, and subsequently notating the performance from the wax cylinder. The phonograph had existed in Turkey since the early 1900s, but was only used as a research tool when Cemal Reşit (Rey), in Paris at the time, sent the director of the Dârü' l-Elhan, Yusuf Ziya Bey, a phonograph upon his request. As Şenel has illustrated, the emphasis in collection was upon the establishment of a large archive, and this was achieved through questionnaires and field-trips, in which the collectors would either use a phonograph or would rely on their hearing to transcribe from performance.[44] Early collection was thus a rather muddled compilation of songs of which the notator had no direct experience, songs which had been notated by hand as the singer sang, and more accurate transcriptions taken from wax cylinders. As a result, one song, 'Kozanoğlu', was notated several different times in different versions using different methods of collection and transcription. Bartók insisted on a field-work methodology which emphasized the careful selection of representative material and notational techniques in which every aspect of the performance

[42] Behar 1987, 94–5.
[43] For an account of Bartok's research trip to Turkey, see Saygun 1975 and Reinhard's introduction to Bartok 1976.
[44] Şenel 1987.

was notated objectively in as much detail as possible. Bartók's assistant, Adnan Saygun, subsequently followed his example, and the principal institutions of research in Turkey today still insist on detailed and 'objective' transcription for their archival material. The prestige that Turkish folk music gained from the attentions of such a figure was undoubtedly of high significance at the time.

The establishment of the machinery of a system of Western musical education and performance was the task of the German composer Paul Hindemith, who was invited by the Turkish government to supervise the foundation of the new Ankara school of music in 1935. In co-operation with the principals of the school, Ernst Praetorius and Eduard Zuckmayer, his task was to oversee the establishment of a Western style conservatory, producing a symphony orchestra, soloists, and composers. Hindemith launched himself into the task with characteristic energy and success. However, he left Ankara feeling vaguely dissatisfied. Having collaborated with Brecht on some early projects and founded the *Gebrauchtmusik* ('music-for-work') movement, he was highly conscious of the organic relation of music to society, and keenly aware of the problems of this kind of musical colonialism. The answer to the musical problem in Turkey was not simply to teach his students to write symphonies in a harmonic/contrapuntal idiom (although he had claimed at one point that this was the only direction in which music could progress), but to encourage them to produce the music that people wanted to hear. On this subject his 1936 report stated: 'They [his musicians] should be sent to the provinces to listen to the music of their own people, living amongst them for a period of months. They know nothing of the needs or capabilities of the populace.'[45]

Hindemith's sentiments ran counter to the spirit of the music reforms, which continued their two-point attack on the musical values of the nation. This consisted of recording, archival collection, and education in techniques of Western composition, working towards an eventual synthesis along the lines of the Russian 'Five'.[46] The invitation of Western *alim* was a symbolic expression of a Turkish notion of Western scientific and technological superiority. The *alim* themselves, men such as Hindemith who were searching for employment outside Germany and Central Europe during the years of Nazi power, often found their own understanding of their roles to be at

45 Cited in Skelton 1977, 136.

46 Mussorgsky, Rimsky-Korsakoff, Borodin, Cui, and Glasunov.

odds with those of their hosts. The rational organization of the music reforms was a notion cherished by the Ottoman and Turkish bureaucracy from the Tanzimat era on. An understanding of the institutional organization and philosophy of these reforms can best be understood in this context, and not in terms of the leadership provided by Western scholars. Sentiments such as those of Hindemith cited above were simply ignored; musicians studying Western music at the State Conservatory today are required to know little else, and are certainly not expected to conduct field trips in order to qualify as professional musicians in the State Orchestra.

Collection was initiated by the Ministry of Culture in 1920, but the official task of the collection was in the hands of the Dârü' l-Elhan. A group from the conservatory set out on the first collection expedition to the provinces of Adana, Gaziantep, Urfa, Niğde, Kayseri, and Sivas, the day after receiving Rey's phonograph from Paris on 31 August 1926. Following the successful publication of their results, four more trips followed between 1927 and 1932. The idea of establishing a national archive in the capital was mooted in the 1930s and the Ankara Musiki Muallim Mektebi (music teachers' school), later the State Conservatory, directed the research. Musicologists and composers such as Alnar, Akses, and Erkin, three of the Turkish version of the Russian 'Five', were involved in this process of collection and archival documentation, using the results to work tentatively towards the desired synthesis of Turkish folk and Western art-music techniques.

The responsibility for the collection of archival material at the Istanbul Conservatory and the State Conservatory at Ankara passed in 1966 to the National Institute of Folklore (Milli Folklor Enstitüsü), which is currently the National Folklore Research Bureau (Milli Folklor Araştırma Dairesi, or MIFAD) administered by the Ministry of Culture. The state continues to maintain institutions whose aim is to collect and document halk music. A more important overt function of these institutions is music education. The emphasis in the State Conservatories is on producing specialists (*uzman*) to lead research, and performers, teachers, and instrument makers to maintain the impetus of the Atatürkian music reforms. The organization of the State Conservatory in Istanbul, affiliated to the Istanbul Technical University at Maçka since 1976, is typical. There are seven principal schools within the conservatory: *Temel Bilim* (Basic Knowledge for music teachers), *Müzikoloji, Kom-*

pozisiyon, *Enstruman Yapım* (Instrument Construction), *Ses Eğitim* (Vocal Education), *Çalgı Eğitim* (Instrument Education), and *Halk Oyunları* (Folk Dances). These offer education to the level of *lisans* (for three or four years) in halk or sanat music. Each course requires participation in at least one instrument class. Of approximately 800 students, some 200 take classes in the *bağlama*, considered by teachers and pupils alike the most logical and representative Turkish folk-music instrument.

The State Conservatory only accepts pupils who have gained the top category of marks in their final *lise* examinations. Numbers are kept down to such a great extent that graduates of the conservatory can expect to find high-prestige jobs in the Turkish Radio and Television, or in other conservatories or teaching institutions. This maintains a core of élite musicians in the city, which defines itself and is defined in terms of the state project and the music reforms. Most, as well as performing, teaching, and collecting, work on 'experiments' (*denemeler*) in polyphonic arrangements of songs, the application of new instruments to song performance, the standardization or 'scientific' (*bilimsel*) development of musical instrument construction. In all this they identify themselves closely with the agendas of music reform. However, reformers realized at an early stage that the construction of a national music could not be restricted to a small group of specialists working in university departments. The media had an important role to play.

There is no doubt that, in their separate ways, television and radio transformed the music reforms. Collection and notation became directed towards the broadcast of the collected and notated music according to the canons of performance exemplified by the choirs, orchestras, and soloists of the Turkish Radio and Television (TRT). These, even though monophonic and not polyphonic as originally intended, in themselves embody radically new principles of performance. Indeed, the TRT soon took over as the dominant institution of research. Thus research, collection, performance, and state media policy became tightly interconnected. Seminal in this process was the formation by Mustafa Sarısözen of the *Yurttan Sesler* ('Voices from the Homeland') chorus for a radio programme of that name in 1948. Sarısözen had been connected with the Ankara State Conservatory archives from the late 1930s, and used these archives as material for his teaching and performing repertoire at the state radio station in Ankara. When Gültekin Oransay took over from Sarısözen as director of the Ankara State Conservatory in 1967, he transferred the archives in their entirety to the TRT, which had been founded four years previously. In 1967 the TRT began to conduct its own research, and by the end of the year some 1,738 melodies had been assembled.[47]

The funds controlled by the TRT have turned it into the largest and most effective institutional base of halk-music research and performance in the country, rivalled only by MIFAD. Popular interest in halk-music has been generated largely by the increased air space given to halk music programmes from the early 1970s onwards. There is a regular intake of new and youthful solo artists, male and female, every year. In Istanbul, TRT resources are at present distributed evenly between sanat and halk music. The *Halk Müzik Bölümü* employs some forty *kadrolu* (full-time) *sanatçı*, a smaller number of *mahalli* (regional) *sanatçı* employed on shorter contracts to provide authentic regional interpretations of the music of particular areas, and a group of *saz sanatçısı*. Most of these instrumentalists are *bağlama* players (who tend to alternate playing different sizes of this instrument which forms the central body of the orchestra), with three *kabak kemane* players, a *tar*, a *mey*, one *Karadeniz kemençesi*, and five players of *def*, *davul*, and other rhythm instruments. Radio and television programmes range from performances involving the entire body of TRT halk-music performers (such as the *Yurttan Sesler Korosu*) to smaller groups employing just one soloist and a smaller group of instrumentalists. These are increasingly filmed on location in an immediately identifiable rural setting. Recordings are seldom used more than once, necessitating a constant round of rehearsal, recording, and filming for TRT employees. Collection of new songs is thus fed immediately into exemplary performance. The polyphonicization (*çokseslileştirme*) of Turkish folk music on the model of Western technique has been relegated to a goal on a distant horizon, to be tackled when the pressing tasks (in the view of State Conservatory and TRT spokesmen) of collection, and the education of musicians who know and are able to perform their own music, have been completed.

A high level of media exposure involving young and personable performers has ensured an enthusiasm for halk music across wide sections of Turkish youth. However, successive Turkish governments have not seen the population of Turkey as passive consumers

[47] Markoff 1986.

of reformed culture. Simply to play a version of familiar songs regularly over the radio, using massed *bağlama* and huge choruses where one voice and one *bağlama* usually suffice, would not achieve anything. Listeners would simply switch off when they heard anything (in particular Western music) they did not like, as Szyliowicz pointed out in his study of Erdemli.[48] In the 1930s and 1940s, when battery-powered radios were first used in Turkish villages, the popular alternative was Egyptian radio, which used a more powerful frequency and was easier to pick up anyway. This had important consequences in the formation of attitudes and tastes in Turkish popular music.

Grass-roots reform was stressed by Atatürk through his own highly publicized popular lecture tours of rural Anatolia. Photographs prominently displayed in schools and public buildings throughout Turkey show him discussing politics with village notables, or teaching the new Latin script to the people at the Gülhane Park in Istanbul. The official institutional agent of provincial reform were the *Halk Evleri*, the People's Houses, which were established in all cities and many large towns in 1932. In an attempt to mobilize local-level reform, the *Halk Odaları* (People's Rooms) were established in many small towns and villages in 1944 and 1945. These had a dual purpose. They provided the means by which the precepts of reform could be mediated to townspeople and villagers. They also provided a centre for regional research activity, providing peripheral data for ideologues at the centre. As Karpat pointed out, the *Halk Odaları* affected relatively small numbers of people. Some 17,000 members were government workers and 10,000 were teachers. Approximately 27,000 were farmers.[49]

Folk-music education and instruction on the *bağlama* were often important aspects of the Village Institute's activity. Birdoğan notes that in a number of villages, locally and subsequently nationally well known *aşık* were co-opted as teachers. Aşık Dursun Cevlani taught *bağlama* at the Village Institute in Cılavuz, in the province of Kars, Aşık Talibi Coşkun taught at Yıldızeli, Sivas, and Aşık Veysel provided occasional tuition at Hasanoğlan, Sivas.[50] But the *Halk Evleri* and *Odaları* were closely identified with the policies of Atatürk's political party, the CHP, and in the early period of democratic experiment became a focus for rural opposition to these policies. As a

[48] Szyliowicz 1966, 100.
[49] Karpat 1963, 61.
[50] Birdoğan 1988, 16.

result they were closed by Menderes in 1951, after Atatürk's party was voted out of power in 1950. They were reopened in 1960 as the *Türk Kültür Dernekleri*, when a military *coup* led by General Gürsel sought to check the reaction to the Atatürkian reforms perceived to have been instigated by the Menderes government. Local institutions have not as a result functioned consistently in mediating reform.

2.6. *Dernek* and *Dershane*

In all Turkish cities today, *Halk Eğitim Merkezleri* provide cheap tuition or training in a number of skills. Whilst the teaching of music is limited by the funds that would be required to provide instruments, *folklor* (regional folk dancing) is a particularly popular option, requiring only one teacher (*çalıştırıcı*), and a *zurna* and *davul* combination to occupy thirty or forty dancers for most of a Sunday. These institutions do not generally contribute actively to tuition in music and musical instruments in Istanbul. The main focus for instruction on musical instruments and singing are private institutions known as *dershane* (indicating any informal place of learning) or *dernek/cemiyet* (club, society). Through the agency of these clubs, which function entirely without state support, the philosophy and practice of the music reforms are transmitted to professional musicians and amateur enthusiasts throughout Istanbul. Many of the proprietors and teachers in these private *dershane* are current or past employees of the TRT or graduates of the State Conservatories, who teach in the way they were or continue to be taught at these institutions.

Extra income is earned from their *dershane*, but the considerations that lead musicians to open up a *dershane* vary, and may embody a number of strategies. These include enabling the owner to participate in wider social networks, providing employment for musician friends and instrument makers, or supplying the owner with a source of material, technical, and moral support for their other professional activities as musicians. Most are situated close to the centre of the city, allowing TRT musicians to commute easily from their *dershane* to the TRT centres in Kuruçeşme and Harbiye, or to the State Conservatory in Maçka. In this way they are able to keep in touch with channels of information throughout the day, and are on the spot to reply to offers for performances at weddings, circumcisions, or concerts, which provide the most lucrative source of extra income to TRT employees. The owners interpret their activity in ideological terms. *Dershane* and *dernek* offering classes in *folklor* or halk music stress the contribution they make to national culture, maintaining the music and dance of the halk, providing the public with able players, and representing Turkey successfully on international competition stages. Those offering classes in art music stress the Turkish contribution to a rich 'Eastern' musical heritage, which arabesk threatens to debase and eventually obliterate. In each case, the language of the music reforms as embodied by the TRT and the State Conservatory prevails, in which the same themes are constantly reiterated: the maintenance of a Turkish cultural heritage, the threat of arabesk, the development of a systematized (*sistemleştirilmiş*) and scientific (*bilimsel*) approach to musical practice, and the education of musicians fit to lead the reform of Turkish music.

Members of the clubs undoubtedly respond positively to this kind of language, as a survey of two such clubs in 1990 clearly demonstrated.[51] One specialized in teaching the *bağlama* in the centre of the old city at Aksaray, close to the public-transport routes to the *gecekondu* to the west of the city walls, and I myself had participated in it as a student for nine months in 1987. The other, in Beşiktaş, ran classes in halk and sanat music, and also provided some tuition on the guitar and electric organ. I had taken lessons here on the *bağlama*, given classes in *solfej* (notation of Turkish halk music) in return for countless favours, and was on friendly terms with the two owners, both graduates of the State Conservatory. The response in both *dershane* to questions about their musical preferences showed the extent of the participant's commitment to halk music. In both clubs, a great deal of informal music-making took place outside the formal classes, which also provided a public arena for discussing music. Recent recordings and television programmes, musical plans and ambitions, research and collecting trips, compositions and experiments were recurrent topics of conversation, and transcribed

[51] With the assistance of the teachers and members of the Yavuz Top Halk Müzik Oğrenim Merkezi and the Ada Müzik Merkezi I received replies to 77 questionnaires detailing backgrounds, education, parental backgrounds, musical experience, and musical preferences. Whilst the results expressed as figures are unreliable and often misleading, the act of distributing these questionnaires was useful in enabling me to meet and discuss the issues that arose with a far wider range of people in the clubs than I had hitherto met.

notations of songs were circulated and photocopied for collection in individual archives.

This degree of enthusiasm might be considered surprising if the view is taken that cultural reform has little popular support. The numbers involved throughout Istanbul are large, although difficult to estimate. The two *dershane* discussed above attracted about 200 members at the beginning of the school year, in September. This number tailed off significantly, leaving about fifty continuing classes throughout the summer. Most members would stay for about two years, often promoting themselves through the classes when they wanted to move to more complex techniques. The membership of the clubs would thus renew itself every two years. The social base of membership is also extremely wide. Membership of the *dershane* or *dernek* depends critically upon its location, and relation to public-transport routes. At the first *dershane* discussed above, most members (58 per cent of the survey) lived in the *gecekondu* squatter towns to the west of the city walls. Their occupations ranged from professional (including accountants, lawyers, and doctors) to skilled or semi-skilled labour (including musicians, nurses, window-fitters, cooks). Approximately a third were students.[52] Their family backgrounds were significant. Virtually all of their parents had been born outside Istanbul, and 68 per cent had migrated to Istanbul from the east and south-east of Turkey, with a further 10 per cent migrating from the East Black Sea area. Of the total, only 14 per cent indicated that their fathers had professional or clerical occupations. Of the rest, 29 per cent indicated skilled labour in their own small businesses (such as garage mechanics, tailors, cobblers, lorry drivers), 38 per cent were unskilled labourers or farmers, and 19 per cent were unemployed. The use of a questionnaire to gather data from the students I could not get to know in person was far from satisfactory, but the figures indicate a membership of generally successful but not yet well established second-generation migrants from poor backgrounds. In the other *dershane*, the position ensured a slightly better heeled clientele, living for the most part in the Bosphorus area, including a higher number of students with parents born in Istanbul and working in professional occupations.

What both *dershane* had in common however was the age of its members. Folk-music clubs and societies draw largely on people

[52] The proportion of students is much higher at the beginning of the academic year in Sept.

between the age of 16 and 36, most of whom are unmarried. The appeal of *dershane* or *dernek* participation lay not so much in providing an opportunity to learn and participate in reformed, state-endorsed traditional music and dance, but in membership of what is in effect a youth club. Music, and talk about music, provided an idiom through which a particular form of sociability could take place. For many young men, the *dershane* provided an acceptable alternative as a locus of social activity to life in the café, which all felt was a waste of time and money. This aura of legitimacy ensured the membership of a number of female participants. In spite of the fact that the *bağlama* was perceived by men in the club to be an instrument suitable only for males and that the mobility of unmarried women in the districts to the west of the city walls was highly restricted, a third of the members at the club in Aksaray were women. All of the women who responded to the questionnaire were unmarried and had full-time jobs. They attended classes at the *dershane* after work, and left for their homes immediately the classes ended. Lengthy breaks for tea and cigarettes during the classes meant that there was still a heavy emphasis on the function of the *dershane* in providing a place in the city where young unmarried men and women could meet informally and inexpensively, without the latter being compromised in any way.

The activities of many *dernek* are geared towards participation in national competitions, in which winners qualify to participate in international events throughout Europe and the Middle East. Those who are not so successful make great efforts to contact competition organizers who would be prepared to finance a visit by a Turkish group. The time spent and energy invested, particularly in folk dancing, ensures a high degree of success on the international competition stage, meaning that funding is not difficult to find for some kind of trip for the smallest clubs, even though it might be to what are seen as more mundane destinations closer to home: Egypt, North Cyprus, Yugoslavia. Success in international folk festivals contrasts markedly with Turkey's continued failure in such events as the Eurovision song contest, and international sports events, which increases the sense of participation in a meaningful and worthwhile activity through the *dernek*. The cost of visas, passports, and contribution to housing funds[53] ensures that travel outside Turkey is restricted only

53 All Turks leaving Turkey are required to pay a contribution of $100 to the *Konut Fonu* (Housing Fund).

to the wealthy. Involvement in *dernek* provides young people, particularly women, with an opportunity to travel which they would not otherwise have.

This contrasts markedly with the sense of powerlessness and frustration often expressed by the same people. In conversation with individual members, a number of themes recurred, particularly the immediate costs of marriage in Istanbul, which include the provision of gold and the setting up of a home (and so prohibit marriage until both man and woman are in their late twenties). The tortuous process of graduating from university often takes many years, with no job guaranteed at the end. Travel, even within Turkey, has become an expensive luxury at the same time as the popular press in Turkey portrays tourism as a way of life to which all can aspire. Lack of opportunity to travel, sexual frustration, employment insecurity, and the poor image of Turkey resulting from what are seen as humiliating failures in an international cultural and sporting arena, form a tight knot of subjects. The language of powerlessness amongst this section of Turkish youth is focused sharply upon these themes. Informants and friends, even in the *dernek* and *dershane* in which I studied and worked, were highly articulate on these subjects. But involvement in these organizations was considered a positive step, a way of 'doing something' with one's time. In a narrow sense, it is certainly true that informal participation in these clubs widens circles of friends and contacts. I observed from beginning to end the process in which one particularly close friend met, courted and eventually married his present wife through involvement in his local *dernek*.

Widespread enthusiasm for and identification with official discourses of halk music should therefore not be seen simply in terms of the successful institutional organization of the music reforms. Official attempts to mediate the reforms to 'the people' resulted in the establishment of institutions which, as Karpat has illustrated, became quickly identified with local political factions.[54] Abolished and reinstated in the sway of macro-political change, these institutions could not provide a coherent and consistent programme of education with any success. For the most part the reforms only succeeded in creating a new élite (defined in opposition to an old élite) of musicians sustained by and sustaining in turn the State Conservatory and the TRT. Outside an organized official context,

[54] Karpat 1963.

however, the language generated by these institutions has been taken up and used in different ways to justify and make sense of participation in informal music clubs and societies throughout Istanbul.

What is perhaps most significant is that the employment of these discourses in the *dershane* and *dernek* does not invariably exclude an active interest and involvement in arabesk. Many *bağlama* students at both *dershane* were keen to progress to the *elektrobağlama* (or *elektrosaz*), an instrument ideally suited to playing arabesk. A number of professional *elektro* players attended courses at Yavuz Top's *dershane*, who were working as *müzisiyen* playing 'market' folk and arabesk music in the Taksim area of Istanbul in which most of the city's night-life is concentrated. In their questionnaires, a great many mentioned an active interest in the music of arabesk star Orhan Gencebay, whose virtuoso *bağlama* playing is highly rated by all except the most zealous ideologues. Taking into account the fact that responses to questionnaires can present an idealized version of how the respondee wants or feels constrained to represent themselves, attitudes towards arabesk were not as critical as I had expected. I quickly identified arabesk enthusiasts who were happy to talk about arabesk, but they would do so in a slightly conspiratorial manner, knowing that they would be letting themselves in for a lecture if they were overheard by any of their teachers. An interest in halk does not therefore exclude arabesk, or vice versa.

The overt aim of the music reforms was to displace 'popular' tastes in music, seen as Eastern and reactionary, in favour of a reformed Turkish folk music. Those connected with these reforms see their job in terms of resisting the all engulfing threat of arabesk. However, the conditions of local-level music-making in the city impose their own patterns. Members of *dernek* and *dershane* align themselves with the official representations of 'the folk' and the principles of TRT and State Conservatory performance practice for quite different reasons, which do not necessarily exclude an involvement in arabesk. Perhaps the most significant example of the reinterpretation of these discourses is the use of the *bağlama*, an instrument which continues to be used as a symbolic marker of all that is 'Turkish' in music, as a symbol of protest through politicized singer-musicians once connected with the TRT such as Arif Sağ. As with the reform of language, the music reforms have provided an additional rather than an alternative register of discourse. At some level or another, most professional musicians outside the TRT continue to play both folk music and arabesk to make a living. The music reforms have provided a language which can be used by musicians to represent, criticize, negociate, justify. To see how this is done it will be necessary to shift the focus from the ways in which halk music is talked about to the ways in which it is performed.

3

'Rule, System, and Technique': Reconstructing Turkish Folk Music

Many folk musicians claim that the value of their music lies in the fact that it is free from abstract and arbitrary rules. For Gökalp, 'Turkish music consists of melodies, unfettered by rule, system, and technique (*kaidesiz, usulsüz, fensiz*), of sincere songs which express the heart of the Turk'.[1] At the same time, rules, systems, and techniques are not only implicitly recognized, but explicitly taught. A way of talking about music as though it were systematic has been created under the social and historical circumstances described in the last chapter. The relationship of this language to what it purports to describe is complex, but provides an important key to the arabesk debate. Halk and arabesk must be seen above all as different ways of talking about music, rather than different ways of performing or experiencing music. To understand this relationship of language to practice it is necessary to look at the construction of a folk-music theory parallel to that of sanat music. This theory is based on the definition and systematization of a body of modal structures, instrument tunings, and rhythms, established through collection and notation, which are inextricably bound up with the role of the Turkish long-necked lute, the *bağlama*.

3.1. Defining Boundaries: *Makam* and *Ayak*

Turkish and Western musicologists have based their distinctions of rural folk music and urban art music on their respective modal structures (referred to as *ayak* and *makam*), reflecting the usual preference for evidence in research which is objectively measurable and supposedly beyond question. The attempt to define a pure and un-

[1] Gökalp 1923, 24.

contaminated 'Turkish' culture owed much to Kulturkreise ethnology. Certain remote rural areas were assumed to have been left behind by the passage of time, like rock pools at low tide, allowing the researcher to look back into his own past. On the basis of this, research was able to determine cultural influence in other more 'contaminated' areas. What 'the Turkish' was, however, had been decided in advance as the organizing and legitimizing myth of the Turkish state. In the case of music, it was assumed beyond doubt that the most original and basic modal structure was a gapped pentatonic scale.

The idea of pentatonicism is of vital significance in Eastern European musicology. Soviet ethnomusicology has taken as axiomatic the evolutionary primacy of pentatonicism as the universal folk mode from which all subsequent modal structures developed.[2] In Turkey this idea owes its existence to Bartók, who considered that the link between the 'old core' of Hungarian music and Turkish music could be seen at the level of the pentatonic melodies common to both repertories.[3] The idea that such links should exist in the first place was in turn motivated by current theories about the Ural–Altaic linguistic group. Thus, 'remote' areas provided relatively simple pentatonic modal structures. It could then be assumed that in any given repertory manifesting a range of modal structures, those melodies which came closest to pentatonicism, or which could be analysed in terms of a vestigial pentatonicism, could be considered the oldest and purest part of the repertory. Evidence for this argument was provided by the relatively simple fretting of the rural *bağlama*. Picken has pointed out the process in which frets were progressively added to the rural and urbanized *bağlama* in imitation of the classical long-necked lute, the *tanbur*.[4] Various sizes of the instrument have been found in Eastern Anatolia whose fretting is still pentatonic, but very few *bağlama* today are not fretted with seventeen or more notes to the octave, allowing players of the instrument to play 'in' *makam* if they wish.

For the Western musicologist the question of the relation of sanat-music terminology to halk music was relatively straightforward. Use of *makam* meant subsequent cultural influence from outside the village. Bartók, interested in the historical and cultural links between the 'old layers' of Hungarian and Turkish music, realized that all such manifestations of urban art music had to be kept clearly to one

[2] Belaiev 1963. [3] Bartok 1976, 38–41. [4] Picken 1975, 291.

side, although intellectual honesty required him to record their existence. When Adnan Saygun asked whether he should include instrumental *taksim* in their collection of Turkish folk music, Bartók replied: 'You are right, if it is a matter of genuine improvisation, then one cannot consider it to be a "Folk Melody". However, if improvisations of this kind are in vogue among peasant musicians of the villages, one must collect them from the folkloristic viewpoint . . .'.[5]

Later researchers have also been unable to avoid the use of the term *makam*. Reinhard, who had attempted to root out the most 'uncontaminated' Turkish culture among the Türkmen of the Toros Mountains, noted the use of the term *makam* in the sense of 'style' or 'genre'.[6] Needless to say, these 'makam' bear very little relationship to their urban counterparts. Tewari included a recording of a *taksim* in 'Hüseyini *makamı*' in his recording of music from Anzahar, an Alevi village in the province of Sivas.[7] A transcription of this shows clearly that, whilst there is some similarity in the tonal construction, there is little observance of the typical 'arch' of the classical *taksim*, or the *seyir*, the cadential tones and melodic figurations relevant to the *makam* as it is performed in the classical repertory.[8]

In the examples cited above, it is often hard to tell whether we are dealing with an attempt to absorb admired techniques of urban art music on the part of *bağlama* players, or the use of technical terminology from non-indigenous musical styles to increase the kudos of the indigenous music or musicians, in the way Afghan musicians described by Baily make use of Hindi music vocabulary.[9] The use of such terms is often problematic to observers who insist on a precise fit between theoretical language and that which it claims to explain. The issue is further complicated by the insistence of many ethnomusicologists on defining a bounded rural musical culture in opposition to a more volatile and international urban culture, represented by the notion of *makam*. This view receives a great deal of official encouragement in Turkey in spite of the fact that it is now less

[5] Bartok 1976, 8–9. [6] Reinhard 1962, 15–16. See also Neubauer 1971.

[7] *Turkish Village Music* recorded in Turkey by Laxmi Tewari, Explorer Series, Nonesuch Records. Picken criticizes Reinhard for introducing *makam* into his discussion of the nomadic Türkmen of the Toros, finding the term 'dangerous to use in the presence of folk musicians' (1962, 186).

[8] See Touma 1971. The most detailed account of the Turkish *makam* tradition and its relation to modal improvisation in English is Signell 1977. For a historical perspective, see Wright 1990.

[9] Baily 1981.

possible than ever to talk about a self-contained world of village culture, separate and distinct from that of 'the outside world'.

Turkish musicologists viewed this distinction in terms of the Turkist theory of culture outlined in Chapter 2. Difficulties of a different order arose for them in the definition of boundaries, particularly with respect to the modal structures of art and folk music. The difficulty lay in the terminology at hand to describe the findings of their research. In a series of articles in the *Türk Folklor Araştırmaları*, Arseven and Yönetken attempted to analyse the folk modal system without recourse to the terminology of the urban and 'Islamic' *makam*.[10] It is largely due to their efforts that the construction and codification of the system of *ayak* ('foot'), the 'folk' counterpart of the *makam* was achieved. This work was hindered by the fact that the Turkish musicologists available to carry out the task had been brought up in the urban art-music tradition and were seemingly unable, or at least reluctant, to abandon the terminology of the system in which they had been reared. Adnan Saygun, who assisted Bartók on his trip to Anatolia, was a typical example. He stated explicitly that the persistently 'flat' intervals in Turkish folk music, marked by Bartók with arrows to indicate inflexions of a simpler tonal framework, were in fact related to the micro-intervals of the classical *makam* system. His annotated edition of Bartók's research contains a list of pieces which he believes to have links with *makam*, and he uses the complicated sigla of art music in order to notate them.[11]

Today the problem is somewhat more complicated. Whilst the system has recently gained much currency, it is still common for folk musicians to make use of the terminology of classical theory. Amongst Turkish folk-music researchers and scholars this switching of codes depends on the context in which the statements are being made.[12] Use of art-music terminology potentially renders academic research in folk music acceptable and legitimate to a wider range of music scholars. In contexts in which wider interests are represented, the vocabulary of sanat music is deemed appropriate. What is at issue is a matter of explanatory power. The vestigial power of sanat-music theory can be seen in the diglossia which pertains to halk-music theory but not to that of sanat music. Folk-music performers and theorists are obliged to 'convert up', whilst those connected with

10 Arseven 1958, Yönetken 1961, 1962.

11 Saygun 1975, 251.

12 See Markoff 1986, 105, for a full discussion.

sanat music perceive no such need. The power of sanat-music theory resides only partially in an implied social disequilibrium. Art music still maintains an air of urban sophistication and élitism. But more important is the asymmetry in the way the two theories are viewed. In sanat-music theory, halk music exists as nothing more than a simplified version of the urban style. In the taxonomy of musical style put forward by Karadeniz, 'Halk music constitutes the third part of Turkish music . . . it is a simplified version of it, and not different from sanat music'.[13] It is this that allows sanat-music performers to include arrangements of rural *türkü* in their concerts, often as finales or encores. The peripheral relationship of halk to sanat music, as far as the latter was concerned, is demonstrated in one of the earliest collections of Turkish music, the seventeenth-century *Mecmua Saz-ü Söz* of Ali Ufki.[14] Art music dominates the centre of the page, whilst folk music is fitted round the sides. And yet the inclusion of both in the same collection, using the same system of notation, indicates that at some level they are commensurable. So at a theoretical and academic level the terminology of art music has continued to invade the space of folk music long after it was deemed to have lost its efficacy. The *makam* system continues to provide a more powerful mode of analysis.

The use of art-music terminology by many professional *bağlama* players and amateur enthusiasts outside an academic context has more of a rhetorical than analytic significance, appropriating the power of the *makam* as a symbol of logical and systematic musical organization. *Bağlama* methods, which generally have the quality of a treatise on Turkish halk-music theory, frequently contain lists of *ayak* and their *makam* equivalents.[15] In demonstrating their skills as *bağlama* players to me on first meetings, a number of musicians showed an encyclopaedic knowledge of regional style (*tavır*), plectrum movements, and regional tunings. An important part of this exegesis was a demonstration of short *taksim* on *makam*, introduced by 'this is Rast . . . , this is Hüseyini . . . , this is Uşşak . . .', and so on. The precise structure of these *makam* cannot be exactly rendered on the *bağlama*. The one-comma B flat required by most *makam* can only be played as a two-comma B flat. The concept of *seyir*, an

13 Karadeniz 1969, 177.

14 A fac. ed. of Ali Ufki's MS, ed. with a commentary by S. Elçin (1976) is available in Turkish.

15 See e.g. Yener 1987. A list of *ayak* and their 'equivalent' *makam* is contained in App. A.

integral part of *makam* theory, was generally not known. But in most cases *bağlama* players, particularly those working as professional arabesk musicians, were more familiar with the art-music terminology than the terminology of the *ayak* system. Most were reasonably familiar with Kerem and Garip, and would be able to refer these respectively to Uşşak or Hüseyini and Hicaz. Only conservatory teachers, however, were familiar with *ayak*, such as Kesik Kerem, or Kandilli Kerem, and their efforts to teach these terms to their *dershane* students were unsuccessful. Most of the students were if anything more familiar with the names of the basic *makam*. On one occasion, presented with the task of identifying the mode of a *türkü* in a class at Yavuz Top's *dershane*, a couple of people identified the piece as being in Karçığar (not a familiar *makam*), but were unaware of the *ayak* equivalent, Yanık Kerem. Many students at *dershane* in Istanbul could demonstrate a handful of *makam* on the *bağlama*, including Rast, Uşşak, Hüseyini, Hicaz, and occasionally Segah. The terminology of *makam* has both an analytical dimension, in that it provides a framework in which music is still largely perceived and explained, but also a rhetorical dimension, in that the presentation of *makam* theory by urban *bağlama* players signifies a scientific and systematic approach to musicianship and musical knowledge.

3.2. Individuality and Invention

In spite of this, halk music has continued to create and define its own discursive space. It has done so not just by analogy with, but also in opposition to, sanat-music theory. Halk music thus remains dependent upon that which it opposes. Gökalp implicitly established the principle that the pure culture of Turkey was the diametric opposite of high palace culture. Thus if the *şarkı* of art music was a composed, individual product, then the virtue of the *türkü* lay in its anonymity. One is the product of a composer (*bestekâr*) and the other is the product of the halk. Collected pieces are rejected by the *İcra Denetimi* (Performance Control) of the TRT if the pieces are held to be 'compositions' (*beste*). In other words, if the person from whom they were collected is known or thought to have made them up, then they cannot be considered as true folk music. Any suggestion of *makam* or *usul* is taken as evidence of individual composition. The labels *yapma* (construct) or *uydurma* (invention) are often used in this context. Their meaning is hard to pin down, since selection relies to a large extent upon the personal whims of the *İcra Denetimi* at the time. Many TRT musicians claim privately that a number of blatantly 'made up' pieces passing as folk music flood through the hands of the *İcra Denetimi*. There is great pressure on young musicians and singers at the TRT to get their pieces accepted, since their names are included in the repertoire and are often announced when they are performed on radio or television. Stories of sums of money being handed over to rural musicians to invent songs and claim that they heard them from their grandparents when they were children in their village are not uncommon.

The problem is particularly aggravated with regard to the question of musicians whose individual creations are known as such in the general repertoire of musicians in a particular locality. Songs of the *aşık* poet-musicians invariably include reference to the poet in the text. Whilst some commentators argue that individually composed songs can be sung as long as the name of the composer is not remembered, in practice there is little chance of this ever happening. At present, the policy of the TRT is thus not to include pieces which are known to be compositions of a particular individual if that individual is still alive. In this way there can be no suspicion of financial profit resulting from radio or television performance of their songs. This argument takes up a long-standing disapproval on the part of Muslim jurists of music-making for financial profit, but locates it in an entirely different ideological context.[16] The result is that whilst the songs of the Kırşehir *bağlama* player and composer Muharrem Ertaş are included in the TRT archive and frequently performed on television and radio, those of his son Neşet Ertaş, whose songs are equally well known through private market distribution, and are held by many to surpass those of his father, are not. By incorporating the work of the dead, the repertoire is allowed to expand, even though 'innovation' as such is denied.

Since evidence of *makam* suggests to the TRT that a piece has been composed, a difficulty arises over the inclusion of folk music from Azerbaijan into the TRT repertory. This has been popularized relatively recently by the current *tar* teacher at the State Conservatory in Istanbul, Dr Şenel Onaldı, and a handful of singers from the north-east of Turkey and Iranian Azerbaijan, notably Hüşenk Azeroğlu.

[16] See Ch. 7, s. 1.

Opinion is divided over its status as 'Turkish' halk music. Its supporters appeal to the unity of the Oghuz Turks. Its detractors point out its resemblance to art music in that it is constructed and performed around a set of eight modes known as *mugam*, bearing a loose resemblance to the *makam* of Turkish art music.[17] This by implication is the result of individually thought out composition and not the anonymous product of the folk. Rigid adherence to rules is held to be the determinant feature of the *beste* or *şarkı*, whilst true folk music is considered to be free from such restraint. According to this logic, the improvisations upon *mugam* which are common in Azeri music differ from art music *taksim* improvisations in not being bound by complex rules. Being free and natural, they are thus able to communicate more directly with the listener. For this reason, a TRT *tar* player pointed out to me that the *taksim* of Turkish art music does not have the ability to 'burn' him in the way that Azeri music does. These arguments create and defend the interest of cliques within the TRT. The popularity of Azeri music at a time when Soviet Azerbaijan was receiving much sympathetic news coverage in Turkey represented a direct threat to the amount of television and radio air time that musicians specializing in other regional interests could control. This air time not only ensured employment at the TRT in itself, but provided advertisement for their more remunerative activities as freelance singers. For singers and instrumentalists with claims to Azeri connections, it created a new regional field to appropriate and occupy. Terms such as *uydurma* and *yapma* are manipulated in these kinds of battles for symbolic capital.

The word *uydurma* (invention) covers two sides of a spectrum in the performance of Turkish music today. On the one hand, as we have seen, it covers the over-determinism of the *makam*; on the other, it can cover excessive freedom. Markoff has illustrated this with reference to a particular well-known chromatic 'variation' in the middle of a solo instrumental performance of the *türkü*, *Şeker Oğlan*, by the virtuoso *bağlama* player Arif Sağ.[18] While the variation is modest by the standards of virtuoso improvisation in the concerto cadenza of classical Western music, this is *uydurma* which verges in the opinion of Sağ's critics, upon *fantezi*. *Fantezi* suggests

[17] The *mugam* system as it is known in Turkey differs from its use in Azerbaijan (see Memmedov 1981). Few professional *tar* players in Istanbul have any connections with Azerbaijan, and those I knew had taught themselves the *mugam* from recordings imported from the Soviet Union.

[18] Markoff 1983, 204.

self-indulgent excess, implying a performance of halk music which brings it close to arabesk. Arabesk musicians however use the term to distinguish 'artful' arabesk from *koy*, 'heavy' (literally 'dark') arabesk. In one case the term *fantezi* is entirely negative, in the other positive. Both cover a form of *uydurma*, in which the issue is an element of obtrusive individuality.

3.3. Notation

We have seen the way in which the construction of a folk-music discourse has proceeded by analogy, creating a modal theory parallel to the organization of the *makam* system into modal groups and families. It has also defined itself in rigid opposition to the discourse it has sought to supplant, asserting anonymity rather than individuality, and planing off the eccentricities of virtuoso performance. The most important aspect of theory, which cements the whole discourse together, is notation. Notation is often taught as an exercise in logic (*mantık*), a way of thinking that relates closely to the nature of the *bağlama*. Notation is bound by that which can be played upon the *bağlama*, and the *bağlama* is bound by that which can be represented in notation. Notation has two principal functions for urban musicians which are seldom clearly differentiated. It allows for the preservation of collected music, being more durable than the perishable low-quality tapes that are generally used by collectors. It also serves as the most convenient method of transmission, allowing pieces to be memorized and learnt for performance.

Notation is taught from the beginning at the State Conservatory *Lise*, and is an essential part of the curriculum in all private music *dershane* in Istanbul. Of the three official classes a week at Yavuz Top's *dershane*, one was devoted entirely to *solfej* and notation skills. In the small music shops concentrated around Şehzadebaşı, which constitute a third area of informal music tuition and socializing, each establishment had a small sign proclaiming that lessons were given 'with notes' ('Nota ile saz dersleri verilir'). My first *bağlama* teacher at one such shop in 1983 had some familiarity with musical notation, but had immense difficulty writing down even the most elementary tunes. He earned his living playing 'market' halk and arabesk music in the *gazino* and *pavyon* in the area, and was employed by the owner of the shop (who could not read music) to give lessons every evening as the shop closed. Most of my half-hourly sessions were taken up by a laborious process of writing down tiny exercises which would take a matter of seconds to play. My offers to do the writing were brusquely dismissed, since this would have confused the teacher's control of the written representation of his trade. Seeing the notation of music as a practical rather than symbolic form of activity, this frustrated me immensely at the time.

The teachers at Yavuz Top's *dershane* were graduates of music conservatories and were highly proficient in reading and transcribing music. Teaching at the *dershane* begins with exercises in the recognition of the names of notes and the temporal values of the notation system. This rapidly progresses in the first year to work on individual pieces. First the notes are 'read', that is, sung to the names of the notes. Short fragments of a bar or two bars are repeated in strict time, until they have been memorized by everybody. When the end of the piece has been reached, it is repeated as a whole until a degree of fluency has been attained. At this point the words are then added and sung by the group. The aim of this exercise, which would usually occupy a two-hour class, is to increase fluency in reading notes and to develop the repertoire of the student. For both reasons, little-known *türkü* are chosen.

At a higher level, the exercise turns to the dictation of completely unknown pieces. In the *dershane* at which I studied, this exercise began in the third group (one lower than the top stream at the time), and was considered a necessary preliminary to the collection of original material in the field. The teacher sings and then plays the *türkü*. The class is required to work out the *ayak* and the *usul* (time signature of the piece). Dictation then proceeds bar by bar until the notes of the whole piece have been covered. The words are then added as a separate exercise. Defining *usul* involves recognition not only of recurrent rhythmic patterns but also of the distribution of words over melodic and rhythmic groupings. In a dictation exercise in which the *usul* might be one of two things, the position of syllables determines the matter. In one such exercise, most of us wrote out a section of a *türkü* as if it were in 4/4 (see Ex. 1). Ligatures have to follow the metrical division of the bar, and this cannot contradict the underlay of the words. Our teacher objected that a 4/4 *usul* meant that the word 'aman' in the second bar was split over two ligatures. We were instructed to arrange it in such a way that the metrical structure of the bar was reorganized from 2 + 2 + 2 + 2 to 2 + 3 + 3

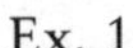

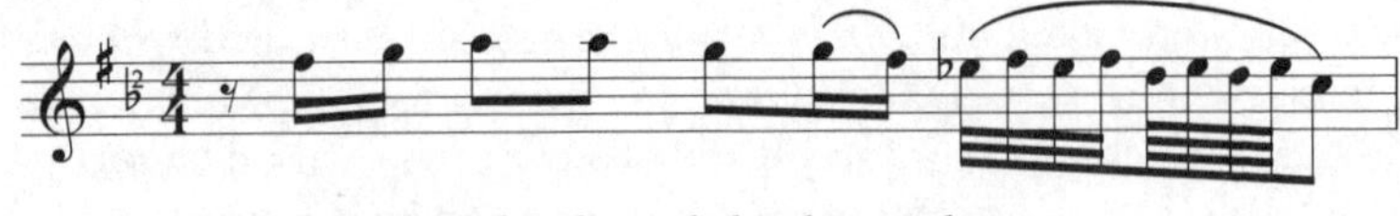

Ex. 2

(see Ex. 2). This therefore required an *usul* of 8/8 rather than 4/4, since a 4/4 *usul* would mean that a main beat would fall in the middle of a word.

Usul is held to fall into three categories, *basıt* ('simple', i.e. 1 + 1, 2 + 2), *karma* ('mixed', i.e. 2 + 3, 2 + 2 + 2 + 3), and *birleşik* ('combinatory', i.e. 3 + 2 + 2 + 3, 7 + 8), and are articulated into the smallest possible units of two and three.[19] *Usul* indicates this breakdown of values through a binary principle of performance on the *def*, *davul*, *darbuka*, or what ever instrument is providing the rhythm for an urban halk-music ensemble. Beats in the middle and edge of the instrument provide two tones, referred to respectively as *düm* and *tek*. A combination of *düm-tek* indicates a unit of two and *düm-tek-tek*, *düm-teka-tek*, or *düm-tek-teka* indicate three. When *usul* is being taught, students are required to move their hands as if conducting, in order to demonstrate their understanding of the rhythm by breaking it down into its constituent rhythmic cells. After renotating the piece discussed above, we were instructed to sing it

[19] Sarısözen 1962.

through, indicating the *usul* by conducting, in order to correct our mistake.

Notation imposes a way of perceiving the rhythm which might have little to do with the way the rhythm was perceived, if at all, by the person who originally provided the music. Our class would have performed the song dictated to us as if it were in 4/4, with a rhythm instrument supplying regular crotchet beats throughout. However, notational practice created a situation in which 4/4 was wrong and 8/8 was right. The authority of the teacher and his control of transcriptional technique would be backed up by the authority of the TRT, whose rhythm players spell out clearly the *usul* determined by the process of notation in broadcast versions of the song.

During classes I noticed a particular difficulty experienced by competent but musically illiterate musicians in differentiating the irregular and asymmetrical rhythms known as *aksak* ('limping') from simple regular *usul*. Having hoped to discover that *aksak* rhythms came as 'naturally' to Turkish children as regular rhythms, this both surprised and slightly disappointed me. The notation of *usul*, and the analysis of rhythm implied by it, may have been contradicting or running counter to a substantially different way of perceiving rhythm. Western staff notation enshrines the principle of the analytic breakdown of temporal values into the smallest possible units which articulate the rhythmic pattern. Let us take an *aksak* rhythm consisting of one 'weighted' value and one 'lightened' value. The weighting of the lightened to the weighted is not regular, that is to say, the lightened does not fit into the weighted on a regular whole number basis. Western musicologists have dealt with all *aksak* rhythms in transcription on the principle of a reduction to the smallest relationship between the units of 2 and 3. Thus the notation of the simplest *aksak* rhythm gives the lightened beat a value of 2 and the weighted a value of 3, creating an *usul* notated in Turkey as 5/8. More complicated ratios can be generated through the addition of cells (see Fig. 1).

After this the binary division of a weighted and a lightened value begins to break down into smaller units. Whilst a case may be made for the applicability of this system to Anatolian folk music in general, in that an analytic breakdown of this order may be arrived at through plectrum movements on the *bağlama*, a clear exception is the *kemençe* music of the Eastern Black Sea area. Amongst Black Sea musicians, particularly in the highland area above Şalpazarı in which

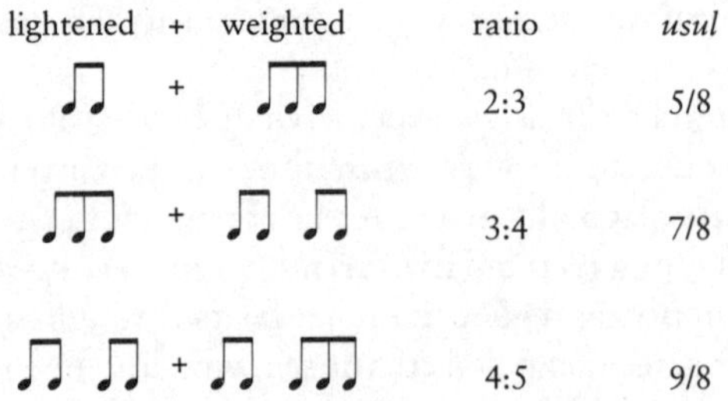

lightened + weighted	ratio	*usul*
♫ + ♫♪	2:3	5/8
♫♪ + ♫ ♫	3:4	7/8
♫ ♫ + ♫ ♫♪	4:5	9/8

Fig. 1. *Aksak* rhythms

I carried out field-work in 1987, *aksak* rhythms are executed and perceived as unequal binary patterns. Although no terminology exists to differentiate these from non-*aksak* rhythms, their binary quality can be demonstrated by the movements of the dancers in the *horon*, and by the left–right swaying, accompanied by the tapping of left and right feet, during improvised singing to *kayde*. The fact that the music is played on a bowed instrument also means that small rhythmic units are not articulated by separate movements, as they are when a *bağlama* is plucked. Typically the bowing technique of *kemençe* players in Şalpazarı makes only two movements for every rhythm, across the strings and back. This does not allow us to break down *kemençe* rhythms into clear subgroups of 2 and 3 as notation requires. Turkish collectors have consequently found Black Sea rhythms particularly enigmatic: not only is the *usul* hard to establish, as a result of the great speed at which the *kemençe* is played, but a given piece seldom settles down in one *usul* for any length of time. A typical improvisation over a melodic pattern (*kayde*) lasting about twenty minutes may change its *usul* (viewed purely in terms of notation) three or four times.

Since it is axiomatic for TRT notation that a piece has a single *usul*, unlimited scope is left for argument over exactly what the *usul* of a particular piece 'is'. This argument reaches particular intensity when it comes to the acceptance or rejection of notated folk music from the East Black Sea area for the TRT archives. The present director, Yücel Pasmakcı, pointed out to me that early collection of Black Sea music was marred by the fact that all *kayde* were considered to be in 5/8 and were notated accordingly. As a consequence of this he had been obliged to go through the entire Black Sea repertory in the archive in order to check and reinterpret what he felt was inaccurately notated material. The 'problem' of the rapid and complex Black Sea *usul* was doubly complicated. Firstly, simple *aksak* rhythms were chosen as the best way of representing these *usul*. Secondly, the use of Western notation ensures that the flexible unequal binary rhythms of Black Sea music remain submerged under an inflexible system in which each rhythmic value can be reduced to a single combination of 2s and 3s. In view of my research in the Black Sea area, I was frequently asked to check or actually write out transcriptions of Black Sea material by TRT vocal artists, either for inclusion into the TRT archives or for circulation amongst session musicians involved in commercial recordings. Here, as before, the main point of argument always lay in deciding upon *usul*. TRT musicians apparently chose the most complicated *aksak* rhythms that could be made to fit, in order to maximize the notational complexity of the music.

This probably resulted from a feeling of inferiority amongst professional Black Sea musicians in Istanbul associated with the TRT and State Conservatory. For them, Black Sea music had suffered as a result of the image cultivated by Mustafa Topaloğlu, whose version of an extremely simple song, 'Emine', had been a commercial success in Istanbul in 1986. One maintained that all *türkü* from his native Beşikdüzü were in a 9/8 *usul*. Working through transcriptions with him, my opinion was that the *usul* changed quite palpably from 5/8 to 7/8 to 9/8, whilst maintaining the same uneven binary pattern in strict time throughout. This was somewhat complicated by pauses for breath, coughs, forgetting the words, and so on. In spite of this he applied an inflexible 9/8 throughout. In this case the collector had recourse to the argument that his informant was musically illiterate (she was in fact his sister), and that he alone was in a position to know what was really intended. TRT researchers are obliged to regularize mistakes since their notations serve a dual purpose, as records and as texts for subsequent TRT performance.

The argument that Black Sea music performed on the *kemençe* embodies totally different principles of rhythmic organization, and that these principles cannot be coherently rendered through the use of Western notation, can be demonstrated clearly. A number of common tunes are played on the *kemençe*, in the upper reaches of the valley, and on the *bağlama* in the coastal regions which are more closely in touch with the central, urban domain of TRT halk music. The high pasture migration festivals in this transhumant society,

Ex. 3

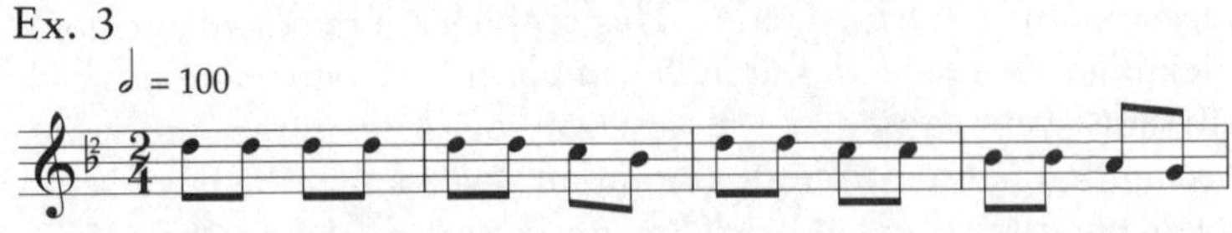

notably at Kadırga, Sultan Murat, and Sis Dağ, bring coastal and upper valley regions together, attracting large numbers of Black Sea migrant workers from Istanbul and Germany. Tunes thus pass up and down the valley, from *kemençe* to *bağlama* and vice versa. *Bağlama* and *kemençe* versions of the same tunes can be compared with one another. Performance upon the *bağlama* slows the tune down and imposes an inflexible pattern of plectrum movements which materialize as a single *usul*. The *kemençe* however maintains a fluid binary rhythm in which the same pattern of notes might materialize as something resembling 5/8, 7/8, or 9/8. As the tune moves down the mountain valley the rhythmic fluidity of the highland style freezes. A corollary of this is that what might be regarded in the upper valleys as aspects of the same *kayde* might be rendered as two quite different tunes when played on the *bağlama*, as in the case of the Beşikdüzü 'Saat Kaydesi' and the Görele *türkü*, 'Püskülüdür, Püskülü' (see Ex. 3). Very few *kemençe* players play *bağlama* at all. Upper and lower valley styles will perhaps continue to be kept apart by the rhythmic principles embodied in performance upon both instruments.[20]

The performance of music in the East Black Sea region is polyphonic, with a melody being played mostly in parallel fourths using the two top strings of the instrument. The bottom string is sometimes used to provide a drone and short figurations indicating the end of a phrase (see Ex. 4). TRT notation requires the music to be

Ex. 4

[20] See Stokes n.d. for a more detailed discussion of the circumstances in which *kemençe* and *bağlama* players in the East Black Sea region do exchange their repertoires.

thought of as monophonic, and notations therefore must reduce the complex interplay of polyphonic textures and inner rhythms of the *kemençe* to a single dimension. The figuration illustrated in Ex. 4 would be notated in full, but in such a way that its status as an ornamental figuration would not be immediately apparent to a TRT instrumentalist with little direct experience of *kemençe* music. The kind of reorchestration typical of commercially recorded folk music isolates fragments of the musical text in 'arrangements' referred to by studio musicians as *partisiyon*. In Ex. 4 the phrase was rendered in such a way that the ornamental figuration was taken up by the full orchestra, turning it into a major surface feature of the studio-recorded sound (see Ex. 5). Transcription thus flattens out the relationship between base structure and ornament. Commercial reorchestration subsequently allows for the possibility of a total reversal of their role.

Ex. 5

The process of collection and transcription also involves substantial modifications to the words. The first process has been the Turkification of the language.[21] For this reason the TRT archive has closed its doors on the substantial Greek repertory of the Eastern

[21] See above, Ch. 2, s. 3.

Black Sea, along with the Kurdish repertory in South-East Anatolia, although a number of these exist in translation. Similarly, words of foreign origin, though not 'dialect', are replaced when possible with Turkish equivalents. As many commentators have pointed out, this has resulted in some absurdities. A song from the north-east of Turkey beginning with the words 'Prahoda mindim sürdüm seyrana' ('I boarded the train and set off on a trip') exists in the TRT repertoire as 'Gemilere mindim sürdüm Samsun'a' ('I boarded the boat(s) and set off for Samsun'). Since the Russian word *prahod* is unacceptable, and no pure Turkish word for train exists, a boat trip is substituted for a train journey.[22] The conscientious collector has changed *seyran'a* to *Samsun'a*, on account of the Arabic origin of *seyran*, and later changes the destination of the trip from Baku (the capital and principal port of Soviet Azerbaijan) to Iğdır (a small city in the centre of Eastern Anatolia). The boat trip that results is highly improbable.

Whilst the language of the text is made to conform where possible to what has come to be thought of as pure Turkish, an effort is made to notate and stabilize regional accents. These however conform to urban stereotypes. The awareness of a 'Laz' dialect from the Eastern Black Sea goes back at least as far as early Ottoman times—a conclusion we can draw from the existence of a 'Laz' character in the Karagöz shadow play.[23] The inhabitants of the Eastern provinces of Trabzon, Rize, and Artvin are considered by Western Turks to belong in their entirety to this ethnic category, whereas in fact only a few do. It is thereby assumed that they all speak Lazca and the same variety of heavily accented Turkish, characterized by the reversal of voiced and unvoiced consonants, a regular shift from /g/ to /dz/ and mutations of vowel harmony. In Trabzon, however, the existence of at least five different dialects is recognized by everybody, and only one of these, namely that of Of and neighbouring Çaykara, conforms remotely to the 'Laz' stereotype. Thus non-Black Sea collectors will tend to interpret what they hear in terms of the stereotype even when entirely inappropriate. İbrahim Can, who was originally employed as a *Mahalli sanatçı* from the Black Sea area, once remarked to me that he was always encouraged to sing in 'correct' Istanbul Turkish in the *dernek* and *cemiyet* in Trabzon in which he participated. Now, ironically, as a representative singer from this area, he is required to sing in a made-up accent which only faintly resembles one which he never spoke in the first place.

22 Birdoğan 1988, 72. 23 And 1979, 73.

Similarly the entire structure of the 'original' is remoulded in the process of becoming a written text for performance. The Black Sea *kayde* is typically improvised, dialogic, and open-ended. Whilst it has rules of procedure, including formulaic introductory openings, relating the song and the singer to the events being celebrated, and individual 'signing-off' motives passing on the improvisation to another singer or closing the *kayde*, an abstract concept of form can be said to be lacking. This can only exist where there is fixed text. Anatolian *türkü* are known as fixed melodies with fixed texts. Black Sea *türkü* thus exhibit clearly the process of formalizing texts from a fund of improvised couplets.

Let us take as an example a common and entirely traditional *kayde* from the Beşikdüzü/Görele region. It was reformulated at the *bağlama* by a young musician from Görele in 1986, who gave the song a regular structure of repeated and non-repeated lines, editing and adding a few couplets to provide the formulaic opening with a more coherent narrative framework for a non-Black Sea audience. The *kayde* itself, sung in the Black Sea area with irregular alternations between its two constitutive elements lasting up to ten or fifteen minutes, was recast into a closed and regularized musical form of three stanzas separated by short instrumental passages, lasting some three or four minutes. It was sung in this form at the request of İbrahim Can, who recorded it, notated it, and submitted it to the TRT archives, and it was eventually sung by the TRT singer himself to a mass media audience. Two mixes of the master tape were made. The first was used in a commercial cassette using a core of Turkish instruments supported by Western percussion, guitar, and synthesizer. In the second mix, the Western instruments were dropped, leaving an 'authentic' performance of the song which was accepted by the *İcra Denetimi* of the TRT. Becoming something of a hit in the city of Trabzon, it filtered its way back to the area from which it came, but having effected the change in status from *kayde* to *türkü*, it had lost some of its currency and was only sung as it had been heard on the radio (see Ex. 6).[24]

The process of transformation is not always as successful as this. The same team constructed a *türkü* from another well-known

[24] Place-names in Ex. 6 (the full text of which can be found in Appendix B): Kadırga is the main focus of the high pasture migrations in the valleys to the west of Trabzon; Sis Dağı is the mountain which lies above Beşikdüzü and Görele. Like Kadırga it is the site of a large annual festival celebrating the migration.

Ex. 6 'Atmacayı Vurdular'

Speed ♩ = 98, voice transposed an octave up from the version recorded by İbrahim Can.

kayde. This had already enjoyed some popularity amongst Black Sea musicians in Istanbul, having been recorded as a *kayde* accompanied on the *kemençe* by Erkan Ocaklı. The words praise the beauty of a young boy, which earned it the nickname of the *ibne türküsü* ('buggers' song'). The same *bağlama* player took the *kayde*, along with some of the formalized expressions of the Ocaklı version, but restructured the melodic form and recast the text to create a somewhat more wholesome narrative of a boy torn between the love of two girls. References to the details of everyday life and the dense natural symbolism typical of *kayde* in their Black Sea form are largely omitted in order to address a wider audience, and the text is given a clear narrative structure. Being too obviously a 'construction' (*yapma*), however, the piece was turned down both by the archive and the *İcra Denetimi*, and the sales of the commercial cassette suffered. I was perhaps the only person who directly benefited from this song. Having first heard the song as it was being assembled by its collector, I learnt it in its invented form and, when in the Black Sea region later that year, sang it to great approval, unable to persuade anybody that I wasn't actually making it up on the spot myself.

In both cases we can see the same processes at work. The Black Sea *kayde* is essentially improvised dialogue over a fixed, but open-ended melodic ostinato. The *türkü* required by the TRT is a formally closed, repetitive, and monologic verse–chorus structure. In the process of transformation from one to the other, what is officially deemed to be the same song has radically changed its nature. It is no longer an improvised demonstration of social wit and verbal skill, but an anonymous product of 'the folk'.

Musicians in the Eastern Black Sea area do recognize that a process of mutation and modification is taking place in the appropriation of Black Sea music by the centralized urban discourse. This recognition was expressed to me in terms of the difference between the *kemençe* and the *bağlama*. The reason that trained and professional musicians from outside the Black Sea could not understand Black Sea music was that the *kemençe*, unlike the *bağlama*, 'does not have notes'. In their view, this comment reflected the difference between urbanized TRT folk music and what *kemençe* players were fond of referring to as the 'living' musical culture of the Eastern Black Sea. Being a fretted instrument, the *bağlama* is closely associated with the concept of notation. The very word for the instrument itself, meaning 'tied' or 'bound', refers to the frets that are tied onto its neck. Pitch thus has a clear spatial referent which can easily be named. The *kemençe* has no frets and thus 'no notes' in a very direct sense. Also, as we have seen, its music puts up some resistance to the steady encroachment of the values of TRT folk music, in which the *bağlama* and notation play a vital role.

3.4. The *Bağlama*

As Picken pointed out, 'the importance of the *saz* [*bağlama*] in the Turkish folk-musical tradition cannot be overestimated'.[25] Indeed today the *bağlama* has come to represent the very soul (*gönül*) of the musician; it is held to weep, to sob, to lament. It was mentioned originally as the *kopuz* in the fourteenth-century book of Dede Korkut, and is to be found in various forms throughout the Turkic world. Representing all that is Turkish in music and all that is musical in the Turk, it has a vital role to play in halk-music education. It is used to teach acoustics and instrument construction as well as folk-music theory, notation, and performance. In the opinion of most musicians, including those from the sanat-music genre, a stranger who wishes to understand Turkish music must begin with the *bağlama*. Having made my first steps upon this instrument, friends said in jest that I had become 'even more Turkish' than them.

Precise details concerning the complex processes of *bağlama* construction will be found in Picken's organological study.[26] The *bağlama* is roughly 80–90 cm in length. The body is typically of about 36 cm in length and 20 cm wide, either hollowed out (*oyma*) of a solid block of chestnut, mulberry, or hornbeam, or carvel-built from curved planks (*yapraklı*) and covered with a table (*göğüs*, 'breast') of soft coniferous wood. The neck (*sap*) is made most commonly from hornbeam, to which are bound a series of nylon frets. Today these are chromatic, with seven microtonal frets, giving seventeen notes to the octave.[27]

In its various lengths and sizes, ranging from *meydan* and *divan*, through *tanbura* and *bağlama*, to *cura*, the *bağlama*, frequently referred to just as the *saz* or 'instrument', forms the core of all folk-music ensembles and orchestras. The TRT *Yurttan Sesler* orchestra accompanies a chorus of some twenty-six men and women with four *divan* (D), seven *divan/bağlama* (B), and usually only one *cura* (C). These provide the central body of orchestral sound, and are placed centrally in relation to other single instruments in order to provide regional colour and a sustained bowed or blown sound to the ensemble (see Fig. 2).

[25] Picken 1975, 272. [26] Ibid. 200–94.

[27] The 17-note octave is as follows:

a b♭ b♭[2] b♮ c c♯ d e♭ e♭[2] e♮ f f‡ f♯ g g‡ g♯ a a

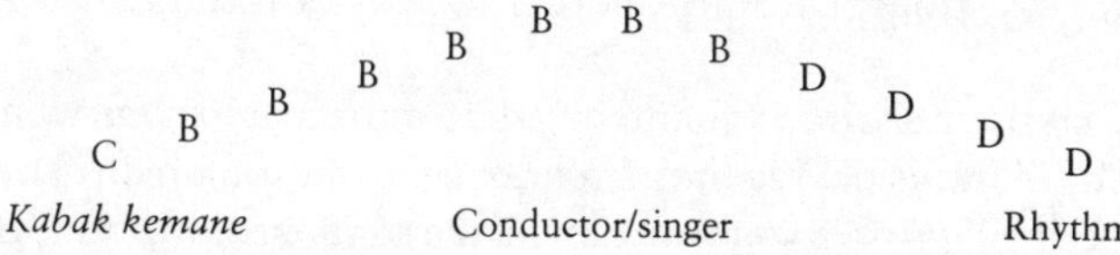

Fig. 2. The arrangement of a *Yurttan Sesler* orchestra, showing the relative positions of *baglama* (B), *cura* (C), and *divan* (D)

Smaller forces are used when halk music is performed in clubs and *gazino*, but the *bağlama* remains central in terms of numbers and the spatial organization of the *müzisiyen*. A TRT singer performing at a wedding celebration may bring along three or four electronically amplified *bağlama* ('elektrosaz'), of which one often has an octave bass doubler, one *kaval* or *kabak kemane*, and usually just one *darbuka* player, sometimes augmented by a *davul*, to provide the rhythm. Numbers are limited mainly by funds. A well-known TRT singer could expect fees of 2–3 million TL for a night's work in 1990,[28] but they would be expected to supply a band and pay for their transport. Depending on the quality and experience of the band, up to 1,000,000 TL would be distributed to the *müzisiyen* as fees and expenses. Even though one *elektrosaz* would do the job as well as four, the visual effect of a group of *bağlama* dominating the centre of the stage is considered desirable. The singer stands in front of the *müzisiyen* that he or she has brought along for the occasion. The *bağlama* occupy the middle space, flanked by a solo melody instrument on their right (i.e. to the left of the stage) and the rhythm on their left.

An important element of the rhetoric which surrounds the playing of the *bağlama* is its logical and systematic organization as a musical instrument. Golden Section proportions govern the construction of the body of the instrument. The positioning of the frets are worked out arithmetically from frequency ratios. Teaching upon the instrument stresses logic (*mantık)* at every turn. The fingering, that is, left-hand movements up and down the fretboard, is not left to chance or individual whim but systematized according to precise rules. Whilst the details of these rules are the subject of much discussion, the emphasis remains very much on the reduction of *bağlama* technique

[28] The exchange rate in the summer of 1990 was approximately 5,000 TL to the English £.

to basic, inflexible principles in order to provide a simple workable system.

It is first necessary to point out that movement from what we would describe as the low notes to the high, that is, 'up' the scale, is described in Turkish as motion 'down' the fretboard. Motion 'down' the scale is conversely 'upwards' motion on the instrument. There are further confusions for those taking their orientations from Western stringed instruments. The bottom, that is, lower-sounding, string course is described as the 'top' and the top, the 'bottom'. To avoid confusion, inverted commas will be used to indicate that the Turkish is being used. These orientations are based on the position of the *bağlama* relative to the human body, and not on an abstract concept of the 'height' of sounds (see Fig. 3).

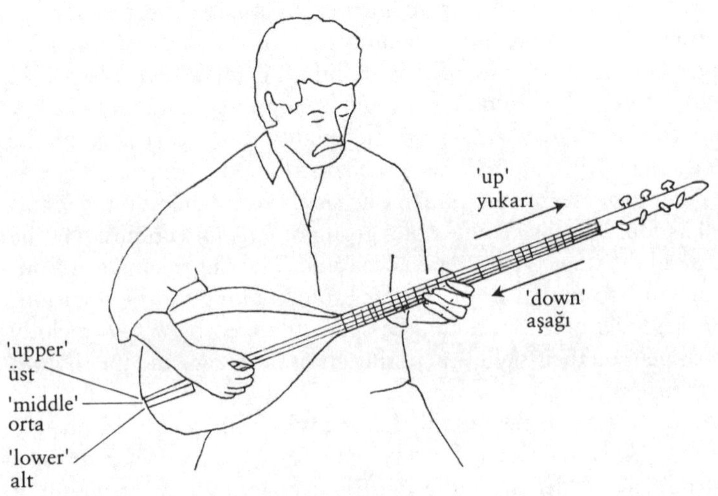

Fig. 3. Spatial orientation on the *bağlama*

Fingering follows the principle that the interval of a whole tone can only be comfortably bridged by the gap between first and third fingers (the index finger is numbered 'one', working upwards to the little finger, with the thumb as 'five'). Intervals smaller than a whole tone are bridged with the first and second finger. Augmented intervals larger than a tone are bridged with the first and fourth finger, by a leap to the second or third finger, or by sliding up the first finger. All of these depend slightly upon the direction in which the melody continues after the interval is played. The overriding principle is to allow the index finger to do the bulk of the work. Thus scalic motion is achieved through continual use of the first finger, sliding up and down to each note and leaving the second and third fingers for the 'echapée' ornamentation typical of *bağlama* figuration.

A small question mark hovers over the use of the little finger. Certain experts regard the little finger as being too weak to be used on its own. When at all possible, it has to be supported by the third finger. The little finger cannot be avoided in certain situations which would result in the excessive and awkward shifting of the first finger. In passages such as that shown in Ex. 7 a fingering of 1 3 4 3 1 might

Ex. 7

suggest itself. Certain teachers concede to the tendency to minimize shifting positions, whilst others apply theory with rigour. Yavuz Top taught his students the inflexible application of the above rule stressing the index finger: the A is approached from the G with a slide on the first finger, leaving the stronger second finger to cover the B flat, resulting in a fingering of 1 1 2 1 1.

A second principle taught in the urban *bağlama* school is the 'systematic' use of all three strings, allowing for the performance of extended scalic passages with the minimum of left-hand shifts up and down the keyboard. The technique of crossing strings to enable perfomance of passages without having to shift the hand is known by the term *pozisiyon* in Turkey. It might be thought of as a 'vertical' technique in that a rendition of a passage involves crossing string courses, as opposed to 'horizontal' technique, which would render the same passage by shifting position up the same string course.[29]

In relation to *pozisiyon*, there are two points to be made about 'rural' performance practice which are in fact more characteristic of non-tutored *bağlama* playing than any particular regional style. In

[29] The distinction made here between horizontal and vertical has much in common with the distinct cognitive patterns described by Baily in relation to left-hand movements on the *dutar* and *rebab* in Afghanistan (1977, 312).

this, ornamentation (*çarpma*) consists of an upper trill executed with the first finger upon the note being ornamented, and the second, third, or fourth finger carrying out the trill, which may or may not be articulated with separate plectrum movements. It is not possible to ornament a note comfortably on any other finger. Rural practice therefore prefers the 'horizontal' movement of the left hand. This allows the index finger to follow the melody up and down the fret-board on the lower string, incorporating as many *çarpma* as possible. The most important difference from urban practice lies in the 'rural' use of the 'middle' and 'upper' strings mostly as drones. The lower string course upon which the melody is played generally consists of two or three strings. If three, two are tuned to the same pitch whilst the other, generally of higher calibre, is tuned an octave lower. The 'middle' course generally consists of two strings tuned to unison, and the 'upper' of two tuned to an octave. If a melody is split up over these differently strung courses a lack of textural evenness results. Many musicians clearly find this unpalatable.

Tutored urban players, however, appeal to the logical character of the vertical technique. It is seen both as a method of solving the practical problem of how to perform a melody from notation, and also as an abstract intellectual exercise. The first stage in teaching the vertical technique consists of the application of the thumb to the 'upper' string course. Tuition always begins in what is considered by most to be the easiest of a number of different *bağlama* tunings, *kara düzen* (see Ex. 8). The outside strings are octave doubled, meaning

Ex. 8

that the interval between top and bottom strings can be interpreted as either two-fifths (i.e. an octave plus one note) or simply as a whole tone. Thus if the first finger is fixed on one fret, the tone lower is available with the thumb (fifth finger) on the top string vertically 'above' it. The vertical position has undoubted advantages in economizing position shifts. This can be illustrated clearly by the opening of an *oyun hava*, Çiçek Dağı, realized both in vertical and horizontal technique (see Ex. 9).

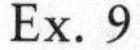

Ex. 9

To this can be added the use of the middle string. Given the wide gap between frets, it is not possible to run up and down scales with complete freedom, except in an oblique way which is only applied in exercises. However, limited use of all three strings is made in scalic passages when the demands made upon the little finger are not too excessive. An *oyun hava* which is used to teach this point of technique in particular is the Azeri Oyun Havası. In this case the piece is in Garip *ayağı* which descends below the finalis by two notes, thus necessitating the use of the middle string when played in its lower transposition. After the first two notes, horizontal technique would require the player to continue up the 'bottom' string, changing position continually. The application of the vertical technique involves no change of position, cutting back instead to the middle and upper strings when necessary (see Ex. 10).

Ex. 10

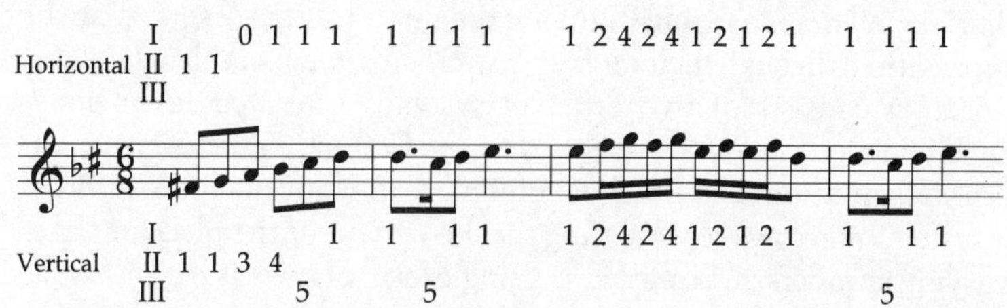

In performance these techniques are compromised,[30] but what is of importance is that the urban tuition of *bağlama* technique involves a process of induction from first principles. Rather than 'How is this passage played by rural performers?' the question asked by teachers is 'How can this passage be played efficiently and cleanly making systematic use of all of the instrument's resources?' The urban tuition of the *bağlama* makes its primary appeal to the Turkish sense of logic, serving as a model of rational thinking. The

[30] See below, s. 6.

application of logic to practical performance problems is held to result in a more efficient and 'clean' (*temiz*) style. Indeed, in many circles this is the highest expression of praise a *bağlama* player can receive.

3.5. Regional Style: *Tavır* and *Düzen*

The *bağlama* is also particularly important in the teaching of regional styles, known as *tavır* ('manner' or 'style'). *Tavır* is a difficult term to define with precision, for it can refer either to individual or to regional peculiarities of performance. Some musicians distinguish carefully between *uslub*, personal performance characteristics, and *tavır*, regional difference. But the flexibility of this concept is vital to its operation, making it a useful term in the context of appraisal and criticism. An evaluation of *tavır* in the context of singing style might indicate correct attention to details of dialect, ornamentation, or vocal production. It is also used as a polite way of suggesting that a rival does not know the correct way to sing a particular song, as in 'He sings well but he has the wrong *tavır*' ('Güzel bir sesi var, ama tavrı iyi değil'). In its wider application, it may perhaps be glossed as 'interpretation'.

On the *bağlama*, however, *tavır* can be reduced theoretically to patterns of ornamentation and plectrum movement which can be defined in terms of notation. These *tavır* provide a musical map of Turkey: all 'regions' (musicians are taught to recognize seven) can be represented through their *tavır* upon the *bağlama*. Complete *bağlama* notation consists of two different systems. One denotes melody, specifying left-hand movements over the fretboard in terms of Western staff notation. The other denotes plectrum movements in terms of a system of arrows representing the movement of the plectrum over varying numbers of strings. Every single facet of *tavır* as regional style is held to be notationally representable in these terms. However, since only a limited number of these exist, and TRT and conservatory-trained musicians are expected to know them by heart, it is common practice to indicate only the region from which the melody was collected in transcription, leaving the performer to select the correct pattern and apply it to the notes. Full plectrum notation is only generally to be found in teaching manuals.[31]

Theory and teaching techniques are based on an inductive process

[31] See Taptık 1977, Yener 1987, and Kurt 1989. Each have devised quite distinct systems of plectrum notation.

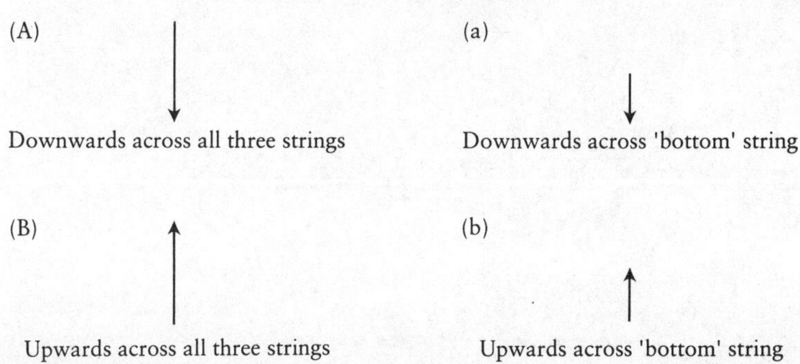

Fig. 4. The four basic plectrum movements in *tavır*

working from first principles towards known and collected *tavır*. Thus *bağlama* students at Yavuz Top's *dershane* were taught that there are in principle four basic plectrum movements, two, a and b, being subdivisions of the other two, A and B (see Fig. 4).

Tavır is held to be theoretically reducible to varying combinations of 'A', 'B', 'a', and 'b'. Until the end of the first year, students play all melodies in combinations of 'A' and 'B'. The differentiation between 'A' and 'a', 'B' and 'b'—crucial to *tavır*—is not covered until the next year, when graded exercises in *tavır* are introduced, taking the student up to the end of the third year. The final year is dedicated to more isolated regional styles. The more simple *tavır* taught in second and third years generally include Azeri, Zeybek, Teke Zotlaması, Tek Tezane, Konya (see Ex. 11).

It will be noted that these *tavır* are in effect templates which can be applied to various rhythmic and melodic situations. Here and there the pattern may be broken, especially to accommodate *pozisiyon*, but it is applied wherever possible throughout the piece. To these may be added more complex *tavır* applied only in specific situations, notably Derbeder, for the Eskişehir tune 'Kervan', and Fidayda or Hüdayda, associated with the *oyun hava* of that name. These *tavır* were generally taught in the last year of *dershane* tuition, although what is considered difficult and easy varies greatly from school to school. For example, Konya *tavır* was taught to third-year students at Yavuz Top's *dershane*, but only to final-year students at the State Conservatory, under the personal supervision of its director, Nida Tüfekçi.

The desire to systematize the differences in regional *tavır* in terms

Ex. 11

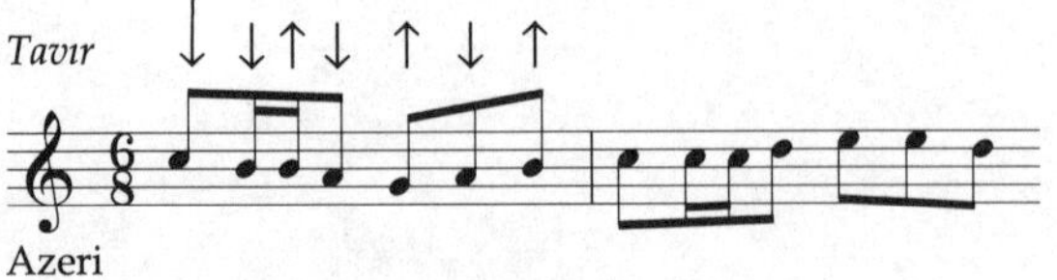

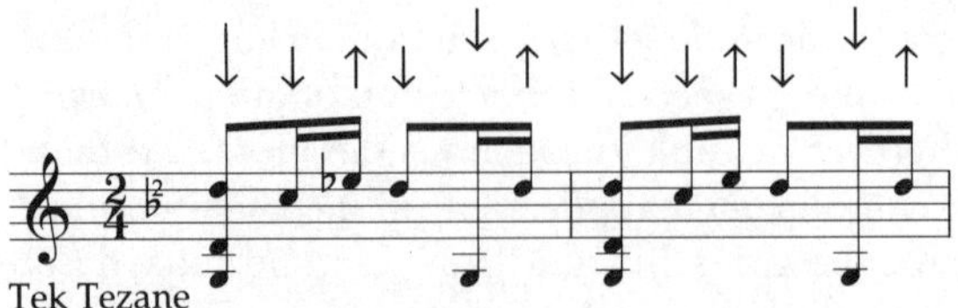

of *bağlama* plectrum movements is so strong that what many recognize as patently made-up *tavır* have recently come into existence. An example of this is 'Karadeniz *tezenesi*', the Black Sea plectrum pattern. This simply consists of adding a *çiftleme* ('doubling') to any *aksak* rhythm (see Fig. 5). It is agreed by all, and particularly by *bağlama* players in Trabzon and the Eastern Black Sea lowlands, that no such thing exists, even though it has been granted the status

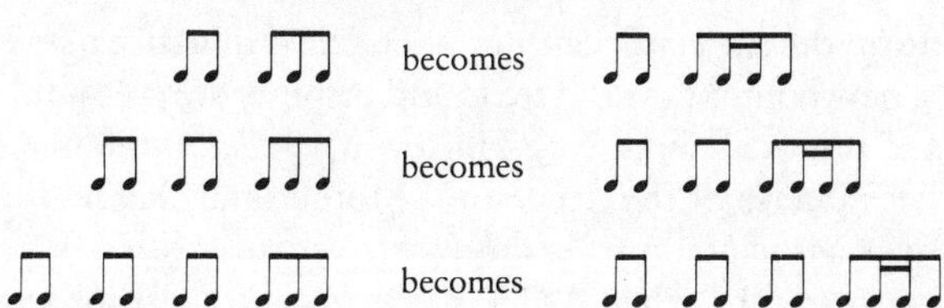

Fig. 5. Karadeniz *tavrı*

of *tavır* by Yener's recent *bağlama* method[32]—the first in fact to make any mention of it at all. What is of interest is that Black Sea musicologists such as Yener are clearly concerned with 'converting' traits of Black Sea musical style as played on the *kemençe* into the national currency of *bağlama* style.[33] A *dershane* that opened in Istanbul in 1988, specializing in Black Sea music and *folklor*, saw the development of a suitable *bağlama* representation of Black Sea music as one of its primary musical objectives.

The attempt to systematize the rural folk music of Turkey in terms reducible to *bağlama* figuration can be seen in another aspect of *tavır*: namely *düzen*, tuning systems. *Düzen* articulate the most important bifurcation of regional styles in Turkish folk music. Although a number exist, they divide themselves into two central tunings and a variety of peripheral tunings of more limited application. After 'Kara' or 'Bozuk' *düzeni*, the next most important is 'Aşık' or 'Bağlama' *düzeni* (see Ex. 12), which is particularly associated

Ex. 12

with the music of the *aşık*, the poet-musicians formerly referred to as *ozan* who principally come from the predominantly heterodox Alevi provinces of Sivas and Erzincan, Alevi communities in Istanbul and Ankara, and the mainly Sunni provinces of Kars and Erzurum. The recent popularity of their music owes something to the current perceived political affiliations of the Alevi who express a history of oppression and social protest in their music from the time of Pir Sultan Abdal, an Alevi musician and *pir* (saint) hanged by the Ot-

32 Yener 1987, 271. 33 See Stokes n.d.

toman state in the sixteenth century. The social injustice of every age provides a new context for old texts and inspires the creation of new ones. In the political climate of Turkey in 1987, dominated by the free-market policies of the Anavatan (Motherland) Party, this style of music was associated unshakably with leftist politics. It came as no surprise to anyone when Arif Sağ, the *bağlama* virtuoso and one of the foremost proponents of this style, became a candidate and was duly elected as deputy for the left-of-centre Sosyal Halkçı Partisi (Social Populist Party) in Ankara at the beginning of 1988. Bağlama *düzen* is rapidly becoming known as 'Arif *düzeni*'.

Even though it can be characterized under the heading of a handful of relatively simple melodic and cadential formulae, the extensive use of the middle string and the power of the emotions associated with Alevi music create an impression of technical difficulty. In Yavuz Top's *dershane* and most others, teaching always begins with Kara *düzen*. Not everyone agrees that the Aşık *düzeni* is more difficult. Nida Tüfekçi begins his students at the State Conservatory in Istanbul with this tuning, since it requires less movement of the hands up and down the neck of the instrument, and calls for close attention to the horizontal patterning of notes across the gamut. The ability to work out the horizontal relationships of notes on the fretboard is considered to lie at the heart of the logical character of the intrument. Most *dershane*, however, have to contend with a lower calibre of student, and the Kara *düzen* is the point of entry. In my experience, most students were particularly keen to progress to Aşık *düzeni*. There was thus always a certain tension between the teachers, who insisted on a thorough grounding in Kara *düzen* and left Aşık *düzeni* until the final year, and those students who wished to progress to Aşık *düzeni* as quickly as possible. Whilst I was studying at Yavuz Top's *dershane*, the more pushy students promoted themselves from first- to third-year groups in a matter of months, resulting in the lowering of standards in the third-year group and the exodus of the better players to the rival *dershane* of Arif Sağ, only a few minutes walk away in Aksaray. Since then, apparently, the situation has been reversed.

Apart from Kara and Aşık *düzeni*, numerous variations in tuning exist. Those which TRT musicians are expected to know are 'Misket', for tunes in Misket *ayağı* with an F sharp finalis (see Ex. 13); Müstezat, which has two tunings depending upon the particular finalis, F or C (see Ex. 14); and Fidayda, which like Fidayda *tezenesi*

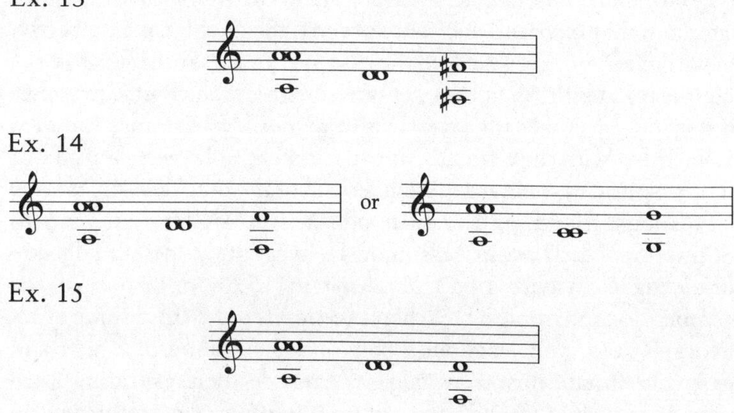

is only used in the *oyun hava* of that name (see Ex. 15). Picken and Markoff note a number of rural variants on these tunings, but these have no currency in Istanbul.[34] Of more interest is a tuning invented in Istanbul which has no currency in the rural area it claims to represent. 'Karadeniz *düzeni*' (see Ex. 16), in which the middle string

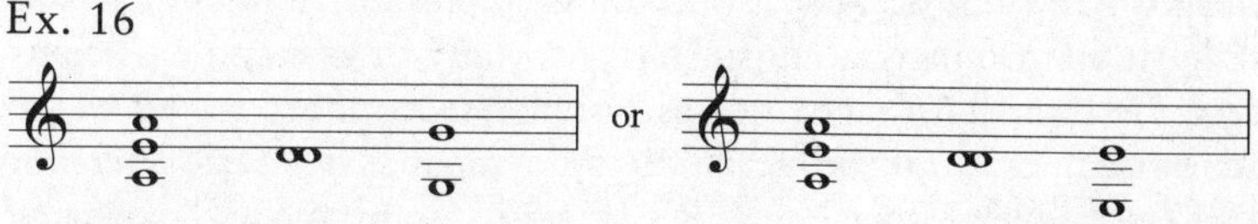

of the 'bottom' string course is tuned so as to leave an interval of a fifth and a fourth between the outer strings, replicates the parallel fourths of the Black Sea *kemençe*. Even though no musicologist would consider Karadeniz *düzeni* to be anything but an *uydurma* of the most blatant kind, this tuning has been used on numerous TRT recordings of Black Sea music, and appears to be gaining some currency.

3.6. The *Elektrosaz*, the *Piyasa*, and the Polyphony Debate: Live and Studio Performance of Halk Music

Outside the TRT and State Conservatories, these systematized techniques are known but seldom incorporated into the playing style of amateurs or musicians working in the commercial market (*piyasa*) in

[34] See Picken 1975, 256–88, and Markoff 1988.

Istanbul. *Dershane* impose a strict system of tuition in which they can claim that *tavır* and *düzen* are covered thoroughly and correctly. As we have seen, this is seldom the case in practice. Students promote themselves at will when they get bored with dull technical exercises in easy *düzen*, lower the standards in higher level groups, and then either leave with their friends or cause others to leave as a result of the disruption in standards. Membership of the *dershane* and *dernek* is thus highly fluid, and even though it is possible for students to follow the 'curriculum' assiduously, very few people do so. Returning to Yavuz Top's *dershane* in 1990, only one of the members, apart from the teachers, recognized me from three years before. Those who leave with some understanding of *düzen* and *tavır* can actuate this knowledge as exercises demonstrating a tutored approach to the *bağlama*, but not in other contexts of music-making. This knowledge is used in an iconic fashion to demonstrate participation in a milieu of musical learning.

Musicians who leave the State Conservatory might be lucky enough to find employment in the TRT. This is particularly desirable not just because it is in itself a prestigious and stable source of employment, but because it puts a high premium on the musician's skills in the commercial music market. Many singers and musicians describe their TRT activities as nothing more than a *reklam*, an advertisement, for more lucrative employment as live performers. In 1990, as a live performer, a TRT singer in Istanbul could expect to make between 1 and 2 million TL profit (after paying the *müzisiyen*) from an 'evening' at which he or she was appearing as the main star, whilst the monthly wage as a TRT *Kadrolo sanatcı* was only 2,200,000 TL. Musicians often perform at occasions at which they will receive either nothing or very little pay, as a favour to friends, or to establish themselves or repay debts to others. For most of my aquaintances at the TRT, these extra earnings would at least double their monthly income, and usually more. The informal performance of halk music, mixed as it often is with arabesk, in *gazino* or at any public social occasion requiring music, has necessitated the electronic amplification of the *bağlama*. Since the use of microphones is both costly and unreliable, the cheapest and most efficient form of amplification has been the development of a *bağlama* with an inbuilt pickup, known as the *elektrosaz*. It is difficult to establish who developed the 'elektro', but many *bağlama* makers and players cited Ragıp Akdeniz and Kazım Alkar as being separately the first musicians to popularize the *elektro* on commercial recordings in the 1970s. Even though most TRT musicians hardly regard this as a musical instrument at all, and certainly not as a legitimate object of research, it is a practical and generally cheap instrument which can be plugged straight into the PA system provided. The *elektro* belonging to Metin Eke, a State Conservatory trained *bağlama* player working as a backing musician in Istanbul, actually cost about half as much as the acoustic *bağlama* he used informally.

The *elektro* is thus an indispensable part of the urban musician's equipment, and provides the instrumental sound that accompanies singers in most contexts outside of the TRT and State Conservatories. Because the sound of the instrument is electronically generated, it only needs one string for each string course, making rapid figuration easier on the *elektro* than on the *bağlama*. There is very little note decay, allowing the *elektro*, unlike its acoustic counterpart, to sustain a tone almost indefinitely without the musician having to reiterate each note in the style characteristic of the *bağlama*. This has resulted in the development of a technique of *elektro* playing which is quite different to that of the *bağlama*, and one which is not taught in urban *dershane*, but acquired when an instrument is purchased.[35] The instrument is usually played in Kara *düzen*, but tuned in G so that the finalis is played on the middle string 'G' rather than the 'A' or 'D' of the 'bottom' string. Musicians therefore depend upon both 'bottom' and 'middle' strings more or less equally. Each note has to be damped after it is played, either with the left hand as it moves to the next note, or with the palm of the right hand if the melody requires a change of string. This makes any effort to reproduce the *tavır* described above totally impossible. An attempt to do so results in *çorba*, 'soup', a muddled and indistinct sound. The fact that the *elektro* has become the most practical and efficient instrument for urban *bağlama* players, whether they are involved in halk, arabesk, or, more commonly, both, has meant that the notions of *tavır* and *düzen* taught at the *dershane* and State Conservatory have very little practical application outside this situation of learning.

The gulf between theory and practice is most clear in the context of the debate over the 'polyphonicization' (*çokseslileştirme*) of Turkish music. The model for the polyphonicization of Turkish halk

[35] The term *keriz* ('messing about') is musicians' slang for the highly ornamented monophonic style used when playing *elektro*.

music is the *bağlama*. A number of Turkish musicologists have argued that Turkish folk music, as opposed to the monophonic art music, is essentially polyphonic.[36] The parallel fifths heard in *bağlama* performance particularly in Aşık *düzen* provide a model for a Turkish, rather than Western, theory of harmony based on the dominance of the perfect fourth. This is referred to as 'dörtlü', quartal harmony, and is based on the idea that a Turkish harmony should be allowed to develop according to principles already latent in Turkish folk music. Experiments in this kind of polyphony are often undertaken in an academic context, or in 'serious' concerts given by orchestras and choirs connected to academic institutions. These use orchestras of the kind developed by the TRT, consisting only of Turkish instruments. A noteworthy example of this is an arrangement of 'Ötme Bülbül' by my teacher Yavuz Top, on a commercially released cassette (*Deyişler*) which did not achieve wide sales, but was possessed and discussed by most of those professionally involved in Turkish folk music during my field-work in Istanbul.

This concept of polyphony contrasts with *üçlü-beşli* ('with-thirds, with-fifths'), which makes use of elements of Western functional harmony, based on an ordered progression of chordal sequences. This form of polyphony has been developed primarily in commercial recording studios, making full use of sixteen-track recording equipment and the availability of electric basses, electric guitars, and synthesizers. Many recent commercial cassettes contain at least one track of fairly heavily arranged songs in *üçlü-beşli* counterpoint, involving a second composed contrapuntal voice (*ikinci ses*), followed by simpler 'monophonic' (*tek sesli*) renditions of other songs. In these the arrangement only extends to the alternation of voice and instruments in carefully worked out *partisiyon*, accompanied quietly by bass and organ or guitar chords. It should be noted that the presence of a quiet chordal accompaniment, which is often mixed so low that it is virtually inaudible, is not taken in itself to imply polyphony. The musician or musicians supplying the organ, guitar, and bass parts work out the chordal pattern (*şifre*)

[36] See Arseven 1959 and Birdoğan 1988, 21–35. Birdoğan simply points out quartal and quintal counterpoint in Turkish folk music and advocates a policy of non-intervention. Musicians are inclined to change their minds on this issue. Yavuz Top's version of 'Ötme Bülbül' on *Deyişler* was perhaps the most elaborate arrangement of its time, but in 1990 he had come to feel it was somewhat contrived. He produced a follow-up (*Deyişler 2*) in which he sings on his own to the accompaniment of one *bağlama* in what was regarded as the traditional style.

amongst themselves, without consulting the singers or producers, who rarely have any understanding of Western harmonic techniques anyway.

Orchestration consists of synthesizer, electric bass, the basic ensemble used in TRT recordings making use of only two or three musicians doubled on different tracks, and a solo instrument of bowed or sustained sound, such as *kemençe*, *zurna, tulum, kabak kemane*, or accordion. The composition of the rhythm section in commercial recordings of halk music reflects that of arabesk, namely a *darbuka*, a *hollo* (a frame drum of Egyptian provenance), and a *def*. Two mixes are made, in one of which the Western instruments are omitted. Songs from this mix are then submitted to the *İcra Denetimi* of the TRT for possible radio and television performance. If the songs are performed, it is not only beneficial for the musician's career within the TRT, but provides an effective advertisement for the cassette. The cassette, in turn, rarely provides significant income for the singer, but is considered to act as effective publicity for his or her services as a live performer.

The distribution of instruments across the channels of a sixteen-track studio for a commercial cassette of Black Sea music recorded in August 1990 ('İşte Karadeniz' by İbrahim Can) was as follows: (1)–(2) blank, (3)–(6) *bağlama*, (7) blank, (8) voice, (9) blank, (10) *darbuka*, (11) *hollo*, (12) *def*, (13) blank, (14) *kemençe* or *tulum*, (15) electric bass, (16) acoustic guitar.[37] Simple counterpoint and chordal backing contribute in the view of singers and producers to a more 'contemporary' sound, one which has become familiar through studio-recorded arabesk and, to a certain extent, with Greek popular music. *Üçlü-beşli* counterpoint in which the second contrapuntal part follows the main voice in simple parallel motion is the only form of polyphony which is suited to the demands of 'the market'. Anything else falls immediately into the category of an experiment, and producers are reluctant to become involved. This became starkly clear when I was asked by one TRT singer to write polyphonic arrangements of a couple of songs which were to be included in his second commercial cassette. He asked me to keep them simple, so as to allow for performance under awkward studio conditions. One

[37] A synthesizer is usually used. On this occasion, when the musicians were working to a very tight schedule, the keyboard player had not turned up. As a last resort, I had been asked to play on a borrowed keyboard. The bass player then volunteered to try adding chords with the guitar he had brought with him for a concert later that evening. The producer and singer were both delighted with the result.

was an Artvin *türkü*, which I arranged in *üçlü-beşli* counterpoint. The other was an Ordu *türkü* whose chorus I arranged in three-part *dörtlü* harmony. I duly wrote out my arrangements in score and in parts, and had them ready for the recording session. The producer however had decided, apparently over the singer's head, that he was in principle against the idea. Even though he would have welcomed experimentation under different circumstances, he said, it was a matter of what people wanted to hear. Counterpoint just 'does not suit' Turkish music ('Türk müziğine yaraşmiyor'). The first arrangement was abandoned without further ado. The second was to go ahead as planned, but I was only given ten minutes to rehearse the small chorus which had been assembled for this purpose. On the first run through, the second vocal part missed its entry as a result of misreading a full bar's rest during which the other part entered. The producer immediately waved his hands in the air and informed us that we would do this one unarranged as well.

My ready acquiescence to this was met with some relief and surprise, since it was probably assumed that these arrangements were offered in the spirit of international co-operation, of my own free will. In fact I had been dragooned into producing them in return for numerous favours. My involvement was reluctant from the start and I was highly embarrassed at the prospect of my work, actually dashed off in a hurry in the reasonably sure knowledge that they would not be used, being subjected to critical examination by his TRT colleagues. But the experiment was the subject of some brief discussion, which added weight to rumours in the TRT that the singer in question was working on 'polyphonic experiments'. His dedication to musical progress was thus established beyond question.

There were several reasons for my reluctance to involve myself in his 'experiments'. As an outside observer, my opinions were held to be of value, and one of the first questions acquaintances high in the TRT and official halk-music hierarchies would ask me was where I stood on this particular issue. Generally our commitment to the principle of monophony was the same, even though our motivations were entirely different. For them, radical change in the performance practices associated with the TRT in the direction of polyphonic folk music would have rendered the music upon which they had based and continued to base their careers obsolete at a stroke. They were also overtly committed to the belief that the Turkish people would never approve of any musical ideas which had their origin outside Turkey. An artificial and hastily induced polyphonicization would do nothing but damage.

For my part, I did not want to accelerate change in the monophonic music in which I was interested. I had also expressed my views on several occasions in public, and did not want to be seen contradicting myself. These utterances reiterated a variety of received 'statements' with which I had become familiar as I absorbed, actively and passively, the habitus of TRT music-making. Given my shaky command of the Turkish language in front of a microphone, it was invariably the safest and easiest procedure to stick to what I knew I could express simply, clearly, and uncontroversially. I argued that Turkish music was essentially monophonic, and that changing this would change its identity as the music the folk created and understood, that the Turkish contribution to Western culture lay most effectively in what Turks knew they were capable of doing well, and not in cheap imitations, and so on. In musicological circles I frequently cited the fascination with 'oriental' monophony in the works of composers who shaped twentieth-century Western musical thought, from Wagner and Debussy to Messiaen, and the self-conscious return to monophony as part of the general economization of technique in the work of the American Minimalists, notably Terry Riley, and more recently in various pieces by Howard Skempton, Piers Hellawell, and Christian Wolff. Privately, my involvement in Turkish music had been motivated by a desire to immerse myself in a radically different kind of music; the difference between the severe monophony of Turkish sanat and halk music and the overweight polyphony of the musical traditions in which I had been brought up, namely late nineteenth- and early twentieth-century Anglican choral music, was as great as I could conceivably imagine at the time.

Polyphonic experiments took place in circles in which these experiments would be understood, but would not disrupt the canon of musical performance propagated by the State Conservatory and the TRT and the jobs associated with it. Halk music could not move too far from the starkly 'monophonic' performance style of arabesk, since this would alienate urban halk-music performers from the majority of their listeners and patrons outside the TRT, upon whom they were highly dependent. In 1987 there was much to suggest that this starkly monophonic style, both in halk (typified by Belkis Akkale) and arabesk, completely dominated the commercial cassette market. The notion of 'experimentation' extends the language of system and logic applied to the *bağlama* in such a way that the instrument provides a model for the future evolution of Turkish music. Systematic *bağlama* playing and a theory of Turkish harmony based upon the *bağlama* remain important ideas about halk music, which are mobilized in particular situations in particular ways, but only tangentially affect its practice in live performance and studio work. This practice can only be understood in terms of other representations of urban musicianship, and these are inextricably bound up with arabesk.

4
Arabesk

The ethnographic present refers to 25 August 1990, when I attended a *Halk Konseri* (People's Concert) featuring Müslüm Gürses, one of a series of free events organized for the Gülhane Park festival. The park is a small wooded area on the slopes between the Topkapı palace and Saray Burnu, the 'Seraglio Point', containing a zoo and a number of tea gardens, all of which are packed on summer weekends. The park is a popular destination for afternoon excursions, since it can be reached easily by train from the outlying suburbs and *gecekondu* areas to the west of the city walls.

The programme is due to start at 7.00 in the evening, with the main act appearing at 9.00. Knowing that this will be a popular concert, I arrive at about 5.00, by which time it is already difficult to find a space on the wooden benches close to the stage. Shortly after I find a place, people are already occupying spaces on the beaten earth slopes opposite the stage, climbing up trees, and clinging to the scaffolding supporting the lighting system. The audience is predominantly male and between 15 and 25 years old, well but cheaply dressed, arriving in groups of four or five. Maltepe cigarette smoke fills the air. Vendors of *simit* bread rings, sunflower seeds, 'Kola', and *ayran* circulate amongst the steadily accumulating crowd. The programme begins with a burst of disco music over the PA system, which precedes about fifteen minutes of advertisements. One of these features the arabesk singer Emrah. A chorus of boos erupts from the audience. The disco music continues when the advertisements stop. In the auditorium in front of me, about three young men have stood up on the bench, and dance to the music, watched now by a crowd of tens of thousands. The music comes to a halt just before 7.00, and a chorus of 'Müslüm, Müslüm' begins.

The lights go up, and a man walks to the centre of the stage to a roar of applause, but it is a false alarm; he adjusts a cable on the floor, and walks off to laughter, ironic clapping, and a renewed chorus of 'Müslüm, Müslüm'. The MC finally arrives, a young and well-known comedian. He explains that he normally does a short show at this point, but since he knows that everybody is impatient to see Müslüm, tonight he will just introduce the programme. The first number on the programme is provided by a light-music singer, better known amongst an older generation than those present to hear Müslüm, accompanied by a keyboard and rhythm box. The second part of the show, preceding the main act, is supplied by Okay Temiz, a drummer associated in Turkey with progressive jazz and experimental music. His huge set of Western and assorted African drums is accompanied by a band of sanat-music performers, who provide a continuous backing music for a series of acts, a magician, two belly-dancers, and two halk-music singers, Arif Şentürk and Süreyya Davulcuoğlu. Attention is hardly on the show, but on the steady flow of arrivals packing the front benches, causing sporadic scuffles, and on the increasingly dangerous acrobatics required of those climbing to the few available tree branches with a view of the stage. In spite of the heavy amplification of the music, it is possible to hear chants of 'Müslüm, Müslüm' from all sides. The main source of entertainment is the crowd itself. Nobody seems to notice when Okay Temiz suddenly stops playing as the next belly-dance act is due to start, and walks off stage. There is feeble applause and a pause. A man walks to a microphone at the front. He explains that Okay Temiz refuses to play to such an inattentive audience, and that everyone would now have to wait for three-quarters of an hour without entertainment until Müslüm arrived.

The band, consisting of eight violins, *ney*, *ud*, *kanun*, electric bass, synthesizer, *darbuka*, *def*, and *davul*, tunes up. A silver suit is spotted moving towards the stage, and the announcer's introduction is scarcely audible above the roar of voices. As he takes his place on the stage, chants of 'Müslüm, Müslüm' give way to 'Müslüm, *buraya!*' ('Müslüm, look this way!'). The only way to see now is to stand on the bench, but people remain in their places. Without addressing the audience, Müslüm begins a forty-five-minute set, singing his best-known songs to ecstatic applause as each one begins. Each song gives way to a better-known one. Most people are standing up and moving forward. Two young men behind me are sitting down, both holding their heads in their hands, and occasionally rolling backwards and forwards on their seats. Tears pour down their faces. Someone to my left holds a cardboard placard, on which the words '*TRT'e hayir! Magic Box'e hayir! Müslüm Baba . . .*' ('No to the TRT! No to Magic Box![1] Daddy Müslüm . . . ') are just legible. The singer, who has hardly spoken a word up to this point, thanks the crowd and says that he will sing just one more song. Everybody around me leaps to their feet and races forward. The man with the placard is now in front of me, on somebody's shoulders, in the gangway between the benches. One of the many policemen who have appeared, apparently in order to keep the gangway clear, taps the man with a baton and orders him to get down and move out of the way. He refuses. The policeman moves forward to grab him, but they lurch forward out of his grasp. The policeman gives up and walks back, shaking his head and smiling to himself.

An article in *Güneş* the next day describes crowds of 60,000 *Müslümcü* at Gülhane Park under a headline proclaiming 'Arabesk'e Zafer!' ('Victory for Arabesk!'). Most papers report the angry words of Okay Temiz with sympathy, and his discourteous treatment at the hands of an unruly crowd. Accounts focus on the heavy police presence and the large number of 'incidents'. Once again, it would appear, a generous attempt to provide the Turkish people with interesting and experimental music is rejected in favour of arabesk.

Arabesk lies at the heart of this problem, in which the music is perceived as an aspect of a wider situation. A number of Turkish observers have pointed out that arabesk can no longer be seen just as music, but as a form of social and cultural existence.[2] The idea that 'everything is arabesk' now has wide currency. From a variety of critical perspectives, arabesk has attracted widespread condemnation. These critical discourses have dominated the way in which arabesk has been represented. Indeed, it might be argued that arabesk has no voice of its own, no way of representing itself, which does not at the same time condemn it out of hand. But what constitutes condemnation from the point of view of certain critical discourses is, to those who listen to arabesk, simply the subject-matter of all good music, an upside-down, unjust world, in which the only certainties are emotions connected with loneliness and alienation. There is thus a certain fit between the negative view of Turkish

[1] 'Magic Box' is a privately-owned television channel which began broadcasting non-stop Western popular music shows and videos in Turkey in 1990.

[2] See Belge 1989, Güngör 1990.

commentators on the subject of arabesk, and the views of the people who listen to arabesk.

A useful starting-point in this chapter will be some of the musicological, sociological, and political commentaries on the subject of arabesk. Musicians associated with arabesk negotiate their professional identities in terms of these discourses. On the one hand they use the all-embracing concept of arabesk to make sense of their experience of the city; a complex, uncertain, and apparently disintegrating social environment. On the other hand, they construct categories within arabesk, defining themselves as representing more positive interests than that represented by 'real' arabesk. In other words, these representations are not just passively accepted, but manipulated and used.

4.1. Musicological Critique: Arabesk and Arab Music

Musicologists see arabesk as the end result of a process of *yozlaşma* (degeneration, literally, 'becoming wild') affecting Turkish art and folk music. This is seen as having its roots in the development of an Arab popular music, associated particularly with musical films. Concurrently, in this view, Turkish art music had been undergoing a long process of simplification and relaxation of the strict rules of classical *şarkı* form. Towards the end of the nineteenth century, the 'romantic' song school of Haci Arif Bey established a 6–8 line *şarkı* form called *nevzemin*, accompanied by texts written in a more simple and direct language. The implication, for writers who have discussed arabesk from a musicological perspective, is that Turkish sanat music has failed to provide an effective counterweight to Arab film music.[3]

Turkish musicologists have represented Turkish art music (*Türk sanat musikisi*) as a cosmopolitan, Middle Eastern music, which is the result of a centuries-long fusion of Arab, Persian, and Turkish musical styles in the Ottoman palace in Istanbul. Arel has stressed the Turkish contribution to the theory, instrumentarium, and teaching of this music, mediated through the presence of Turkish teachers in the most prestigious conservatories outside Istanbul, in Damascus and Baghdad, such as Mesut Cemil, Refik Fersan, Muhiddin Targan, and Çevdet Çağla.[4] The reaction to this cosmo-

[3] See in particular Öztuna 1987. [4] Arel 1969.

politan style began in Egypt towards the end of the nineteenth century, but it was not until the 1920s that film and radio reformulated and popularized the new Egyptian music. The Egyptian film industry began its activities in 1927, but the new reputation that Egyptian film was soon to enjoy started from 1933, with the production of *Al-warda al-bayḍā*, which was made by and starred Mohammed Abdulwahhab. Following the success of a musical film by the Syrian singer Nadirah in 1932, it was a light musical drama, constructed around the vocal skills of the central protagonist. The music for these films was eclectic, combining Western operatic and dance music techniques, Egyptian folk music, and the *makam* of the art-music tradition. In conformity to Egyptian tastes to this day, the film music was essentially vocal; the talents and skills of the vocalist dominated the music and the films which served as their vehicle. In spite of this, the orchestras that accompanied the singers in these films were large and cosmopolitan, using instruments drawn from the art-music instrumentarium (*ney, kanun, ud*) and Western instruments (violin, flute), with a particular emphasis on percussion (*def*, cymbals, *zilli maşa*, castanet, *darbuka*). The combined effects of a well-established, largely foreign-owned recording industry, which began producing Egyptian music as early as 1904, the Egyptian National Radio station, opened in 1934 and subsequently dominated by the music of Umm Kulthum, and the musical film made Egyptian music highly popular throughout the Eastern Mediterranean.[5]

The effects of Egyptian film and radio began to be felt in Turkey in the 1930s. Kocabaş and Güngör have argued that this was directly attributable to the ban imposed upon the radio broadcasting of Turkish art music between 1934 and 1936.[6] In 1935, 8,082 officially registered radio receivers existed in Turkey. Of these, 2,838 were to be found in rural areas. Unable to hear music that they enjoyed, they either turned off their sets, as Szyliowicz has described in Erdemli,[7] or tuned into Egyptian radio, which was easily available as a result of its high broadcasting frequency. It is impossible to identify with any accuracy the amount of time people spent listening

[5] For an account of the early history of commercial recording in Egypt see Danielson 1988.

[6] See Güngör 1990, 55. Güngör draws upon Kocabaş U. (1980) *Şirket Telsizden Devlet Radyosuna* (Ankara, SBF Yay) for figures concerning the numbers and distribution of radio sets in Turkey during this period.

[7] Szyliowicz 1966, 100.

to Egyptian music from this period on, but Turkish translations of the songs of Abdulwahhab dominated the commercial recording market in Turkey. Translations of 'Ya Dunyā, Yā gharāmī; Yā dam' i, Yā ibtisāmī' ('O World, O My Love; O My Tears, O My Laughter'), 'Aḥibbu īsht al-ḥurriyya ziyy al-ṭuyūr fawqa al-aghṣān' ('I Long to Live Free, like the Birds on the Branches'), and a number of songs from Abdulwahhab's musical film *Aşkın Gözyaşları* ('The Tears of Love') sung by Hafız Burhan Sesyılmaz became the most highly selling records in Turkey during the 1930s.[8] Other Arab music stars associated with Egyptian films, such as Leyla Murad, Farid al-Atrash, and his sister Asmahan al-Atrash, became famous in Turkey in much the same way.

Official attempts were made in Turkey to check the popularity of Egyptian film and Egyptian radio, which by the 1940s must have been an essential part of the cinematic and musical experience of rural and urban Turks. In the twelve years between 1936 and 1948, 130 Egyptian films were shown in Turkey.[9] In 1948, both the importation of films from Turkey and the performance of Egyptian film music in Arabic were banned by the Matbuat Umum Müdürlüğü (General Directorate of the Press). This initially had the effect of creating a secondary industry in Turkey of translating and imitating Egyptian film. Öztuna emphasizes a common critical theme when he points out that the real damage was done by a heavy-handed and insensitive bureaucratic reaction to undesirable trends in popular tastes. Arabic songs, being in Arabic, were neither fully understood nor entirely appropriated by the Turkish audience. In Turkish, however, the same songs were memorized, and the same film plots, circulated in cheap written and pictorial publications, became more firmly established than ever before. Furthermore, a team of twelve musicians who worked in this secondary translation and performance industry had their work broadcast frequently on the national radio.[10]

Early Turkish cinema followed Egyptian models closely, as in Muhsin Ertuğrul's film *Allah'ın Cenneti*, with songs by Münir Nurettin Selçuk, released in 1939. This team worked on a number of highly popular films, including *Kahveci Güzeli* of 1941 and *Halıcı Kız* of 1957. However, it is argued by a number of people involved in the film industry at that time that Egyptian musical films were not the only models for early Turkish musical film. The first Turkish film

[8] Öztuna 1987, 54. [9] Ibid. 50. [10] Ibid. 51.

with sound, *İstanbul Sokakları* (*The streets of Istanbul*), produced by Muhsin Ertuğrul with the Fitaş company in 1931, was closely modelled on the American film, *The Jazz Singer*. Turkish film directors were able to draw on Arab, Indian, and American popular cinematic traditions, but soon began to develop in their own directions. All of these made extensive use of music. *Hac Yolunda* (*On Pilgrimage*) was the first of a series of religious films produced by Hürrem Erman, which achieved wide popularity in Turkey at a time when pilgrimage was all but impossible. This shaped a taste for historical subjects filmed in exotic locations by the Erman brothers, particularly Baghdad, for many of which the music was provided by the art-music composer, Sadettin Kaynak.

In 1946 the first of a series of musical 'village films' ('Köy Filmleri') was produced by Baha Gelenbevi, *Yanık Kaval* (*The Burning Flute*). Later, the films of Hüseyin Peyda, such as *Söyleyin Anama Ağlamasın* (*Tell Mother, Don't Let Her Cry*) of 1950, were set in the south-east of Turkey and followed this trend, but adopted a more self-conscious 'realism' in spite of a heavy reliance on the 'musical' format. A particular feature of his films was the musical graveside lament, but the 'realistic' portrayal of village life was deemed subversive and *Söyleyin Anama Ağlamasın* was banned. One of the most striking pieces of 'realistic' cinema was produced by Lütfi Akad with Kemal Film in 1952, *Kanun Namına* (*In the Name of the Law*). This related the true story of garage mechanic Nazım Usta (played by Ayhan Işık) whose marriage is broken up by his sister-in-law Nezahat and a man, Halil, who is in love with Nazım's wife Ayten. The plot involves the introduction of Nazım to a *femme fatale*, Perihan, with whom he eventually falls in love. In this way his marriage is successfully destroyed by the plotters. When he learns the truth, Nazım kills Nezahat and Halil and wounds his wife. Chased by the police, he flees to his garage, but eventually surrenders. In its use of tragic narratives and crimes of honour, this film provided a model for arabesk cinema of the 1970s and 1980s.[11]

It is certainly incorrect to see arabesk cinema as nothing more than a pale imitation of Egyptian musicals, since by the 1950s there was an entrenched tradition of Turkish language musical films on exotic, religious, and rural subjects, as well as the kind of *verismo* plots typified by *Kanun Namına*. In the same way it is impossible to

[11] See Scognamillo 1987. For brief discussions of Turkish popular cinema in English, see Dorsay 1989 and Özgüven 1989.

describe arabesk as nothing more than Egyptian music with Turkish words. The musical models with which arabesk musicians are familiar today certainly include but are not limited to Egyptian music and musicians. Indian music enjoyed a brief period of popularity in the 1950s. Even though Orhan Gencebay rejects the idea that his music is arabesk, preferring instead the description 'Türk Müziğinin özgür icraası' ('the free performance of Turkish Music'),[12] his music is decidedly eclectic, drawing upon his experience as a halk-music performer, Western popular genres, and Indian music. He plays the sitar himself on *Aşk Ben Yaratmadım*, and a widely circulated promotional postcard of him shows him sitting on the floor in front of a vase of flowers, surrounded by *bağlama*, playing the sitar. Ali Osman Erbaşı, a well-known producer and *bağlama* player in the commercial music market, mentioned that he had bought a sitar from a penniless 'European hippy' returning from the East and very much wanted to use it. In spite of studying a Ravi Shankar video at length he lamented that he had still not been able to teach himself to play anything on the instrument. Whilst arabesk *darbuka* players often cite Egyptian musicians as their chief source of inspiration, such as Hambuda, Setrak, Sait Artis, Hasan Evvel, and Muhammed el-Arabi, many that I met had an equal fascination for Indian *tabla* players. Reyhan Dinlettir, bongo player for Ferdi Tayfur, showed me a variety of *tabla* playing techniques on the bongos that he had learnt by studying videos of the Indian *tabla* virtuosi Hüseyin Rahmani and Muhammet Rafi. Knowledge of Indian music and musicians marks a certain 'cosmopolitan' sophistication amongst arabesk musicians. This constitutes one of the ways in which arabesk musicians distance themselves from the notion that their music is simply an imitation of 'Arab music'.

But for most musicologists, arabesk is simply a Turkish version of Arab popular music, itself only a degenerate form of Ottoman Turkish art music. The vehicle of this music and the cause of its degeneration was the cinema, which made it available to a mass audience. Güngör sees the process of degeneration beginning with Sadettin Kaynak's involvement with the films of the Erman brothers in the 1950s. She cites Kaynak's knowledge of the folk music of south-eastern Turkey, a religious musical education as a *hafız* and *mevlidhan*, and a deep knowledge of the music of the Arab world.

[12] Interview with Gülsün Karamustafa, 'Arabesk Türkiye'de en çok dinlenen müzik', *Gösteri*, 16 (1982), 76–7.

His wide experience of music outside the Turkish art-music conservatories and quest for an individual, popular style led to a 'breaking of the shell' ('kabuğun çatlaması') of the classical forms.[13] From this the arabesk of Orhan Gencebay and Ferdi Tayfur directly follow. In her analysis, the weakening of the hold of classical forms had begun with what Turkish musical historiography defines as the 'Romantic School' of Turkish art music, the new *şarkı* form developed by Haci Arif Bey and later popularized by Şevki Bey. Thus weakened, Turkish music was unable to withstand the changes wrought by the popularization of the genre through musical film. Whilst many musicians would disagree with this low evaluation of the music of Sadettin Kaynak, considered by many to be the last great *usta* of Turkish classical music, the relation of the degeneration of the genre to mass media circulation is accepted by most musicologists in their written and verbal denunciations of arabesk.

For Öztuna, arabesk is the *alter ego* of sanat music; the one standing for that which characterizes the Arab style (*uslub*) and the southern mind, with its self-indulgent immersion in all that comes easily and naturally in music, the other for the intellectual rigour and sense of balanced decorum, backed up by the weight of imperial tradition, in the cold north of the Islamic world. As a respected musicologist, Öztuna is typically ambivalent in finding much to praise in the Arab style as characterized by film music. Particularly praiseworthy is the 'length and calm clarity of the voice' ('Sesin uzunluğu ve berraklığı'), its 'sparkling quality' ('parlaklığı'), its 'fullness' ('tokluğu'), its 'depth and vocalise' ('davudiliği ve gırtlak nağmeleri'), the large and cosmopolitan orchestras, the advanced use of 'light counterpoint' ('hafif çokseslilik'), and a musical atmosphere which 'immediately absorbs and bewitches one' ('insanı derhal saran ve cezbeden').[14]

He deplores, none the less, the lack of historical consciousness and the general ignorance of the rules of classical composition on the part of the composers. This, he suggests, is a result of an overindulgence in vocal skills, the lack of attention to details of composition and the failure to cultivate adequate instrumental skills. He points out that such composers as Şeyh Selame Hicazi and Seyyid Derviş only became famous by riding on the coat-tails of the singers they wrote for. Most composers simply did not understand music ('hiç bir musiki sistemini bilmiyorlardı'—'they did not understand any

[13] Güngör 1990, 58. [14] Öztuna 1987, 48–9.

musical system at all').[15] As we have seen, Turkish instrumental playing in art- and folk-music genres stresses the importance of system and logic. The *bağlama* provides a model of logical thinking to such an extent that a good player is often said to play with the precision of a machine. This high evaluation of logic, system, and 'science' (*bilim*) can be extended to cover not just performance but composition and the entire programme of 'modernizing' Turkish music. In general it might be said that to criticize the actions of anybody in Turkey as unsystematic (that is, without *usul*, implying order, logic, system, decorum) is to criticize them very severely.

Most tellingly, Öztuna criticizes the Arab style as being exaggerated, possessing an excess of uncontrolled emotion ('his mübalağası').[16] Transplanting itself to Turkey this music ironically took firmest root in the very city which created the imperial style of Ottoman art music, appealing most to those of 'degenerate taste' ('zevki bozulmuşlar').[17] To summarize the terms of Öztuna's criticism, the Arab style and arabesk are overindulgent to the voice at the expense of compositional and instrumental technique; this musical laxness, coupled with the exaggerated means of expressing emotion, resulted in it appealing to the lowest of tastes. It is, in short, a degenerate version of all that is good in Turkish sanat music. The principal framework of the criticism of Öztuna, Güngör, and others is one in which arabesk is represented as a manifestation of the negative values associated with the Islamic cultural heritage of the Turks. In this respect this view bears an affinity to the comments of Ziya Gökalp,[18] but Öztuna has the additional problem of defending sanat music. He succeeds in doing this at the expense of arabesk, representing sanat music as an international musical high culture to which the Turks have made a recognized contribution, and arabesk as a deviant version of this tradition.

Indeed, for many of its critics, arabesk expresses a negative and essentially 'eastern' aspect of the Turkish psyche about which something has to be done if the Turks are to be saved from themselves. Arabeskçi have of course used this discourse of Easternness to their own advantage, explaining (to me amongst others) that the popularity of arabesk owes its existence to the fact that the Turks are inextricably and essentially an 'eastern' people, and therefore much given to melancholic introspection and emotion (*duygu*). Record producers have also made use of this argument, when it suits their

[15] Ibid. 47. [16] Ibid. 47. [17] Ibid. 47. [18] See s. 4 below.

purposes, to explain their—to many utterly unacceptable—business practices. A brief article published in 1987 in the Turkish daily *Milliyet* describes the first recording contract of an 11-year-old girl, Küçük Demet, due to last for life. In the course of an interview with the recording company the following exchange apparently took place:

> 'In order to earn money, you are playing around with the future of a tiny little girl. You don't think about her at all . . . If this was a Western country, you would be in gaol . . . '
>
> 'Mr Recording Company' gave the following reply:
>
> 'Well, I'm a business man you know, and of course I have to worry about my money. It's not me that's responsible for Demet's future, it's her family. Anyway, this isn't the West.'[19]

Güngör and others see arabesk in terms of a peripheral reaction to heavy-handed centrist reform, in which arabesk simply filled the gap left by bureaucratic insensitivity to the 'real musical needs' of the people. Öztuna dismisses arabesk from a quite distinct perspective, in which the music is seen as popularization of a high art genre in which the qualities of balance, order, and decorum are sacrificed in the process of meeting mass demand. Both share the view that the process of degeneration results from inadequate direction from above.

4.2. Sociological Critique: The *Gecekondu* Problem and '*Dolmuş*' Culture

In Turkey, sociology provides the principal framework for criticism of arabesk. It associates the ill effects of arabesk with its perceived audience, a wave of migrants who poured in from the countryside to settle in the *gecekondu* (squatter towns) on the peripheries of the large cities in the west of Turkey from the 1950s onwards. In this critical discourse the emphasis is on the stresses and strains in Turkish society which have resulted from Turkey's perceived over-rapid and unplanned development. This contrasts with the critical viewpoint outlined above which sees in arabesk a timeless expression of an Eastern passivity and pessimism. It emphasizes instead the relationship of arabesk to a historically specific state of social and

[19] *Milliyet*, n.d.

demographic imbalance arising from the transition from the old order to the new, however imaged. This state of imbalance has created the conditions of a mass society excluded from the processes of production, who address their problems in the language of arabesk, a language of alienation and fatalism.

Migration in Turkey has certainly had a history which long precedes the policies of the Menderes government between 1950 and 1960. But in 1950 the 'democratization' of the political process and a massive programme of foreign loans transformed the Turkish rural and urban economy. This simultaneously generated huge surpluses of manpower in rural Turkey and an uncontrolled demand for labour in the cities, directly contributing to the rural–urban migration which has dominated Turkish society, and the concerns of Turkish sociologists, over the last three-and-a-half decades. Sociological explanations tend to focus on rural demographic 'push' or urban 'pull' theories,[20] but the city also has an ideological force, a pull on the rural imagination. This continues to make migration to the city an antidote to perceptions of exclusion from the 'democratized' post-Menderes economy, even though opportunities in the city can never succeed in matching the hopes and expectations of most migrants. In spite of the fact that alternative destinations opened up for Turkish migrant workers in the late 1960s, principally in West Germany, Libya, and Saudi Arabia, the pressure of internal migration continues to put a strain on the infrastructure of Turkish cities, posing a problem of an entirely practical kind to urban planners. Even official statistics indicate a sixfold increase in the population of Istanbul between 1950 and 1985, and an increase of 1.1 million in the five years between the censuses of 1980 and 1985.[21] Popular perceptions suggest a city with a rapidly growing population and an inadequate infrastructure, rendering the day-to-day difficulties of coping with the urban space increasingly less managable.

The focus for migration and perceptions of migration is the *gecekondu*. *Gecekondu* means 'put up at night' (literally, 'night-it-was-placed'). The image associated with this expression is one in which settlements of tiled, single-storey accommodation, appear suddenly on the outskirts of the city, according to no apparent logic.

[20] See Beeley 1983, 8, and Keleş 1990, 31–6.

[21] The handbook of official statistics (Başbakanlık Devlet Istatistik Enstitüsü 1988) gives the following population figures in Istanbul for the years in question: 1950, 1,166,092; 1960, 1,882,092; 1970, 3,019,032; 1980, 4,741,890; 1985, 5,842,985.

The reality of the situation is far more complex. Keleş identifies three broad phases of *gecekondu* development.[22] The first, from the late 1940s to 1960, was marked by hurriedly built constructions on unoccupied areas of Treasury or *vakıf*[23] land, in which labour was provided by individual families or by village groups migrating together, as Karpat and others have described. The second, from 1960 to 1970, was a period dominated by *gecekondu* entrepreneurs, using their own labour to put up *gecekondu* buildings to rent out to newly arrived migrants. The third, from 1970 to the 1980s, was a period of 'commercial' *gecekondu* construction, in which firms secured building sites and put up large numbers of buildings for migrants to rent. The location of the *gecekondu* is also far from random and uncontrolled. *Gecekondu* settlement in the initial years of *gecekondu* development in Istanbul was centred around factories in Rami, Kocamustafapaşa, Ümraniye, and Kartal, with the aid and co-operation of the factory owners, for whom the *gecekondu* dwellers constituted a vital and easily manipulable labour supply.

The legality of the *gecekondu* is similarly a matter of some complexity. Successive Turkish governments have attempted to control the *gecekondu* problem by legislation and planning. A series of five-year plans, put into action in 1963, 1968, and 1973, demonstrated the ambivalent attitudes of the state towards migration. On the one hand, uncontrolled settlement put an intolerable strain on the urban infrastructure. On the other hand, migration provided a vital pool of labour for urban industrialization. The first plan stressed control of the number of migrants. The second endorsed migration, but sought to reduce disparities in regional wealth leading to intense migration from particular areas. The third followed the first in attempting to restrict movement to cities for those with no prospect of employment. The model for the legal control of the *gecekondu* was provided by the Gecekondu Kanunu (Law) 775, passed in 1966. The three fundamental aims of this law were *iyileştirme* (improvement), *ortadan kaldırma* (removal) and *önleme* (prevention). Improvement has meant the extension of the urban infrastructure, in the form of surfaced roads, refuse collection, and public transport. *Gecekondu* which could not be 'improved', as a result of dilapidation and squalor, particularly those which could be deemed to be detracting from the beauty of buildings of historical value, were to be demol-

[22] Keleş 1990, 375–6.

[23] *Vakıf* are donations to religious foundations now administered by the state.

ished and their inhabitants resettled. The 1966 law intended to remove about 30 per cent of existing *gecekondu* in Turkey in this way. Prevention involved both the forceful destruction of newly established illegal *gecekondu*, and the provision of lands and funds to the local *belediye* to build new housing for low-cost rented accommodation for the migrants. Land was provided to local councils from remaining unused Treasury land, and capital came through the establishment of '*gecekondu* funds' financed by the Ministry of Public Works and Settlement and by revenue from local council budgets. Since 1985, state control of these funds has passed into the hands of the Public Construction Administration (Toplu Konut Yönetimi).

In practice, official attempts to deal with internal migration remained a step behind efforts to rehouse the migrants. The distribution of title-deeds (*tapu*) to *gecekondu* dwellers has become a powerful political tool. Governments have repeatedly bought support by means of general 'pardons' (*af*), the most recent of which took place in 1984. This supplied all present *gecekondu* dwellers with title-deeds, but promised to provide no more. The dramatic action of bulldozing a *gecekondu* to the ground will only be taken when no political capital is to be gained and the land is required for other purposes. On 24 July 1987, the mayor of İzmir, Burhan Özfatura, gave the order for the destruction of the *gecekondu* of Kuruçeşme in the Buca district of the city. This event attracted a great deal of unwanted publicity when a certain Abdülhadi Güneş, a migrant from Kars (in the north-east of Turkey) took his young daughter as a hostage on the roof of his *gecekondu* home and threatened to throw her off the roof if the bulldozers came near. His protest was unsuccessful.[24]

There is thus a constant process of assimilation, in which the *gecekondu* is, if allowed to stand, provided with legal title-deeds and the benefits of city services, all the time attracting kin and fellow villagers from the countryside. Istanbul spreads outwards like a many-limbed animal up the shores of the Bosphorus and along the 'Ankara' and 'London' roads, respectively to the east and west of Istanbul. The oldest *gecekondu*, such as those established around the industrial areas of Zeytinburnu and Rumeli Hisarüstü, are indistinguishable from older legally settled parts of the city, apart from a few streets of the older, single-storeyed tiled housing which exist behind the apartments and smart shops on the main streets. Saran

[24] *Cumhuriyet*, 27 July 1987, 1.

noted that Çağlayan *gecekondu*, in which he conducted research, possessed doctors, dentists, and shops long before *tapu* were distributed to the squatters in 1966.[25] Even in more recently settled *gecekondu* areas, the relationship of housing types to *tapu* ownership is complex. In Dolayoba in 1987, many houses built in a typical *gecekondu* style had in fact possessed *tapu* for thirty-five years. One such house belonged to the family of a Black Sea musician with whom I worked. They had made provision to build an extra storey, but unfavourable financial circumstances made this impossible. More modern two- and three-storey buildings close by, indistinguishable from the kinds of small apartment block to be found all over Istanbul, actually did not possess *tapu*.

From a legal point of view the definition of a *gecekondu* area has always been a highly complex matter. From a sociological perspective, however, what the *gecekondu* 'is' and what it represents is less problematic. The *gecekondu* is the urban locus of internal migration, whatever its legal status. It represents a transition from rural to urban life, in which processes of urbanization could be examined in detail, and the extent of Turkey's ability to modernize itself could be demonstrated. As such, *gecekondu* in Istanbul, Ankara, and İzmir were the focus of major sociological research projects throughout the 1970s. The extent of 'modern' attitudes towards participation in a national planned economy rather than a village economy, literacy, involvement in national political organization, and the right of the individual to choose their occupation, spouse, and use of leisure time were measured in wide-ranging statistical surveys designed to calibrate the extent to which the process of transition from villager to city-dweller had taken place. Karpat, for example, focuses on attitudes towards the media, such as newspapers, cinema, and radio, as an important aspect of the research he and his assistants carried out in the Nafibaba, Baltaliman, and Ahmet Celaleddin Paşa *gecekondu* in Istanbul.[26] Kongar looks at the extent to which children are allowed by their parents to choose their own careers and spouses in the Altındağ *gecekondu* in Ankara and various *gecekondu* in İzmir.[27]

Even though the early results of this research indicated that for the most part *gecekondu* dwellers still saw themselves as villagers (*köylü*) rather than as city-dwellers,[28] the *gecekondu* was represented by Turkish sociologists as essentially a beneficial environment of social

[25] Saran 1974, 330.
[26] Karpat 1976, 146–51.
[27] Kongar 1976, 209.
[28] Karpat 1976, 144.

change. The *gecekondu* allowed the migrant to maintain close ties with his native village and to organize his domestic life in much the same way, whilst participating in a national political and economic framework. The ability of the migrants to adapt to the exigencies of their situation was a common theme, allowing the squatter town to be seen as a rich source of future entrepreneurial dynamism. In spite of difficulties of access to educational and medical services resulting from the marginal location of the *gecekondu*, many Turkish sociologists stressed the high level of absorbtion of migrants into the formal economic activity of the city. In spite of arguments that the Turkish pattern of internal migration was creating social and economic divisions both on a national and a local scale,[29] the dominant representation of the *gecekondu* throughout the 1970s was positive.

But this rosy picture of a healthily urbanizing society was shattered during the two years which immediately preceded the military coup of 12 September 1980, in a period of widespread political, social, and economic disorder that is often referred to as the 'period of anarchy'. In contrast to the sociological literature, popular perceptions see the *gecekondu* as a problem relating directly to the perceived collapse of the city in the late 1970s. For a friend of my *kanun* teacher, whose views were highly typical of those who saw themselves as established city-dwellers, even if they were themselves first-generation migrants who had previously lived in *gecekondu*, the issue was clear and urgent. He was a chemist, born and bred in Istanbul, and living comfortably in the modestly prosperous district of Bağlarbaşı. His views, delivered weekly whilst he was driving me from my *kanun* teacher's house to give lessons on the electric organ to his son, could be summarized as follows. The problem of the *gecekondu* is that it introduces its inhabitants to a process of rapid and traumatic social and cultural change for which they are ill prepared. Missing their homes, migrants seek to re-create the village environment in the city. Their livestock and horses clog up the city thoroughfares. They sit and eat from the floor with their hands, rather than using chairs, tables, and cutlery. They store their savings under the bed, or buy gold for their wives, and consequently do not participate actively (except as a drain) on the national economy. Not only do the *gecekondu* lack the infrastructural facilities of the rest of the city, but its inhabitants dispose of their waste carelessly, as though they were still in their village, causing pollution, filth, and

[29] See Beeley 1983 for a summary of the Turkish literature on the *gecekondu*.

disease. Even worse, huge numbers migrate directly from their villages to Western Europe 'without even having seen a city', and scarcely give themselves time to change out of their baggy trousers (*şalvar*) and headdresses (*poşe*), thus giving Europeans the 'wrong' idea about the Turks and Turkey. The rapid change to which they are exposed results in a crisis of identity, and this crisis explained the more 'irrational' aspects of urban life in Turkey: the violence of the late 1970s and religious reaction (*irtica*).

In this discourse, the *gecekondu* is seen as a state of movement between two categories of social existence, the village and the city. The *gecekondu* is a liminal zone, neither one thing nor the other. It is not 'fixed' or 'well-seated', to translate the expression 'tam oturmamış', which is used, for example, to describe a fitting which is not properly fixed, or wobbles and is not yet ready or suitable for use. It is also used of individuals if they behave in a childlike or otherwise unstable way, and of social states. In using the language of psychopathology, the squatter towns become an image of urban disintegration and disorder, in spite of academic sociological argument to the contrary. This experience of urban liminality, coupled with the increasingly evident exclusion of large sections of the Turkish population from the 'democratized' wealth-creation proclaimed loudly by the Özal government, has created a peripheral culture identified as the culture of arabesk.

The connection between arabesk and the *gecekondu* is most evident in the concept of *dolmuş* culture. Arabesk is frequently described as *dolmuş* music. *Dolmuş* are a form of shared public transport, which consist largely of 1950s Chevrolets and Desotos inside the city walls, and small minibuses which connect points of departure (particularly the quays at Eminönü, Üsküdar, and Kadıköy) inside the city boundary with the surrounding *gecekondu* districts. With the exception of Üsküdar, which serves the *gecekondu* areas towards Çamlıca and Ümraniye, and Kadıköy, which serves the *gecekondu* along the Ankara road, the nexus of the *dolmuş* routes is the Topkapı garage (see map). Located at the Topkapı gate in the old city walls, near the famous brothels of the dilapidated Sulukule, and surrounded by graveyards, conspicuous with their tall cypress trees through which the *dolmuş* have to pass, Topkapı figures prominently in the urban Turkish imagination. It is a twilight zone in a spatial, social, and moral sense. Within the walls lie the monuments to Ottoman Turkish imperial culture; without, the ephemeral junk

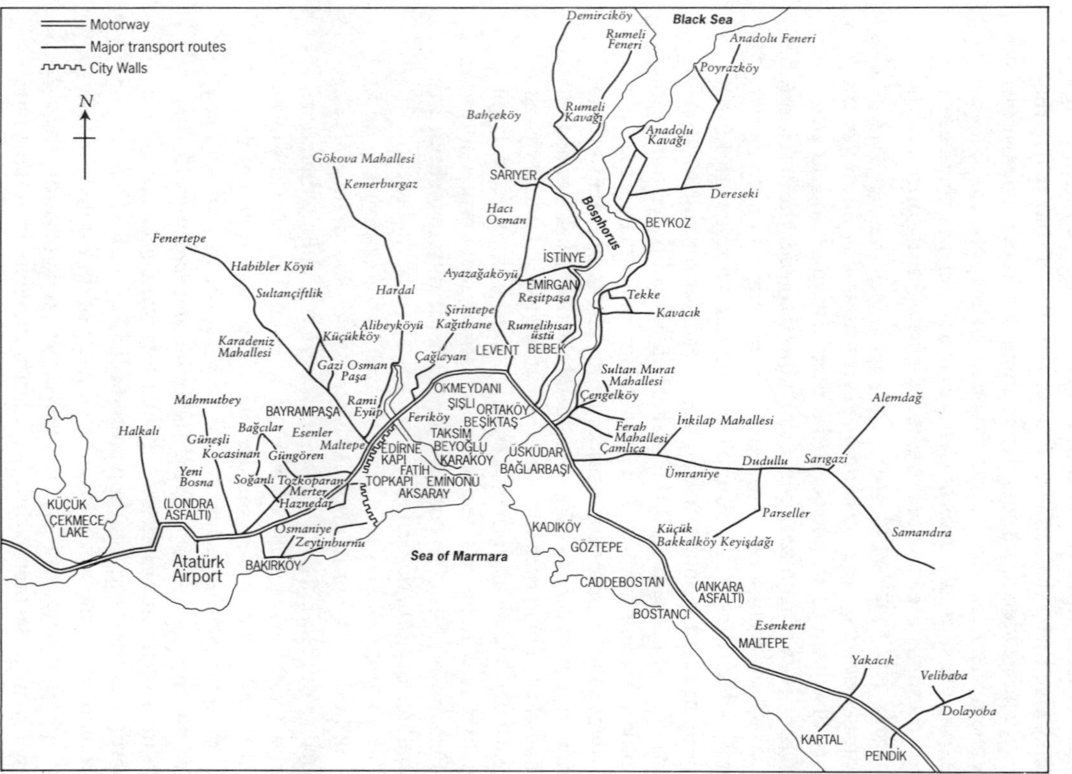

Public transport routes and main areas of *Gecekondu* development in Istanbul (*gecekondu* and old *gecekondu* areas are indicated in italics; lower case letters indicate principal areas of *gecekondu*

of modern Turkey's trash culture; within, the palaces and mosques; without, the beer houses and brothels. Within, order and the living; without, chaos and the dead. It is easy to see the way in which the Topkapı garage and the *dolmuş* driver represent the liminal position and confused identity of the *gecekondu* dweller. Like the *dolmuş* driver, they too are condemned to a peripatetic existence, circling around the walls amongst the graveyards, dogs, mud, and chaotic traffic, but never coming to rest within the city itself.

Arabesk speaks through the films which accompany the music, as well as the texts of the songs themselves. *Dolmuş* driving is an occupation with which many of those migrants who have enough capital to buy a car or minibus involve themselves. Consequently, arabesk stars, acting out the role of the star-crossed migrant, a role they may in fact have acted out in 'real life', portray themselves as *dolmuş* or lorry drivers. Many of the dramas of alienation and oppression are set in the Topkapı bus station itself. The force of the idea of driving, implying both mobility but also the inability to come to rest, draws much of its power from this. The association of arabesk with the *dolmuş* and the *gecekondu* is underlined by the clutter of decoration within the *dolmuş*, the icons of arabesk. Even though the playing of music was banned on public transport at the beginning of my field-work in 1986, the inside of the vehicles are covered with stickers proclaiming messages from arabesk songs: 'Seni Sevmeyen Ölsün' ('May They that Do Not Love You Die'), 'Gurbet Kuşları' ('Migrant Birds'), 'Mavi Mavi' ('Deep Blue'), 'Sus, Gözlerin Konuşsun' ('Be Silent, Let Your Eyes Talk'), 'Şoförüm' ('My Driver'). These accompany brief prayers and invocations written in Arabic and Roman script on the same multi-coloured reflecting plastic stickers, 'evil eyes', plastic flowers, pictures of arabesk stars, and other representations of arabesk sentimentality: a little boy with a huge, glistening tear rolling down his cheek and a little girl praying in front of a picture of the Kaba at Mecca.

The notion of *dolmuş* culture is many-faceted. For Eğribel the *dolmuş* shares with arabesk and the *gecekondu* the quality of being a popular response to needs which have not been met by the state. The *gecekondu* is a response to the problem of migrant housing, and the *dolmuş* serves the migrant transport needs with which the official public transport system cannot cope. Similarly arabesk is a response to ill-conceived attempts by the state to construct an official (at root, Westernized) culture which does not answer the cultural needs of the populace. All of these are described as a culture of *alternatifsizlik*, a lack of viable alternatives.[30] But Eğribel also perceives in these responses a lack of order, which is manifested in the economic organization of arabesk itself. The situation which has encouraged the growth of arabesk is the unofficial economy, in which rampant cassette piracy has made arabesk cheaper and more readily available than ever before. Indeed, it was only in 1989 that the Turkish government responded to the requests of a lobby within the music industry by implementing law 3257, passed originally in 1987, which specifies that every recorded tape carries a *bandırole*, a stamp indicating that tax has been paid upon it. This was intended as a direct move against pirate cassette copying. It is too early to say what the effects of this will be, but what is significant is the perception that it is principally arabesk, as opposed to any other kinds of music, that has benefited from this parasitic relationship on the back of the informal economy.

Through the concept of *dolmuş* culture, a formulation which has gained a certain currency amongst the liberal-intellectual critics of arabesk, the link between the *gecekondu*, social and moral disintegration, and arabesk is made explicit. Thus arabesk comes to be synonymous with all of the pathological symptoms of Istanbul's rapid urbanization. This also includes individual depression and suicide. An article in *Milliyet*, 13 July 1987, makes the point clear:

> In research on the subject of 'The relationship of arabesk culture to suicide' by Faruk Güçlü, it was revealed that the arabesk *gecekondu* culture affected in particular the young population. In research which claims that the films and television programmes which spread arabesk culture are the cause of the increase in suicide cases, it was revealed that 28 of the 681 suicide cases that took place in Ankara between 1980 and 1985 had chosen suicide 'in order to save themselves from those things they had bottled up inside them (*açmazlarından*)', being affected by the cinema, the press, and the films which are broadcast on television.

This association of arabesk with the *gecekondu* links the music with an image of an urban lumpenproletariat dislocated and alienated through the process of labour migration. However, the alienating and negative effects of arabesk also have a more specific political dimension, in which arabesk is seen in relation to religious reaction (*irtica*) and the politics of the Özal government.

[30] Eğribel 1984, 38.

4.3. Arabesk and Religious Reaction

The lyrics of arabesk express, to its critics, a negative set of attitudes about life in language and a style of vocal delivery that is felt to be highly 'Arabicized'. The most sweeping condemnation of arabesk is that its words are *saçma*, that is, 'rubbish', but also something which is scattered and without focus. The words do not speak plainly, but circumlocute. To speak about a matter honestly and plainly in Turkey is 'to speak the Turkish-of-it' ('Türkçesini söylemek'); flowery circumlocutory language and fluent rhetorical skills in general are distrusted and considered an attribute of foreigners. In addition, the tense glottis sound preferred to render the kind of vocal ornamentation associated with arabesk results in a direct distortion of the Turkish language. In the case of a school of singers associated with the sanat-music singer, Müzeyyen Senar, and now represented in arabesk by Bülent Ersoy and Derya Çağla, this distortion is considered by other singers to be highly exaggerated. Particular attention is paid to diction in Turkish conservatories. TRT musicians frequently criticize another's performance by expressing doubts about their *diksiyon* when there is not much wrong with it, but when it is impossible to congratulate them unreservedly, even if only to demonstrate a superior sensitivity to a third party. In vocal delivery and sentiment, arabesk is therefore held to represent a refusal to deal directly with reality, resulting both in sentimentality and fatalism. Many of my informants claimed on the strength of this that arabesk was intimately connected with social and religious reaction, a major issue in Turkey at the end of 1986.

Whilst there is no immediately obvious evidence to suggest that there is any direct link between *irtica* (religious reaction) and arabesk, many people interpreted both as manifestations of cynical manipulations of religious belief and popular culture. This was explained to me in the following terms by my first *bağlama* teacher, condensing his own words, which worked through this particular argument with great regularity. Arabesk inculcates the quintessential but double-edged virtues of stoicism and the passive acceptance of fate. The free-market politics of the present government (the Anavatan Party of Turgut Özal) has benefited a wealthy minority at the expense of an increasingly impoverished and alienated majority. But instead of providing a focus for perceptions of exploitation, which would enable the displaced work-force of the city to take effective political action, arabesk presents political and economic power as facts with no explanation other than fate. Turning the arabesk star from victim to hero is nothing more than worthless compensation for a ruthlessly exploitative situation.

Fatalism (*kadercilik*) is seen in this account as an essential traditional Islamic value. From a theological perspective he was in profound error. Muslim scholars differentiate sharply between a belief in fate and fatalism: the former concept does not deny man free will, but stresses that God knows in advance exactly what that choice will be; the latter is a doctrine of complete passivity. Furthermore, the one kind of music which all religious authorities agreed was *haram* (that is, prohibited) with any degree of unanimity was arabesk, not only on account of its passive fatalism, but because of its associations with drinking and sex.

In spite of this, my teacher would declare that, in controlling an ideology of passivity, those profiting from this situation control the ideological means for the exploitation of the work-force, and are able to rely on the passive acceptance of the people as the system is made to work relentlessly to the advantage of a wealthy minority. For my *bağlama* teacher, there was thus no surprise in the fact that the most rapid beneficiaries of Özal's reforms were, to use his expression, the *haciler* and *hocalar* (pilgrims and teachers) who appeared to run all of the small business and shops in the city.

This idea seemed to have a great deal of plausibility at a time when a series of exposés carried out by the journalist Uğur Mumcu detailed the involvement of the Turkish military and the present government in the so-called 'Rabıta affair'. Initially, the funding of Turkish religious functionaries in West Germany and Belgium by the Saudi-based Rābitāt al-Ālam al-Islāmī was permitted by a decree in 1981 authorized by the government of Admiral Bülent Ulus.[31] This took place at a time when thousands in Turkey were being arrested and imprisoned for their links with 'international communism'. But the links with this international Islamic organization continued through the connections that they had fostered with the two brothers of the Prime Minister, Yusuf and Korkut Özal. Rabıta funded a mosque on the grounds of the parliament and a mosque together with an Islamic centre on the campus of the Middle East Technical University in Ankara. Their activities in Turkey continue through

[31] See Akın and Karasapan 1988, 15. See also Stokes 1989 for an account of its relation to the arabesk debate.

the existence of a number of banks and financial institutions, notably the Faisal Finance Corporation. In addition to their regular commercial activities, these finance the establishment of religious foundations, publications, and newspapers.

The religious affiliations of the Özal government which came to light in the course of the Rabıta affair have incensed their centre-left and secularist critics, who included amongst their number my first *bağlama* teacher and my flatmate. Things appeared so coherently interconnected to them that it was never possible to talk about arabesk without being plunged into long arguments concerning the threat posed by religious reaction and its manipulation in the hands of a cynical government. There were further reasons for the feelings of bitterness whenever this subject came up amongst friends in the halk-music department of the TRT. The TRT was then being guided by a government think-tank known as the *Ocak* ('Hearth') committed to the—for many—reactionary concept of the 'Turkish–Islamic synthesis' (*Türk-İslam sentezi*). At that time, numerous changes in TRT programming had been encouraged in ways which symbolically indicated a return to 'Islamic' values, and a distinct back-pedalling on such crucial issues as the language reforms, in which the TRT played, and continues to play, a vital role in generating a certain currency for new words. Texts for newsreaders in 1987 were being guided by frequent lists of 'new' words, which were in fact the 'old' ones that had originally been replaced by the language reforms. The language of newsreaders in 1987 was indeed conspicuously Arabicized. Only five years earlier, the language of TRT newscasters had been a thoroughly reformed Atatürkian *öztürkçe*. The fact that halk music was now being rescheduled and often replaced by sanat music was interpreted by them as a part of exactly the same process. At about this time a number of interviews with arabesk stars, looking at arabesk from a less than critical angle began to be shown. In 1980 a surprise appearance by Orhan Gencebay, singing 'Yarabbim' on the TRT's New Year's Eve programme set the precedent for holiday performances (at the New Year or Bayram festivals) featuring big stars associated with arabesk. For the most part these stars did not sing the songs which had made them famous but pieces from a standard repertoire of halk or sanat music. Zeki Müren, the self-proclaimed 'Sanat Güneşi' ('Sun of Art') who had become a household name as an art-music singer, but had begun to sing arabesk in 1987 with his cassette *Helal Olsun*, was a regular performer on the New Year's Eve show. On the eve of Kurban Bayram in 1990, İbraham Tatlıses, perhaps one of the best-known arabesk stars, appeared on television to sing an *uzun hava* from the TRT halk-music repertory. For halk-music singers at the TRT these occasional incursions of arabesk musicians on peak-viewing-time shows posed a very direct threat to their virtual monopoly of TRT airtime. This was represented as an erosion of Atatürkian values endorsed at the very highest levels.

The close involvement of the Özal family with a number of arabesk stars provided additional fuel for this argument. Early in 1988, Özal appeared in close and apparently friendly conversation with Orhan Gencebay at the society engagement party of Gülşah Koçyiğit (daughter of film star Hülya Koçyiğit) and Selim Soydan. For the music press, 'Prime Ministerial Support for Arabesk' became front-page news of almost scandalous significance.[32] The tabloid press avidly reported Özal's enthusiastic attendance at a series of arabesk concerts in 1988, during which year the Anavatan Party adopted one of the most popular arabesk songs of 1987–8, 'Seni Sevmeyen Ölsün' as its campaign jingle for the 1988 election. The Prime Minister's wife Semrah caused the TRT substantial embarrassment by insisting on the presence of Bülent Ersoy at a televised official reception early in 1989. Until that moment the TRT had refused to acknowledge the existence of the flamboyantly-dressed transsexual, since she had been banned from giving stage performances in Turkey, and effectively banished to West Germany in 1980. Another Prime Ministerial favourite is İbrahim Tatlıses, who was included in the entourage accompanying Semra Özal on her official visit to Soviet Azerbaijan on 12 June 1990.

The culmination of the apparent *rapprochement* of the government and TRT with arabesk took place at the First Music Congress organized in Istanbul in February 1989 by the Minister of Culture and Tourism, Mustafa Tınaz Titiz. The result was the official endorsement of 'Acısız Arabesk'—arabesk with the *acı* (pain) and *keder* (grief) removed. According to a report on the congress in the weekly *Hafta Sonu*,[33] the TRT were prepared to 'recognize' music whose words were not fatalistic (*kaderci*). The first example of this reformed arabesk was a song entitled 'Sevenler Kıskanır' sung by Hakkı Bulut, and composed by the Western-style light ('Hafif') music composer, Esin Engin. In spite of the fact that the cassette

[32] *Müzik Magazin*, 7, 25 Jan. 1988.

[33] *Hafta Sonu*, 7 Mar. 1989.

containing this piece was given the benefit of substantial publicity and a TRT broadcast performance by Hakkı Bulut in the Atatürk Kültür Merkezi in Taksim Square, the experiment was a commercial failure. I was unable to find the cassette anywhere when I returned to Istanbul later that year. The experiment undoubtedly represented an attempt by the government to control and appropriate arabesk to its own ends, and at the same time to demonstrate its active and responsible role in Turkey's cultural development. To critics of the government and of arabesk, the congress provided final evidence of the government's cynical use of popular culture to further its own ends. The politics of the Özal era have come to be described by its critics as 'arabesk politikası', suggesting at once reaction, cynicism, and confusion.

This political critique focused upon the language of arabesk as a symbol of what arabesk expressed in social and political terms. The fact that my Turkish often expressed itself most spontaneously in the slightly archaic language I had absorbed whilst learning Turkish in England was initially something of a joke. When it became clear to the people who felt a special responsibility towards me that I could not so easily 'unlearn' this vocabulary, it became something of an issue and, in the end, the subject of acrimonious arguments. Even when I had learnt to adjust my vocabulary to the company in which I found myself, the fact that I might merely know the meaning of an 'old' word which had come up in a book or crossword provoked comment and criticism. It was as if the accumulation of old words in the mind were exercising a polluting and corrupting influence, whether they were being used or not. This must have explained why I became so obviously animated when the subject of conversation turned to Islam in Turkish politics, the *tarikat*, arabesk, and so on. I was able to understand, as it were, its subversive language. I did not help the situation by regularly arguing against their seemingly uncritical views on the manipulability of language.

Such arguments inevitably ended in bitter recriminations about trivia. My attitude to these issues, in which arabesk played only a small but central role, said everything that needed to be said in the clearest terms about the defects in my character: I was not a 'positive' thinker; I could not 'conform' to either Turkish or English society (they presumed, since that was why I was in Turkey in the first place); I was irresistibly attracted to the things any right-thinking man should be heard to criticize; and in my personal life I was lazy and irresponsible to boot. As they often explained, these defects did not spring from an active misanthropy so much as an immature passivity, and it was precisely this passivity upon which arabesk thrived. State hegemony operates precisely within this domain of 'trivia', in which language, taste, and personal habits and dispositions are the media through which power is negotiated, manipulated, and contested.

Musicological, sociological, and political critique defines musicians and audience, and specifies processes of degeneration and disintegration which have given rise to arabesk, and to which arabesk in turn contributes. These critical discourses have in effect constructed a myth of arabesk which is compounded by the use of a language of alienation, grief, and fate by musicians and audiences themselves to explain the meaning and significance of arabesk. Through the agency of the popular press, radio, and television, official and unofficial representations of arabesk become closely intertwined. The association of arabesk with an identifiable migrant culture needs therefore to be examined in some depth.

4.4. The Musicians

In Istanbul there is a clear picture that the stars of arabesk are migrants from the south-east of Turkey. The life stories of arabeskçis are intimately known and regularly updated in the tabloid and music press. Details of these biographies combine with their coverage in the press and the stories told in the films—in which the singers invariably retain their 'real' names ('Orhan', 'Ferdi', 'İbrahim', 'Emrah', and so on)—to form a fictionalized biography that is essentially bound up with the experience of the music.[34] In the context of arabesk perhaps one of the best-known fictionalized biographies relates to İbrahim Tatlıses, who was one of the most consistently successful arabesk singers throughout the 1980s. Cassettes which include such songs as 'Mavi Mavi', 'Gülüm Benim', 'Allah Allah', and most recently 'Fosforlu Cevriyem' have been amongst the few which have sold over a million copies. It is widely known that he

[34] Cf. Jefferson's comment on the concept of the fictionalized biography developed by the Russian formalist critic Tomashevsky: 'the life is as much a fiction as the poetry and becomes a kind of secondary creation against which the primary one may be read' (1986, 33).

left Urfa, an impoverished province in the south-east of Turkey in which approximately half of the population speak Arabic and half Turkish. On migrating to Istanbul in the early 1970s, he worked for several years as a labourer on a building site, before his voice was 'discovered' (a theme elaborated in a number of films), and he shot from anonymity to fame. His films describe the life of an Urfalı migrant in Istanbul, but here the close resemblance ends. For whilst the fictionalized hero goes on to suffer and eventually be destroyed by the city, in 'real life' most arabeskçi invest their capital and become successful businessmen. İbrahim Tatlıses has made substantial investments in construction and tourism. More typical is the path followed by Ferdi Tayfur and Orhan Gencebay, who have both started their own recording companies, largely but not exclusively dedicated to the production of their own music.

The relationship of 'fiction' to 'fact' in the life of arabesk stars is more complex than many commentators would allow. For Güngör, arabesk fans allow themselves to be deceived by the claims of the stars to be members of 'the halk' when in fact they are living the life of millionaires. For a small number of stars, arabesk is clearly an extremely lucrative business. Ferdi Tayfur earned a record 5 million TL per day at the İzmir Fair in 1979.[35] In 1990, sums of 10 million TL were commonplace for evening performances by well-known stars, contrasting with sums of around 3 million TL for lesser-known TRT and commercial market singers. But the 'fact' of wealth is part of the 'fiction' of arabesk drama. Many films portray the migrant's fatal inability to reconcile a village mentality with the acquisition of wealth through hard work in the city. The existence of a remote and manipulative object of affection, invariably a beautiful woman enshrining 'modern' urban values, brings about a terminal conflict between the aspirations of the migrant in the city and his limitations. The tempestuous and often violent love-life of İbrahim Tatlıses fits in clearly with the subject-matter of the films, and is reported avidly by the press, amongst other incidents. During the year I was in Istanbul, he was detained for a number of offences, including possession of hashish, beating his girlfriend,[36] and threatening behaviour carried out by 'his men' towards the elderly director of a rival cassette firm over an insult. Audiences thus bring to the films and the music a reading of the character which is made up not

[35] Eğribel 1984, 26.

[36] The actress Perihan Savaş.

only of the fictionalized character of the films and songs but also of the actor's story serialized by the popular press.

A close mapping of 'fact' and 'fiction' is to be found in the story of the female arabeskçi Bergen, who enjoyed substantial popularity from the mid-1980s until her death in 1989. One of the most notable aspects of this biography was a violent relationship with her first husband. According to accounts published in newspapers shortly after her death, an unhappy love affair led her to abandon her job in the Post Office at the age of 17. Whilst drinking away her sorrows with girlfriends in the Feyman Night Club in Ankara, she was invited to sing on stage, and subsequently employed by the manager of the night-club as a performer. This began a career as a light-music singer in clubs in Adana, Mersin, and İzmir. Whilst working in Adana in 1980 she met and married a certain Halis Serbest, who, two years later in İzmir, tipped a bottle of car acid over her face in a fit of jealous rage. This resulted in the loss of her right eye. Bergen divorced her husband, and continued with her career as an arabesk singer, now known as 'Acıların Kadını', 'The Woman of Grief'. The story contains the classic elements of the arabesk drama: happiness shattered by immediately understandable sentiments and actions resulting in a permanent disfigurement. Lacking a 'face' in a horrifically real sense, Bergen was condemned to a life of social and sexual marginality as a singer and a divorcee. After constant threats from her ex-husband, Bergen was abducted by him after an evening performance in Kayseri, driven back towards their native Mersin, and shot to death in a roadside restaurant in the Toros Mountains on 15 August 1989.

The most important element of the biography concerns the place of origin of the stars themselves. Most of the main representatives of arabesk throughout the 1970s and 1980s came from Adana (Ferdi Tayfur and Müslüm Gürses) and the neighbouring provinces to the east, especially those characterized by a relatively high proportion of Arabic speakers, in particular Urfa (İbrahim Tatlıses), Diyarbakır (Coşkun Sabah, Emrah, Mahsun Kırmızıgül), and Antakya (Ceylan, Gökhan Güney). The 'Arabic' identity of this area in general, an 'orient' that exists within the national boundaries of Turkey, is highly significant. Its cultural and geographic proximity to Syria and Iraq is held to explain the 'Arabic' nature of this music and its similarity to Arabic musical styles. It is indeed conspicuous that arabesk is not associated with the predominantly Kurdish south, central, or north-east of Turkey, although a number of arabeskçi do, for example, originate from Malatya (Malatyalı İbrahim) and Elazığ (Mustafa Keser).

The association of arabesk with Adana in particular is strengthened when we look not just at the singers but at its composers and lyricists. Arabesk is a music which revolves around star vocal performers, the names of whose accompanying musicians are largely unknown to the general public. In spite of this, a number of composers and lyricists are well-known personalities in their own right. The actual biographies of many of these conforms neatly to the general outlines of the hagiographies of the film stars. Burhan Bayar, who wrote, amongst a number of other particularly popular hits, 'Gülüm Benim' and 'Mavi Mavi', was born in 1955 in Adana. After spending some time in Istanbul as a student of architecture in 1970, he abandoned his studies and began to play *ney* and *kaval* with his brother, first in Istanbul *pavyon* and then in the night-clubs of Ankara. For a period he worked with İbrahim Tatlıses, but whilst in İzmir he was caught in possession of hashish and sent to gaol. Since then his fame as a composer has been associated particularly with İbrahim Tatlıses.

Of the arabesk lyricists perhaps the best known is Ahmet Selcuk İlhan, who as well as being the current director of Ferdi Tayfur's 'Fedifon' studio, has written some 500 songs. He was born in Adana in 1953, and emigrated to West Germany after completing his *lise* education in 1970. He began to write arabesk lyrics professionally whilst living in Germany in 1978. He returned to Istanbul and graduated in German language and literature from Istanbul University in 1980. Hamza Dikeli, who was born in 1950 and worked in a tea-house until his work was eventually 'discovered' by Burhan Bayar, can be added to the list of songwriters and lyricists originating from Adana.

It might be argued that, in the Turkish music business, myth contructs reality, selecting and propelling forward stars whose lives can be made to fit the model. For audiences, the myth is sustained because it enhances their belief that the arabesk drama describes the world 'as it is'. For some singers the myth legitimates their activity as musicians to themselves and their employers. It also provides a model for the way in which musicianship is perceived, by musicians, audiences, and critics alike. In this model, musical training is absent. Singers and writers are simply discovered, possessing 'natural' talents and abilities. Whilst it is true to a certain extent, this argument would overstate the role of the record and cassette industry in selecting and training popular singers. A number of the most famous arabesk singers, whose career paths followed more conventional trajectories, were born and brought up in provincial areas elsewhere in Turkey.

Orhan Gencebay is one of the most notable of these exceptions. He was born in Samsun, on the Black Sea coast, on 4 August 1944. He attended classes in art music at an early age, and learnt the *bağlama* from his father. In 1967 he applied for a place at the Istanbul TRT school (which leads automatically to a highly prized place in one of the TRT orchestras or choruses) and was accepted, but could only study there for some ten months before being called up for his military service. In 1968 he began an apprenticeship with the popular musician Ahmet Sezgin, composing songs and working as a *bağlama* player in a night-club genre dominating the commercial market, which closely resembled but was not yet known as arabesk. The term arabesk was first used by journalists to describe Orhan Gencebay's first solo cassette in 1970, *Bir Teselli Ver* (*Console Me*), which owed much to the commercial urban popular music of Ahmet Sezgin, Sinan Subaşı, Şukran Ay, Sevim Şengül, and others, but used Western electric instruments to a far greater extent. Following the success of his early cassettes, in 1973 Gencebay established his own record label, Kervan Kasetçilik, which continues to produce and distribute his music. His musical education therefore consisted of a combination of parental involvement, local music clubs and conservatories, the TRT school, and an *usta-çırak* (master-apprentice) relationship in Istanbul with Ahmet Sezgin. This mixed pattern of formal and semi-formal learning processes is shared by the majority of professional musicians working in Istanbul today.

Orhan Gencebay constitutes an exception to many arabesk stars in that his music is widely recognized as representing the 'serious' side of arabesk, in contrast to the starkly monophonic and more bluntly sentimental style of Ferdi Tayfur. I frequently heard the joke, in connection with arabesk, that the gangs who roamed the streets in Istanbul in the late 1970s were not so much interested in whether you were on the right (*sağcı*) or left (*solcu*), but whether you were a *Ferdici* or an *Orhancı*. As mentioned above, Gencebay himself has long denied that his music is arabesk at all. In spite of this, most people consider his music to be arabesk, but a high quality of musical workmanship is recognized in both his compositions and performances which makes him acceptable to a number of musicians working in halk or sanat music. Sanat-music performers in a club (*cemiyet*) in Trabzon with which I was connected in 1987 described him enthusiastically as a *bestekar* (composer) and *büyük usta* (great master), terms that would not be used to describe any other arabesk musician. Nuray Hafiftaş, a singer in the halk-music department of the Istanbul TRT, included an old Orhan Gencebay hit in a recent commercial cassette of halk music. The arabesk of Orhan Gencebay has thus gained a certain currency amongst people who otherwise claim to despise the genre as a whole. His exceptional qualities, however, are considered to have nothing to do with the fact that he is not from the south-east of Turkey, but with the high level of his compositional and technical expertise.

The 'grass roots' in the social organization of arabesk are musicians, arrangers, producers, and composers who are professionally involved in different genres. The professional life of Mustafa Keser provides a good example. He began working as a *müzisiyen* (backing instrumentalist) for commercial sanat-music singers in his native Elazığ in 1965. In 1975 he won a place in the İzmir TRT halk-music department as a *mahalli sanatçı* (local artist) on a short-term contract. Finally in 1981 he moved to Istanbul as a full-time (*kadrolu*) member of the TRT as a sanat-music singer. He supplemented his wage by performing his own compositions as a singer in the commercial market, accompanying himself on an 'Arab scale' synthesizer and rhythm box. This style of performance, principally associated with smaller *gazino*, is described as 'Taverna', even though its repertoire overlaps substantially with arabesk. When I met him in 1990, he had released three arabesk commercial cassettes, one of which (*Seviyorum, Çaresizim*) had reached number fourteen in the arabesk charts compiled by *Müzik Magazin*. This popular success enabled him to find evening employment as a singer in one of the larger and more prestigious of the *gazino* and *Müzik Holları* (Music Halls) in Kumkapı.

Mustafa Keser is perhaps an extreme example of a versatile musician who is able to switch from one genre to another when required. A number of arabesk composers also come from within the ranks of the TRT in Istanbul. Esat Kabaklı used composition as a minor source of income, but also as an outlet for an evident enthusiasm for songwriting which he was unable to do in the TRT. Nuray

Hafiftaş, also a TRT halk-music vocalist, provided a piece for a recent cassette by the young arabesk singer Canan Nergis which I watched being produced in 1990. Ali Osman Erbaşı, a well-established arabesk producer and composer of songs for arabesk stars including Müslüm Gürses, is also a fine *bağlama* player who plays in and produces commercial halk-music cassettes for TRT singers. The image of arabesk musicians as rural–urban migrants from the south-east of Turkey must therefore be clearly separated from the actual biographies of arabesk instrumentalists, producers, and composers, many of whom are thoroughly educated musicians with close links with official musical circles.

The mythic biography of the arabesk star as rural–urban migrant from the south-east establishes the singer as a social marginal with a message of alienation from the periphery of Turkish urban society. The fictionalized biography constitutes a text against which the primary text of the songs and films is read. What is most important about this secondary text is not so much the fact of its location in a particular representation of migration and *gecekondu* life, a marginalized geographic space, but the social liminality that this implies. This liminality is also expressed on a moral plane through constructions of gender and sexuality. In Western orientalist discourse it has long been recognized that musicians in Middle Eastern society appear to flout every availably moral code.[37] For entirely different reasons, the orientalist representation of a sensuous and lascivious East conforms in many ways to indigenous representations of musicians in Middle Eastern society. Condemned by overwhelming social and religious strictures, musicians exist in a world of outsidership and poverty, but this frees them to indulge themselves in a world of sensuous pleasures denied to society at large. The protagonist of the arabesk drama moves in a world of wealth and beautiful men and women on the one hand, and poverty and the self-destructive pleasures of alcohol on the other.

The mythic marginality of musicians is expressed in different, and apparently contradictory, ways. Male arabesk stars divide into 'real men' and 'effeminates'. Those that come indisputably from the marginalized geographic space of the south-east and the *gecekondu* conform outwardly to an accepted presentation of masculine selfhood, through dress, speech, and a conventional code of male honour.

[37] See Lane's description of the Egyptian '*Ghawa'zee*' and '*Khow'als*' (1836, 94–102).

Threatening a rival with a gun upon insult may be against Turkish law, but is the action of a man of honour which immediately commands respect. The domestication implied by marriage is rejected. A large number of male arabeskçi live with the women of their choice but do not marry; Orhan Gencebay and Sevim Emre, İbrahim Tatlıses and Perihan Savaş, Ferdi Tayfur and Necla Nazır are notable examples. Their biographies allow for no dilution of their essential masculinity. It is as if those whose credentials of marginality are sufficiently well established are then free to present a conventionally gendered self, even if this presentation is of a studied and somewhat exaggerated nature.

Those that do not marry are obliged to establish their marginality on a different plane. We have already noted that Bergen had, through losing her 'face', lost her womanhood, and thus stood outside a conventional mode of womanly behaviour. A conspicuous number of male arabeskçi are transvestites and transsexuals, who have not only lost their 'faces' along with their moustaches, but their manhood as well. Graphic snipping gestures made by cassette sellers to me on earlier visits (when my stumbling Turkish invariably necessitated a running commentary in sign language) left me in no doubt as to exactly what it was thought these people lacked. Striking but different examples are the camp and well-spoken Zeki Müren and the transvestite-transsexual Bülent Ersoy. More recently a 'new wave' of transsexual singers have achieved a certain notoriety, including Merve Sökmen, Zümrüt Canseli, Ertaç Ünsal, Noyan Barlas, Seyhan Soylu, and 'Mimi' Soner. In contrast to the 'male' south-easterners who have not married but live with their lovers, Bülent Ersoy recently attracted a great deal of publicity by getting engaged to her (male) lover, whom she met whilst making a film during the seven years spent effectively in exile in West Germany. Ironically Bülent Ersoy was originally banned under the 12th article of the Police Vazife ve Salahiyetleri Kanunu (Duty and Capability Law), which states that women and girls can only perform on stage with special permission. In this case permission was refused on moral grounds. This effectively cut off the artist from her main source of income in Turkey. Public opinion on the issue rose to such an extent that substantial political capital was eventually to be gained by granting her permission to perform in Turkey. So 'male' arabeskçi of demonstrably 'normal' sexuality do not marry, whilst 'female' arabeskçi of demonstrably 'abnormal' sexuality do.

The sexual marginality of the arabeskçi has been accompanied by an increasing indeterminacy of the markers of sexual identity in the performance of arabesk. A music teacher in Istanbul once commented that 'at present in Turkey, men sing like women and women sing like men'. He could not say what the reason for this was, although it provided an illustration of the social malaise represented by arabesk: the mixing up of things which ought to be kept separate. The tessitura preferred by male arabesk singers is high, corresponding to a high tenor in Western music, falling generally between middle C and the octave above it. The low register favoured by female arabesk singers, such as Tüdanya, Bergen, and Ayşe Mine, falls into much the same range. It is indeed difficult to tell at times, on the evidence of the tessitura alone, whether a man or a woman is singing, although it is often clarified by details of pronunciation. 'Male' arabeskçi often sing in the dialect of the south-eastern provinces, which is clearly characterized, amongst other things, by a sharp distinction between /k/ and /q/ (corresponding to the distinction between ك and ق in the northern dialects of Arabic), which is entirely absent in 'Istanbul Turkish'. Conversely 'female' arabeskçi tend to sing in Istanbul Turkish. Zeki Müren is often described as one of the best speakers of correctly pronounced and articulated Turkish, even though any attempt to imitate it would be ridiculed as excessively flamboyant and effeminate.

Most folk musicians attributed this merging of tessitura to the popularity of the folk singer Belkis Akkale. For them the problem was not that men sing 'high' so much as that women sing 'low'. Though not herself an Alevi, Belkis Akkale has become associated with the Alevi music of her native Malatya. Singers of this music tend to favour a deep voice, whether man or woman. Whilst representatives of an older generation of female musicians at the Istanbul TRT tend to sing in a higher register, today most well-known female halk-music singers, such as Gülşen Kutlu, Can Etili, and Nuray Hafiftaş sing in deep voices. It seems more likely that the impetus comes from arabesk, in which the merging of male and female tessitura has a correlate in the merging markers of gender identity amongst the arabesk 'effeminates', although this was a possibility my informants from the halk-music department of the TRT were loath to consider. This homogenization of musical markers of gender identity has been given additional emphasis by the relatively recent popularity of the child arabeskçi. Küçük Emrah's spectacular success in the early 1980s was followed by Küçük Ceylan and today by a whole flood of pre-pubescent singers.

The relation of the arabeskçi to their sexuality is equivalent to that of the *gecekondu* to the city and of the south-east of Turkey to the nation. It is a marginalization which is not motivated by ill will or perversity but simply as a powerlessness to change the way things are. Accusations of deviancy (*sapıklık*) or pederasty (*sübyancılık*) are seldom levelled against arabesk, and the remarkable personalities of Zeki Müren and Bülent Ersoy attract less criticism than amused comment. Bülent Ersoy became a liberal cause in Turkey towards the end of 1987, when her exclusion from public life was seen as unfitting for an open and democratic society.[38] When Bülent Ersoy was shot on stage in 1989, apparently for refusing to perform a song upon request, the mother of the would-be killer cursed her son in public, and prayed that 'Bülent Hanım' could find it in herself to forgive their family.

These constructed identities emphasize marginality and alienation, underlining what the music is about. Stage and film personae, cassette covers, journalistic coverage, and interviews combine with the music and songs to construct a composite text, each element of which supports and explains the others. Whilst this undoubtedly provides a language in which musicians can be represented and marketed by the media industry, musicians are not simply passive consumers of this myth. Many musicians are involved in a number of different musical activities, and are obliged to represent themselves in different ways according to the circumstances. Mustafa Keser has created for himself an extremely secure niche in the musical life of the city, complete with an office and studio in a smart and central area of Istanbul. The picture on the front of his second cassette, however, *Bana Kötü Diyen Diller Utansın* (*Let Those that Call Me Bad be Ashamed of Themselves*) portrays him as the archetypal *gariban* of the arabesk film, a solitary figure hunched over a glass of *rakı* with a cigarette burning listlessly in his fingers. The image immediately identifies and sells the cassette as arabesk. In the company of musicians, and especially a foreign researcher, he insists that his music is not arabesk, but 'olduğu gibi Türk Müzik', 'Turkish music through and through'. He pointed out that most listeners are simply too ignorant to recognize the brief *taksim* improvisations and complex modal modulations with which the music is littered. The

[38] See A. Görmüş and A. Baştürk 1987.

relationship of his music to arabesk, whose legitimacy he refuses to acknowledge, is superficial, and should not deceive the more cultured listener. His music is indeed popular amongst a number of people in the sanat- and halk-music sections of the Istanbul TRT. He once commented to me, with a smile, that with his first cassette he had 'broken open a few coffins' ('Birkaç tabutu yıktım'). Much of Mustafa Keser's success has involved the successful manipulation of the arabesk image. He has been able to negotiate his public persona in such a way that he is still able to retain his credibility in art- and folk-music circles as a commercially successful musician who has not simply sold out to the *piyasa*.

Arabesk musicians have recourse to other strategies to distance themselves from the image of arabesk and the arabeskçi. 'Malatyalı' İbrahim Dulkadıroğlu, star of three films and with seventeen commercial cassettes to his name, describes his music as *fantezi* rather than arabesk. This he distinguished in opposition to a category of *koy*, 'heavy' (literally 'dark') arabesk, typified for him by Gökhan Güney. In *fantezi*, the emphasis is upon instrumental composition and not on text, making extensive use of *elektrobağlama* and flute. This contrasts with the extensive use of large choruses of violins in *koy* arabesk. The term *fantezi* has a long history in the sanat-music tradition, implying a light piece in a 'free' idiom. Today it has a particular currency amongst *bağlama* players, such as İbrahim Dulkadıroğlu, who have no formal knowledge of art music but do not limit their use of the *bağlama* to the halk-music repertory or style. The distinction between *fantezi* and arabesk is, however, not one which can be made clearly or systematically by Turkish urban musicians. What constitutes *fantezi* to one may simply be arabesk to another. The term should be seen in a rhetorical context, allowing the musician to be considered by the outside world as an arabesk musician, but to represent themselves in other contexts as serious artists. Musicians thus participate in the construction of the arabesk myth as long as it suits their commercial interests, but have recourse to a variety of strategies to negotiate their musical identities in other circles.

4.5. Audiences

The arabesk narrative so associates the music with the process of migration that both musicians and their audiences are closely identified with the *gecekondu* and rural–urban migrants. Internal migration undoubtedly had a profound effect upon patterns of musical production, patronage, and consumption in urban Turkish society. Güngör, Eğribel, and others have described the ways in which a new class of wealthy rural migrants who had profited from the politics of the Menderes era sought to appropriate and imitate an urban pattern of leisure activity.[39] The focus of this leisure activity was the *gazino*, a form of café providing food, alcohol, and musical entertainment, closely modelled on the cafés known as *meyhane*, formerly run by the Christian minorities in the Beyoğlu and Taksim districts of Istanbul. The popularization of the urban sanat-music genre in the 1950s was clearly represented by Zeki Müren's use of a 'T' shaped stage at this time, allowing him to walk out in front of the singers into the audience. This class of migrant nouveaux riches saw their aspirations represented in the popularized sanat music then typified by Zeki Müren, at a time when the tastes of the settled bourgeoisie were captivated by the revived *şarkı* style of Munir Nureddin Selçuk and the tango of Fehmi Ege.

Arabesk is, however, identified with the labour migration of a later period, associated with rapid *gecekondu* development and demographic growth. Whilst *gecekondu* development tended to keep villagers together, reliant upon one another for support and assistance in building their houses and securing employment, their occupation in factories and proximity to other migrant groups involved the gradual formation of a distinct class awareness. This awareness crystallized around the growing organization of trade union movements amongst migrant factory workers in the late 1960s and early 1970s.[40] The use of *bağlama* in the context of a musical genre which otherwise resembled the popular sanat music of the 1950s therefore had a particular appeal to a distinct class of rural–urban migrants. This music, typified by Orhan Gencebay's *usta*, Ahmet Sezgin, was cultivated in the 'popular' *gazino* clustered around beauty spots in Istanbul close to the *gecekondu*, and disseminated by the increasingly available technology of mass culture. Orhan Gencebay's first single, 'Bir Teselli Ver', produced in 1970, sold 600,000 copies. Mass sales in today's terms, in which top-ranking artists regularly sell a million copies of a cassette, were not achieved until labour migrants in Germany began to bring back

[39] Güngör 1990, Eğribel 1984. [40] Dubetsky 1977.

cheap cassette recorders and the recording industry adjusted to this change in the early 1970s.

It is important to see the early years of arabesk, therefore, in relation to rural–urban migration and a class awareness which cut across 'vertical', regional identities. The situation in 1990 is very different, but arabesk is still seen as being 'the' music of the *gecekondu*, even though the nature of the *gecekondu* and rural–urban migration has changed profoundly. In addition, the mass media dissemination of all kinds of music has created a world of multiple musical contexts, in which arabesk exists everywhere, and is listened to, if only passively, by everyone. According to research carried out in 1988, some 200 million cassettes are produced by the recording industry in Turkey, of which 150 million are arabesk.[41] Consumption of this huge output could not conceivably be confined to the *gecekondu*. Although systematic research on the class distribution of cassette sales figures is lacking, my own casual observation of individual cassette collections indicated clearly that arabesk cassette sales are not limited to any one class or musical interest group within the city. But the power of the image is such that when I was making my initial steps in pursuit of arabesk I was frequently advised to go to the *gecekondu*, preferably by *dolmuş*, and the music would simply be there and ready for me to study and investigate. The fact that arabesk frequently cropped up under my nose in the TRT halk-music department in the centre of the city, and appeared to be absent from the peripheries of the city, where it was supposed to be, was one of the recurrent themes of my field-work.

Two aspects of the consumption of arabesk indicate that it is not listened to in the *gecekondu* any more than anywhere else. Firstly, the proportion of arabesk music to halk and sanat music in the shops of cassette vendors and the trolleys of the *işportacılar* (street sellers) remained remarkably consistent everywhere in the city, consisting of about 50 per cent arabesk and 50 per cent assorted halk, sanat, taverna, and özgün[42] genres. The most significant variant was the

[41] *Cumhuriyet*, 25 Aug. 1988.

[42] Özgün music has become extremely popular since 1989. Ahmet Kaya's self-consciously political songs were described by many as 'protest arabesk' at the time, and subsequently dubbed 'Özgün' by the press. Özgün differs from arabesk in the political content of the lyrics and the more systematic use of guitar-based harmonies. Part of the popularity that this music now enjoys relates to the ready availability of imported guitars, which have only recently been marketed at prices which bear comparison with the cost of a cheap *bağlama*.

amount of Western popular music, which would occupy a far more significant proportion of a cassette vendor's stock around Taksim and Beyoğlu, and be virtually absent at the Topkapı garage market. In addition to costing an extra 1,000 TL (a Turkish cassette was 6,000 TL and a licensed Turkish copy of a Western pop music cassette was 7,500 TL in the summer of 1990), the importance of song texts is such that most young people consider it a waste of time and money to buy cassettes containing lyrics they do not understand. Secondly, the cassette-buying public do not limit their listening to any one genre. The multiple dimensions of listening experience were demonstrated to me most clearly when I attempted to compile statistics of musical preferences in *dernek* in Aksaray and Beşiktaş. An active enthusiasm for one genre in no way precluded an active enthusiasm for another. Whatever other patterns emerged, there was no clearer preference for arabesk amongst participants living in *gecekondu*, or second-generation migrants from the south-east of Turkey, than any other group defined by their location within the city or father's place of birth. Perhaps most significant was the high proportion of people who indicated active preferences for both halk and arabesk. Even though patterns of musical consumption are difficult to pin down and do not necessarily translate accurately into numbers (since somebody who actively listens to and enjoys arabesk may not necessarily have enough money to buy or possess a great many tapes), the evidence from the *dernek* suggests that people concurrently listen to and identify with a number of different genres. Arabesk cannot therefore be defined as the cultural property of a particular group or class existing in the city today.

The association of arabesk with the *gecekondu* should not be regarded as an accurate sociological explanation about who produces or listens to the music, but as a metaphorical statement. If this is accepted, the attempt to seek and define a class of passive music consumers with a culture or habitus neatly conforming to a notion of 'the popular' is sociologically meaningless. A more useful approach would be to define some of the ways in which the myth and music of arabesk is actively used. Putting a tape into a cassette player is not a semantically dead gesture of passive consumption, but an act which constructively defines the self, the group gathered, and the space in which the gathering takes place. Perhaps the most significant of these spaces and groups are the *muhabbet*, usually single-sex gatherings of friends in which food, drink, conversation, and music are shared. In the Turkish context the *muhabbet* is the very essence of sociality itself. Arabesk is an indispensable element of the male gathering around the *rakı masası*, the '*rakı* table', defining an intimate interior in which the operations of the 'real' world are temporarily suspended and friendship can be explored and celebrated. My *kanun* teacher would take advantage of his wife's absence of a few days (to visit her parents in Eskişehir) to prepare a *rakı masası* and get hopelessly drunk with me and a few other friends under the pretext of introducing me to arabesk. In his opinion, any attempt to understand arabesk without the *rakı masası* would be doomed to failure from the start. On both occasions he rendered himself virtually incapable of playing the *kanun* in his *gazino* band later in the evening, but the exercise demonstrated to me the close link perceived between arabesk and the pattern of sociality celebrated by the *muhabbet* of the *rakı masası*. The association of arabesk, exploring themes of grief, separation, loneliness, and alienation, with this pattern of sociality is perhaps surprising, but the *muhabbet* is a bitter-sweet occasion, in which drunken conversation emphasizes absent friends, past times, and the transitory nature of the pleasures of social existence.

The arabesk cassette tape is therefore used to structure and define extremely formal patterns of social activity. This is also largely true of live performance. Evening performances in *gazino* replicate in a public domain the experience of the *muhabbet*. For the most part, an evening in a *gazino* is a fairly rare night out to celebrate a particular event or welcome a friend who has not been seen for a while. The band and singer provided by the countless down-market *gazino* and music halls of Istanbul are seldom well-known and are hardly ever the focus of attention. Groups sit around tables, facing one another and not the stage. Musicians play for a small fee and a brief ripple of polite applause at the end of each piece. What is important is not the star singer, but the *muhabbet* situation, which is defined in part by arabesk. Well-known arabesk stars, on the other hand, perform in established night-clubs which are sufficiently expensive to bar entry to anybody except the extremely rich. An evening in Maksim's, perhaps one of the best-known and most central *gazino* in Taksim Square, to hear İbrahim Tatlıses cost 200,000 TL in the summer of 1990.

The only opportunity to hear well-known arabesk stars in a live performance context are *Halk Konserleri*, 'People's Concerts'. These are sometimes privately run affairs, in which a large marquee is provided and cheap tickets are sold to the public on a commercial basis. Sometimes these concerts are free events organized by the *belediye* (town or city council). The most important of these in Istanbul is the series of arabesk concerts organized as part of the Gülhane Park summer festivities. Every evening for a month a programme of entertainment, featuring light music, halk- and sanat-music singers, belly-dancers, magicians, and comedians culminates with a short programme by an arabesk star. The response to these is so overwhelming that stars are not advertised too far in advance, for fear of attracting unmanageable crowds.[43] The 'People's Concert' attracts a particular age and social group, invariably described to me as 'arabesk types' in explanation of the unruly behaviour which is believed to accompany these events. Boys and young men without the means to be able to afford regular trips to *gazino*, or to buy arabesk cassettes with any regularity, constitute the bulk of the audience, for whom the concert provides a focus for an evening out. It also provides a rare glimpse of the star, the reality behind the omnipresent, mass-produced images of posters and cassette covers. The relationship of the singer as lover to the evasive and remote object of desire (*maşuka*) in the arabesk text is replicated by the relationship of the star on stage to the fan (*hayran*). The individual presence of the musician lies at the very heart of the event. The appearance of the star on the concert stage is an emotional moment of intense semantic density.

It is possible to distinguish the *Halk Konseri* and the *muhabbet* as entirely different patterns in the consumption of arabesk. In the first, the relationship of star to the individual *hayran* is all important. The groups in which people attended the *Halk Konseri* appeared to split up towards the end of the concert as the audience became atomized, each individual becoming lost in an inner emotional world. In the *muhabbet*, the music defines a situation in which attention is focused on the group of people present, on the very notion of sociality itself.

Arabesk is used in other ways, in particular as a mode of self-representation, enabling people to talk about themselves to other people. It was for the most part difficult to get people to talk about arabesk directly. No critical language exists to talk about arabesk in any positive way. Arabesk can only be represented verbally in terms

[43] Ferdi Tayfur's concert at Gülhane Park on 16 July 1989 was attended by 97,000 people.

that condemn it as a threat to Turkish values. One friend, a 16-year-old from Çorum in the north-east of Turkey who was working as an assistant and door-keeper in the *dernek* in which I worked in Beşiktaş, was an enthusiastic fan of a number of arabesk stars. He was extremely reluctant to talk to me about arabesk, particularly within earshot of his employers (both of whom were graduates of the State Conservatory and he knew them to be extremely critical of arabesk). When he did, he presented a shredded and disjointed account of offical discourses condemning arabesk out of hand, and was quite unable to say why he liked it at all. The music was simply 'rubbish' and did not reflect real events (*gerçek olaylar*). Like all ethnomusicologists I had hoped to find informants who would be fluent in the art of talking about the music I was interested in. All of my seemingly simple enquiries about why people liked arabesk seemed to end in confused and contradictory answers.

Without doubt, my manner of questioning in any Turkish context must have seemed blunt, overinquisitive, and often nonsensical. Many people may have assumed that as an 'intellectual', associated with their teachers, TRT musicians, and singers, I could not conceivably be interested in arabesk, and was therefore going to be critical or condescending about their tastes. On the other hand it seemed that people really did have very little to say about arabesk. The dominant rhetoric about arabesk, imparted by schoolteachers and the media, effectively mutes any ability to make a sophisticated and positive verbal response to arabesk. This fact adds a further weapon to the official critical arsenal. A schoolteacher in Güngören once remarked to me that he would have no objection to arabesk if his pupils could find something sensible to say about it. The ability to talk about arabesk might have conferred upon it some kind of social and intellectual legitimacy. The result of arabesk is a numbing of the critical faculties: it just sends them to sleep (*onları uyutuyor*). I found myself agreeing that there was simply no way of 'researching' arabesk, in which the notion of research implied setting up formal situations in which people could be made to talk clearly and directly about the music.

As an outside observer trying to deal with arabesk in question-and-answer situations defined and controlled by myself, I was bound to be disappointed. In retrospect it would appear that my most fundamental methodological tool was friendship. What arabesk represented and the way it was used became accessible to me through my experience as a somewhat ambiguous participant in Turkish family life. In situations defined and controlled by other people, I was involved and implicated in a domain of frustration, unhappiness, and turbulent emotions. Arabesk provides the speaker with a language of self-representation in which the speaker is able to identify with the *gariban* (outsider) of the arabesk drama. A brief anecdote will serve to illustrate this. The younger brother of my first *bağlama* teacher had just finished his military service and was at something of a loose end. We went to visit his *bağlama* teacher, who worked during the day for a small haulage firm and taught during the evening in a local *dershane*. He was keen to impress himself upon the affections of the teacher's daughter, and most of the evening was spent in polite conversation, evidently intended to impress a future father-in-law, around the two subjects which afforded a recognized opportunity for displays of rhetoric: politics and football. The evening was interrupted by the arrival of another friend of the *bağlama* teacher, a middle-aged man who ran a small copper-smithery. He was made welcome, and with tea and cigarettes dispensed, conversation flowed much as before.

During a brief lull, Ahmet, the copper-smith, remarked that he had just been watching a video of one of Emrah's recent films, *Yuvasızlar*. Since I was actually the only one present who had seen it, he described the film to us. At that point the dialogic exchanges of the previous discussion came to an abrupt halt as Ahmet began his monologue. Emrah is marooned in Istanbul, deserted by his parents and left with his younger brother to look after. The younger brother is ill and sickening fast; they are living in a ruined patch of the city walls. Emrah walks past a restaurant and sniffs the smell of kebabs in the air. The owner of the restaurant leaves a kebab on the window-sill for one of the customers on the street. Emrah grabs it instead and runs off with the restaurant owner in hot pursuit. Without taking a bite himself (Ahmet dwelt on this point at some length), Emrah feeds it to his ailing brother and bursts into a song of grief as he does so. The restaurant owner listens in amazement, tears streaming down his face. By this time Ahmet too is openly in tears. He switches to a story from his own childhood, in his village near Samsun. His family had been poor and he was working in a neighbouring village when he was a teenager. One evening his journey back home took him past the village baker. It was a cold evening and there was a pile of steaming, freshly baked bread outside his bakery. It was, he said, the only thing he had ever stolen in his life. He took one loaf to a bridge over a stream, sat under it, and ate the bread.

Ahmet was known by everyone as an 'open' and generous person, much given to extravagance in any form—a 'typical *Karadenizli* (from the Black Sea)'. At the time, what startled me most about this incident was the complete lack of embarrassment at a grown family man talking about things in a manner which completely contravened all recognized codes of male comportment and behaviour. In retrospect it became clear that Ahmet had been using the arabesk narrative to make a complex statement about himself to his friends. Interweaving an episode from his own life with the film, Ahmet was reminding himself and others that everybody carries inside themselves some aspect of the *gariban*, the social outcast, and that this occasionally necessitates complex moral choices whose outcome might not necessarily be 'correct' or desirable. If I had known Ahmet as well as everybody else in the room, I would undoubtedly have been able to construct other readings of his account of the film. Not knowing me well at that time, he was conceivably pointing out to me as a stranger that his current prosperity was the result of work and personal hardship, and that I was to treat him with the respect due to a self-made man. It is also possible that he was making a quite different kind of statement about the inevitability of feelings of loneliness and frustration to Osman, the friend with whom I had arrived, whose introverted moodiness sometimes irritated him. What was clearly evident to me after the event was the way in which arabesk had been used in a performative context to construct a domain of meaning relating specifically to an individual and a small group of friends.

The language of migration, the south-east, and the *gecekondu* provides an idiom in which people are able to identify and present problems, difficulties, and frustrations in their own existence. Whilst the emotions associated with these problems are banished from the realm of official discourses, they are acknowledged and defined in the subversive discourses of arabesk. The propositions made by these discourses at a musical, poetic, and visual level have an internal coherency, tightly binding together recurrent narratives, images, and metaphors. It is to these that we shall turn next.

5
Arabesk Lyrics and Narratives

When people talk about arabesk they do so in terms of the lyrics of the songs and the films to which they belong. In the texts, ideas and images are compressed into a small number of extremely dense lines, extended by melisma and musical repetition. On their own they have an abstract quality, consisting of a displaced rhetoric of suffering and frustration. Whilst the locus of the texts is unquestionably an urban space, a world of taxis, trains, cafés, crowds, and unfamilar streets, the singer, the loved one, and the cause of suffering are seldom specified or described. Even the gender of the loved one remains ambiguous through the use of the unspecified third-person pronoun, 'o'. It is precisely this abstract quality that allows for the texts to be embedded in films and personally constructed narratives in the manner described in the previous chapter. This provides the basis for what I shall tentatively describe as the aesthetic experience of arabesk, the understanding of 'what it means' in relation to one's own experience.

The perception of meaning is a highly significant aspect of the Turkish response to music. I frequently heard a singer's voice being evaluated positively as *manalı* ('meaningful') or *ifadeli* ('expressive'), and what was compelling about arabesk was precisely this *mana* ('meaning') and *ifade* ('expression'). In discussing the clarity of diction of Zeki Müren and reasons for the popularity of certain arabesk musicians, I heard one musican friend, a TRT singer in Istanbul, remarking to another: 'Müzikte önemli olan şey nedir? Anlaşılma' ('What is the important thing in music? Being understood'). In other words, the value of the music and the voice lies in its ability to communicate the sentiments with which arabesk is concerned. I was assured frequently that I would never be able to understand arabesk. As a foreigner, someone who could not have been expected to have internalized the narratives of arabesk, its significance would always remain hidden. It was only after I had been in Istanbul for some time, and was able to draw on the lexicon of arabesk to describe my own early experiences and use arabesk in the way other people did, that I was deemed capable of 'understanding'. There is thus a dense web of metaphor radiating outward from the song texts to the films and other kinds of narrative, and it is this that provides the basis of a communicable understanding of music. These texts and narratives constitute the subject of this chapter. The point of departure and return will be a metaphor of burning which runs through every aspect of music-making in Turkey.

5.1. Predicative Metaphors of Sound: *Yanmak* and *Yakmak*

As a preliminary step it is first necessary to look at the general usage of the verbs *yanmak* (to burn) and *yakmak* (to light) in the Turkish language. The first refers to the passive state of burning, or being alight. Of the seven definitions given in Redhouse, the first four cover aspects of this.[1] Five is 'to be painful, to hurt, to be very thirsty', and describes the use of the word in phrases such as *miydem yanıyor* ('I have a stomach-ache') and *ayaklarım yanıyor* ('my feet hurt'). Definition six gives 'to be ruined, to be done for, to become not valid or forfeited, to lose one's turn in a (game)'. When asked to provide an answer to a question he does not know, a pupil in a classroom will mutter 'Eyvah! Yandım . . .' ('Oh God! I'm done for . . . '). The derived form *yanık* (scorched or burnt) is the name for a card game resembling rummy, always played for money, referring to the object of the game—to get other players out so that they have to buy their way back into the game. The seventh definition is 'to feel grieved or sorry (for); to be consumed with passion (for)'. Thus *yandım Allah diye bağırmak* ('to shout out saying God I have burnt') comes to mean 'to be in great distress or suffering'. To these Alderson and İz add, amongst others, the expressions *canım yandı* ('I have suffered, I was hurt'), *dert yanmak* ('to complain of one's state—*hal*—or circumstances').[2] It is important to establish the use of the verb in reference not only to the experience of suffering, but the communication of this experience as complaint, the pouring out of woes.

Turning to the active principle, *yakmak*, Redhouse provides us with numerous definitions connected with lighting and setting fire, but also 'to blight (vegetation)', 'to inflame with love', '*slang*, to dupe, hurt deeply, to destroy', and finally, as definition number

[1] Redhouse 1976. [2] Alderson and İz 1959.

eight, 'to compose (a folk song)'. Thus in colloquial Turkish, one refers to the singing of a folk song as *türkü yakmak* rather than the more 'correct' *türkü söylemek* or *türkü okumak* (respectively, to say or read a song).

The metaphor of combustion runs through every aspect of music-making in Turkey, in critical language, in the texts, as the name for kinds of music, and, as we have seen, in the very verbs which express the act of music-making. Thus a piece of music, or a singer's voice, either 'sets one on fire' or it does not (*beni yakar* or the negative, *beni yakmaz*). Similarly someone with a good voice will be approvingly said to have a voice which is *yanık*, 'scorched' or 'burnt-up' with emotion. Other terms of appraisal are used to describe singing voices. The expression *kadife sesli* ('velvet-voiced') frequently used to describe a vocal quality which is in many ways the opposite of *yanık*. Mustafa Keser told me that he attempted to emulate the velvet-voiced, 'soft as cotton' (*pamuk gibi yumuşak*), voices of Frank Sinatra and Nat King Cole. In spite of his success as an arabesk singer, this style of singing is one generally more appropriate to Turkish art music than arabesk. The intensity of emotions associated with arabesk mean that a harsh and bitter sound is preferred. Other terms of appraisal applied to the voice are *ayva tadında* ('tasting of quince'), *buruk* ('acrid, astringent'), and *gevrek* ('crisp, brittle'), but the word *yanık* is the most precise and focused in its meaning, referring to peculiarly Turkish musical qualities. Thus it might be said of a Western singer, or a Turk singing in a Western style, that their voice is *tatlı* ('sweet') but it is unlikely to be described as *yanık*. This is an expression of appraisal which resonates fully only in the context of Turkish music.

As a term of aesthetic appraisal *yanık* generally refers to vocal qualities. It might initially appear to describe a high male head voice, in the region of a high tenor with an average tessitura of C to a/b flat, characterized by such popular halk and arabesk singers as İbrahim Tatlıses, Burhan Çaçan, İzzet Altınmeşe, and Mahmut Tunçer. Dialect is also an important factor. The glottalization of the mid /k/ to back /q/, the tendency to render these plosive consonants as fricatives, and tensed glottis vowel sounds are characteristics of south-eastern varieties of spoken Turkish. Along with the high tessitura this results in a distinctive style of vocal production and ornmentation to which the term *yanık* is invariably applied.

In male voices, this contrasts with a quality of voice referred to as *davudî*, 'deep and manly', such as those of Muzaffer Akgün in the 1950s and an older generation of Istanbul TRT halk-music singers such as Ömer Şan and Şahin Gültekin. However, the predominantly Alevi musicians who constitute a popular sub-genre of folk music in Turkey today, including Arif Sağ, Yavuz Top, Muhlis Akarsu, Musa Eroğlu, and Süleyman Yıldız, sing in deep voices, corresponding to a low baritone (AA–C). Female musicians associated with Alevi music such as Can Etili and Belkis Akkale have popularized a style of singing which is particularly low in the female range, overlapping with a high male tessitura (C–a/b). The relationship of this to the low female tessitura in arabesk has been noted in association with the homogenization of gender markers in the music. All of these voices are described as *yanık*, so their 'burning' quality is not confined to pitch alone. In fact, I was told that 'a voice which isn't *yanık* would never catch on with us' ('yanık olmıyan bir ses bizde tutulmaz'). It is clear that there are no obvious vocal markers, in terms of tessitura or vocal tone production, for this 'burning' quality in the human voice, since it can be applied with equal validity to the quite different vocal styles of the south-east and the northern and central eastern provinces. I suggest that what is considered to be *yanık* is not the quality of the voice but the subject-matter of the songs and stories associated with arabesk, and indeed all popular musical styles in Turkey.

If this is the case, a question immediately arises over the use of the verbs *yanmak* and *yakmak* when applied to purely 'abstract' instrumental forms. Whilst the instrumental technique of individual musicians may not be described as *yanık*, the sound of a particular instrument, or class of instruments may be characterized in terms of its burning quality. A TRT player once indicated his preference for the *tar* over its art-music equivalent, the *tanbur*, by saying that the first 'lights' him (*beni yakar*) whilst the other does not.

Instrumental sounds are not systematically characterized. Even though few Turks would admit to not liking the sound of the *bağlama*, it is recognized that preferences are personal and idiosyncratic. What burns one might not necessarily burn another. Perhaps the most extended example of the Turkish characterization of instrumental sounds is a poem by the fifteenth-century poet Ahmadi in Çağatay Turkish.[3] Unfortunately some of the instruments to which he refers no longer exist, in Turkey at least. The *tambura* (a long-

[3] The story is transl. in full in Eckmann 1962.

necked lute) asserts its superiority as the best instrument because of its 'weeping lamentation' which could soften the hardness of stone. The *Ud* claims that it knows all of the musical keys and modalities and 'its lamentation burns the soul'.[4] The *çeng* (a small harp) claims that it has the sweetest sound of all. The *kopuz* (today's *bağlama*), being the 'nightingale in the rose garden of love', knows the secrets of love in all tonalities and makes everybody its slave. The *yatugan* ('a kind of lying harp') contends that 'the fire in its body sends out sparks in every direction').[5] The *rebab* (a fiddle) is pious and the *gıçak* (a small turcoman fiddle) a vagabond. The *kingira*[6] finally 'maintains that it is able to create an uproar like the raising of the dead and is freer than all of the other instruments and is every way equal in rank to the *tambura*'. The *tambura* retorts to each instrument in turn by commenting on their shape and method of producing sound, in an uncomplimentary manner. Finally the tavern-keeper who owns the tavern in which the dispute is taking place rouses himself from his drunken stupor and puts a stop to the debate. At the request of the other instruments, he orders the *tambura* to apologize to its companions for its hostility. This story, highly influenced by Mevlevi mysticism, clearly indicates that from the very earliest written sources the power of instrumental music was expressed by the metaphor of burning so prevalent in the context of music-making in Turkey today.

The word *yanık* is also used to describe a genre of solo *bağlama* pieces from Central Anatolia,[7] a rare *bağlama* tuning,[8] and as a well-known scale formation in halk music, Yanık Kerem. It is a variant of Kerem *ayağı*, differing from it in its substitution of a C sharp for a C natural in the conventional notation (see Appendix A), resulting in an augmented second between the second and third degrees of the scale. The equivalent of this mode in Turkish art music, Hicaz *makamı*, is considered to be emotional and moving (*hüzünlü*), which is thought to make it particularly suitable for use in the call to prayer. But the augmented second is such a commonly heard interval that it appears to have an entirely neutral quality, except for those musicians who are aware of the fact that it has 'oriental' associations for Europeans. In fact, the characterization of

[4] Ibid. 119. [5] Ibid. 120.

[6] Eckmann describes it as 'a musical instrument with two wires' (ibid. 120), but the *kingira* is not known in Turkey today. Nor is the instrument mentioned in Picken 1975 or Ögel 1987.

[7] Picken 1975, 243. [8] Ibid. 288.

modal structures, in the way in which Western musicians are taught to think of the major scale as 'happy' and the minor scale as 'sad', is largely absent in technical treatises and popular wisdom alike.

It is clear that the term *yanık* cannot be pinned down to any easily definable trait of musical style or performance. Like all such terms making 'aesthetic' statements, it is an elastic term whose vagueness permits it to be used in a variety of ways. It is also a response to something that does not lie on the surface of the music, in its technical mastery or style of performance in itself. It is a recognition of the story that lies behind the music, and the process of bringing this inner narrative into the outer world through music and verse. Music, whether vocal or instrumental, is held to be good to the extent to which it brings out the story in a clear and direct manner.

5.2. Narratives of Music: The Arabesk Film

The clearest picture of this story is to be found in the Turkish musical films, particularly those connected with arabesk. The interdependent relationship of film and reality is striking. During my field-work I was conscious as an outsider that public social intercourse always involved the performance of carefully studied roles. Conversely, watching the films, the actors do not 'act', but play themselves. In most films, arabesk stars use their real names, 'Orhan' (Gencebay), 'İbrahim' (Tatlıses), 'Ferdi' (Tayfur), 'Mahmut' (Tunçer), and so on. Whatever the personal circumstances of the viewer, the film is sufficiently 'open' as a text to provide a point of contact with personal experience, a mapping of the past. The arabesk drama is a picture of reality, and not an illusory artifice for the purposes of idle distraction or simple entertainment. With reference to the nineteenth-century *ortaoyunu* and Karagöz shadow plays, the Turkish literary historian Metin And suggests that this is a consistent feature of the Turkish conception of drama.[9]

The film presents a structured plot, of which the majority have a tragic as opposed to happy conclusion. It is hardly necessary to carry out a strict structural analysis of the arabesk film plot to demonstrate the common dramatic and rhetorical gestures that are employed. Instead I will take the outlines of four plots, chosen with their relative dissimilarity in mind rather than their similarity, to show

[9] And 1979, 14.

that within the genre there is in fact a high degree of structural uniformity.

(a) Bende Özledim: Ferdi Tayfur (1980)

'Ferdi' makes love to his fiancée before setting out from his village to work in Libya. He arrives in Istanbul to discover that his application has been postponed for six months in order to get the appropriate health certificates and visa. Dejected, he walks out of the employment agency's office and is immediately hit by a car on the street. He is taken to hospital, but is not badly injured. He relates his story to the man driving the car, who offers him employment as a mechanic in his garage. At this time his grandfather dies leaving him a small amount of money, most of which he sends back to his parents and fiancée. Ferdi's patron lends him enough money to set up his own garage and haulage business. Under the illusion that he is rich, the girl next door forces him to marry her by getting him drunk one night. She soon gets bored with Ferdi's lack of money and prospects, and gets a job first as a model and then as a mistress to Ferdi's ex-boss in order to pay off her gambling debts. Ferdi sees them together in the distance and chases after them in his lorry, crashes, and is taken to hospital. By pretending to be blind on his release from hospital he catches his wife and lover *in flagrante delicto*, kills both, and runs back to his village to see his old fiancée and child. The police catch up with him and surround the house. He surrenders and is taken away.

(b) Mavi Mavi: İbrahim Tatlıses (1985)

İbrahim works as a minibus driver at the Topkapı garage. Whilst driving schoolchildren back in the evening from an expensive private school, he falls in love with the mother of one of his charges, who hires him to drive her to and from the aerobics classes where she is an instructor. İbrahim is first teased and eventually humiliated for his lack of sophistication and awkwardness. Later he gatecrashes a swimming-pool party, pushes most of the guests into the pool, grabs the woman, and drives her, bound hand and foot, to his village. He locks her in a room whilst he goes off to the tea-house to see his family and friends. She tries to escape but cannot. Satisfied that her spirit is thoroughly broken, İbrahim takes her back to Istanbul, but realizes that any future relationship is impossible. After a period of heavy drinking, he takes his mother's advice and marries the daughter of their next-door neighbour. The aerobics teacher has meanwhile had second thoughts and decides to make it up with İbrahim. But it is too late. She rushes back to İbrahim's village just in time for the wedding. She is completely ignored except for an intense passing glance from İbrahim, at which point the film ends.

(*c*) *Ayrılamam*: Emrah (1987)

The arabesk star Emrah is seen relating the story of his life to journalists after a concert, explaining that life has not always been easy for him. When he is a child, Emrah's father, a worker in Germany, dies leaving the family a large sum of money. Emrah's mother is persuaded to leave the village and take herself and both children to Istanbul by his paternal uncle, who intends to seduce the mother and appropriate the money. He puts Emrah to work as a 'partner' in a garage business and creams off the profits of Emrah's hard work. Emrah's sister falls ill, and the uncle intervenes to send her off for specialist treatment in Germany. In fact he sends her off to the home of a friend in Istanbul who uses her as a housemaid until she gets better. In this way the uncle takes the inheritance to pay for the sister's non-existent medical expenses. Having both children out of the way, he is free to seduce Emrah's mother. Emrah discovers mother and uncle apparently making love and runs away, living on the streets until his voice is 'discovered' and he is offered employment singing in clubs. After a *rapprochement* with his mother, at this point living in poverty in a *gecekondu*, he discovers the truth about his sister. His uncle is sent to prison, and his sister dies as a result of the neglect of her illness. However he is soon out of prison, and cannot resist one last attempt on Emrah's mother. Emrah catches him in his mother's house and shoots him dead.

(*d*) *Bırakmam Seni*: Küçük Ceylan (1988)

Ceylan is born of a village woman and a father who has left to work in Istanbul. Whilst she is still a baby her mother is employed by a rich woman as a housemaid. She is informed that her husband has been taken ill and wishes to see her in hospital in the city. In her absence, the baby Ceylan is kidnapped by her employer and husband. They have no children of their own, and need a child so that the good-for-nothing husband can ingratiate himself with his mother-in-law and inherit a fortune to pay off his gambling debts. Ceylan is bought up as their daughter. The real mother returns to her village distraught and goes mad. Years later, Ceylan is on holiday at the large estate of a rich relative, where she sees, but of course does not recognize, her 'real' mother working in a gang on the fields. By offering to help she begins a friendship with her. Finally, an accident happens and Ceylan requires a blood transfusion. Her 'real' but unrecognized mother is the only one at hand with the requisite blood group. When Ceylan returns to her adopted mother, her grandmother dies, and her adopted mother inherits the house, which she immediately turns into a gambling den. Having served her purpose, Ceylan is told to pack her bags and go. The grandmother suddenly materializes; she has suspected her daughter and tricked her by pretending to be dead. With the family lawyer present she leaves all her money to Ceylan, and dies a little later. Ceylan leaves her house to her adopted mother since 'without money she is nothing' and learns from her who her real mother is. Enquiry in the village reveals who her real mother is and the whereabouts of the father who disappeared in Istanbul. He is bought back to the village and the family is reunited.

The recurrent dramatic devices of these stories involve the disruption of the family, migrant labour, alienation in the city, a state of solitude and helplessness brought about by a remote and manipulative 'other', and exploitation most clearly revealed in an opposition between work and gambling. The films are full of complex and often contradictory inner voices, but play with and explore a basic plot, knowledge of which can be assumed on the part of the audience. Given the high proportion of tragic conclusions to arabesk films, the happy conclusion of film (*d*) has an ironic character which in no way challenges or undermines the basic plot formula. In this, the telos of the drama is inexorable. Progressive crises finally put the protagonist in a situation in which their only moral resource is their honour, but this provides no coherent resolution to the situation. The plot presents a sequence of progressive dislocation and disintegration, leaving the protagonist in a state of wretchedness and loneliness.

Since the story is always 'known' and few surprises exist, the focus of the drama is not the ending or denouement. The point of the structural machinery of the drama is to provide a series of focuses, each one a stage in the fall of the protagonist. The flow of dramatic action is suspended and the state of the protagonist is expressed in music. Each film contains some three of four songs, with incidental music being produced by synthesizers or recordings of Western music. Songs which achieve the status of popular hits, giving their name to the film and cassette of the film music with which they are associated, typically occur in the middle of the film. The most successful and well known of these songs coincide with the most intense of these dramatic focuses. These often begin with a short passage of vocal improvisation, in imitation of the *uzun hava* of halk music, consisting of a brief vocalise on the opening line, or title of the song. Film (*c*) conforms to this pattern closely. A critical point in the drama is reached when Emrah's uncle takes his sister away, supposedly to hospital in Germany. This particular dramatic juncture, in which the protagonist is seen at his most exposed, alienated, and exploited, is the cue for the song bearing the title of the film and cassette. The conventional response to the beginning of a known song—applause, whistles, and cries of 'Allah!'—is replicated in the cinema with an extra dimension of intensity added by the visual image and the knowledge that the emotional epicentre of the film has been reached.

5.3. The Arabesk Song Text and the Interior Domain

Turning back to the arabesk song text, it is now possible to see the way in which it focuses a dense cluster of themes connected with the arabesk drama: *gurbet* (living alone as a stranger or foreigner, particularly as a worker), *yalnızlık* (loneliness), *hicran, hüsran*, and *özlem* (sadness and yearning), *gözyaşları* (tears), *sarhoşluk* (drunkenness), *zülm* (oppression), and finally *kader* (fate). Before turning to these themes and separating their individual strands, it is necessary to establish that the song text in Turkish is of an oblique and indirect nature, lacking any clear narrative structure. In the context of arabesk it is easy to see why this should be the case, since the narrative structure is present in the films of which the song is only a part. Each song, connected or not with a film, is part of a drama which everybody knows. In folk music this is not so obvious, but no less the case. The startling juxtapositions and dense imagery are at first confusing. Bartók found Turkish folk lyrics perplexing. Comparing them with those of his native Hungary, he commented that:

> the overwhelming majority . . . [are] much more 'abstract', sometimes reminding the reader of the symbolistic, surrealistic, and whatnot art poetry of

> the beginning of this century. A student in New York, . . . whose native language is Turkish, asserted that the abstruseness is deliberate; in fact, that in Turkish rural poems the harmonious effects resulting from the succession and sound of the words, the rhythms and so forth,—and not the meaning of the text lines or stanzas—are of primary importance. This theory is open to question, for it alone does not account for the abstract character of the texts.[10]

If we look upon Turkish folk poetry as incomplete fragments of wider dramas, the problem of the 'abstruseness' of the song texts which so bothered Bartók disappears. The text does not have the function of imparting a story because the story is already known: a natural disaster, the death of a brigand or the departure of the village 15-year-olds to fight in the war. If this implied narrative structure could in any way be removed, the musical performance would be rendered meaningless.

Somewhat in the manner of Baroque opera, the dramatic action in the arabesk film stops at the moment the musical set piece begins. The effect of this is twofold. It draws attention to a particular dramatic juncture, closely associated with the disintegration of the family unit, and it allows for a moment of reflection on the more generalized themes of the drama in a poetic/musical register which is freed from the dictates of the logic of narrative progression. In arabesk, the outsider is presented with an extremely dense web of metaphor and symbol. The recurrent elements of the text depict the outer aspects of an emotional 'state' (*hal*). The poetics of arabesk are entirely bound up with the description of this state.

The implicit background of the arabesk drama is labour migration, *gurbet*. Since knowledge of this will be assumed by songwriters, direct reference to *gurbet* is not common, but occasionally to be found in the song texts themselves. A notable example is Arif Sağ's 'Gurbet Treni', popularized by İbrahim Tatlıses. Arabesk lyrics concentrate more fully upon the state of loneliness and sadness brought about by the situation of being 'in *gurbet*', as typified by this opening (to Orhan Gencebay's 'Kaderimin Oyunu'):

Ne sevenim var,
Ne soranım
Öyle yalnızım ki

I have no lover | Nor anybody interested | I am so lonely . . .

[10] Bartók 1976, 205.

Musical performance makes a statement about solitude. As Bartók discovered to his frustration when he was attempting to get a recording of villagers singing together in a chorus, music in Turkey is essentially a solitary and individual occupation.[11] Turkish folk-music instruments are designed to be played on their own and not in ensembles, even though the imitation of Western orchestras has led, as we have seen, to the establishment of large folk-music orchestras by the TRT. Instruments are ideally learnt during periods of enforced loneliness. Prison and military service are considered to be particularly fruitful in opportunities for learning the *bağlama*. I once heard an anecdote describing a young man who asks how he can learn the *bağlama*. It is recommended that he goes to prison, partly since most of the best *bağlama* players in the district have wound up there, but also since the enforced solitude and isolation provide ideal conditions for learning the instrument. He steals a donkey, reports himself to the police, and is sent to gaol to emerge years later a virtuoso musician.

In concert, the arabesk singer holds the stage on his own and sings as a solo star and not as a member of a band. In a number of ways, therefore, music is associated at both symbolic and practical levels with solitude. It is not surprising then that the subject of much Turkish folk music as well as arabesk should be associated with the departure of friends and relatives through war, death, or *gurbet*. Whatever the initial cause of migration to the city, the arabesk drama states that the eventual and inexorable result of migration is a self-absorbed emotional malaise whose description occupies most of the arabesk lyric texts. This feeling is accentuated by a dramatic device common to most arabesk films, in which the newly arrived migrant falls in love, as in film (*b*), or is obliged to enter into some kind of relationship with a woman whose remoteness from the protagonist is represented by her 'modernity' and beauty. Since many young men leave their families and migrate to the city as a result of 'boredom' (*can sıkıntısı*) and an urge for sexual adventure as well as a need to find work, the female co-star of the arabesk film is both the perfect symbol and the reality of the aspirations and fears of the urban migrant. Sex provides an idiom of integration and fulfilment. The soft-pornographic character of many arabesk films emphasizes the gap between the viewer and the erotic image on screen in such a way that the viewer's identification with the *gariban* outsider of the

[11] Ibid. 7.

film narrative is doubly reinforced. The powerlessness of individuals to integrate themselves coherently and fully into a society is in the context of the arabesk film the powerlessness to achieve sexual congress. The remote erotic image, often played by actresses who are well known outside the context of the film from photographs in newspapers and pornographic magazines, thus manipulates and finally excludes not only the protagonist of the 'imaginary' drama, but also the male viewer himself. The identification of the female viewer with male stars such as Ferdi Tayfur and Emrah, widely popular amongst female arabesk fans, is also a relationship with a remote and unattainable erotic image, even though it is complicated by the fact that for the most part the films are made by and for men. For both men and women, however, the films assert that the gap between image and reality, isolated self and society, 'Turkish' honour and 'modern' morality, the rural and the urban, is ultimately unbridgeable. Through the attempt to bridge the gap, the protagonist is reduced to his lowest level: his own honour is dragged through the mud, cutting him off from society, forcing him into a series of moral conundrums involving theft, alcohol, and acts of violence which drive him ultimately to self-destruction.

The poetic terms in which this situation is described in the arabesk lyrics can be summarized and exemplified in the following way:

(i) Hüsran ('disappointment', 'sorrow', 'frustration')

Ve hüsran olursa her aşkın sonu
Hatırla sevgilim beni hatırla

And if disappointment should be the end of every love | Remember my love, remember me ('Beni Hatırla', Samime Şanay)

(ii) Özlem ('yearning', 'longing')

Yıllardır bir özlemdi
Yanıp durdu bağrımda

There was a yearning for years | Which burned continually in my breast ('Mavi Mavi', İbrahim Tatlıses)

(iii) Kara sevda ('melancholy')

Umitsız bir aşkın esiri oldum
Öldürecek beni bu kara sevda

I've become a slave of a hopeless love for you | This melancholy will kill me ('Seni Seviyorum', Ümit Besen)

(iv) Hasret ('longing', 'yearning', 'ardent desire')

Aşkın, hasret çölüyüm ben
Bir göz yaşı gölüyüm ben

I am the longing desert of love | I am a lake of tears ('Yanımda olmayınca', Zeki Müren)

Güne hasret yaprak gibi
Suya hasret toprak gibi
Şırıl şırıl ırmak gibi
Seviyorum diyebilsem

Like the leaf longing for the sun | Like the earth longing for water | Like a gurgling river | If only I could say I love you. ('Seviyorum Diyebilsem', Muazzez Abacı)

The naturalistic metaphors of the last two examples amplifying the extremely common word *hasret* introduce the themes of dryness and wetness; the state of *hasret* results in a dryness comparable to that of the desert crying out for water. The strong theme of tears in arabesk gains some of its resonance from this; if the inner being[12] is parched and burnt up like a desert with longing, the futility of tears (*gözyaşları*) is all the more evident. Tears pervade arabesk lyrics, as well as the lurid posters and postcards showing sobbing little boys and girls invariably to be found alongside pictures of Atatürk, the Bosphorus Bridge, and 'Bismillahs'[13] in cafés, lorries, and *dolmuş*.

Silsem gözlerimi kurusun diye
Bahar seli gibi boşanır gelir
Nerde sevdiklerim hani sevenler
Ağlatıyor beni acı gerçekler

If I wipe my eyes so that they may dry | They empty like a spring flood | Where are those I have loved, where are those that love me? | Painful truths make me weep ('Acı Gerçekler', Orhan Gencebay)

[12] See below, s. 5.

[13] A shortened form of the formula *Bismillaharahmanirahim* ('In the name of God, the Compassionate, the Merciful') which is used at the beginning of any undertaking, and whose text is displayed prominently in the interior of houses, public buildings, and motor vehicles.

Uzaktan görenler mesut sanıyor
Bilmezler gözlerim her gün ağlıyor

Those who view me from afar think that I am happy | They do not know that my eyes weep every day ('Benim Hayatım', İbrahim Tatlıses)

Bakarsın anlarsın gözlerime sen
Eğer ağlıyorsam yaşıyorum ben

If you look into my eyes you will understand | If I am weeping, I am living ('Ağlıyorsam Yaşıyorum', Gülden Karaböçek)

Control of emotion at an early age in the family and at school defines and gives expressive form to states of mind and being. Every rite of passage faced by the young Turkish child emphasizes the correct and controlled response to pain and suffering. It is expected that young male children will weep at their circumcision ceremonies, although the ritual is accompanied by exhortations for them to behave like a man and suffer in silence. The Turkish comic writer Aziz Nesin vividly describes how he used to shut himself in the toilet as a child in order to cry.[14] For males, weeping is acknowledged but can only take place in solitude and private space. Public weeping amongst women is confined to particular occasions, such as the departure of a guest, the point at which the bride leaves her parental home in marriage ceremonies, death, and funerals.[15] The gloomy facial expressions in the iconography of film posters and cassette box covers and the obsessive reference to tears in arabesk lyrics thus make clear, socially constructed, statements about the nature of the inner and private self.

More extreme states of suffering described in arabesk lyrics are those of pain and malady (*dert* and, less frequently, *çile*). Along with *hasret*, *dert* is probably one of the most frequently occurring words in recent arabesk lyrics, often paired with *derman* (from the Persian word meaning 'remedy' or 'cure'):

Bir acı gönlüme yeter
Derman olsun dertlerime

One pain is enough for my soul | May there be a cure for my afflictions ('Zoruma Gidiyor', Ceylan)

Derman bana senden gelsin
Bekliyorum dertli dertli

[14] Nesin 1977, 118.

[15] This dourness, at once calculating and full of threatening powers of control and self-discipline has been a significant trope in European travel writing on Turkey. See e.g. Durrell's description of Sabri Tahir in *The Bitter Lemons of Cyprus* (1959).

May the cure come from you to me | I am waiting in anguish ('Dertli Dertli', İbrahim Tatlıses)

References to the unhealable wound (*yara*), physical wounding, and mutilation also abound. This can be external:

Hancer yarası değil
Domdom kurşune değdi

It was not a dagger wound | But a dum-dum bullet that pierced me ('Dom Dom Kurşune', İbrahim Tatlıses)

Or it may be internal:

Dermansız yarası kanıyor gönlüm

The wound of my soul bleeds without cure ('Çaresizim', Ferdi Tayfur)

Gönül yarasından acı duyanlar
Feleğin kahrına boyun eğermiş

Those who feel pain from a wound in the heart | Their necks bent to the blows of fate ('Gönül Yarasından Acı Duyanlar', Alaaddin Şensoy)

Many of its critics claim that the result of arabesk is to drive those who listen to it to despondency and alcohol. The many-levelled connection between alcohol and arabesk must be seen in terms of patterns of leisure activity in Turkish cities. Drinking and music (if only in recorded form) can accompany complete, but public, solitude in *birahane* or *gazino*, or can accompany intensely social *muhabbet* gatherings. Wherever it is consumed, in a predominantly Muslim society, drinking alcohol is not simply recreation but an intensely semantic act. In arabesk lyrics, the emphasis is upon alcohol as a refuge and consolation, its consumption an act of simultaneous self-gratification and self-destruction:

Gönlüm şimdi teselleyi şarapta buldu

My soul has now found its consolation in wine ('Hüzünlü Günler', Müslüm Gürses)

Kadehler elimde her gece yandım
Meyhanelerde ben bir yuva kurdum

I burnt myself up glass in hand every night | I made a home for myself in the *meyhane* (Ümit Besen), in Güngör 1990, 150)

But in arabesk, alcohol is ultimately incapable of sustaining the terms of its own world of make-believe, throwing the quest for the real object of desire into even sharper focus:

Yolum düşer meyhaneler üstüne
İçtikçe aklıma sevgilim gelir

I end up in the *meyhane* | The more I drink the more my lover comes to mind. ('Acı Gerçekler', Orhan Gencebay)

Arabesk lyrics and films portray alcohol as both a symptom and a cause of the protagonists' decline. The resort to alcohol is seen as an image of the passive acceptance of fate, a decision to evade responsibility and not make an active stand against the way things are. Alcohol also provides the protagonist of the drama with a temporary means of escape and transcendence, but renders him less capable of dealing with a situation which has worsened through neglect. In the view of its critics it is precisely this emphasis upon alcohol that encourages the audience of arabesk to do nothing and to accept fate, even though the films and lyrics point continually to the futility of alcohol as a means of escape (note film (*b*) in particular), and provide a sustained critique of modern Turkish society.

5.4. Arabesk and Protest: The Social Domain and the *Gariban*

Arabesk broadly divides society into two categories of wealth, 'haves' and 'have nots', and two moral categories, corrupt and honest. Minor characters exist in the films who are rich but honest and honourable (for example, Ceylan's adopted grandmother in film (*d*)) and poor people who are either corrupt or corruptible (for example, Ferdi's wife in film (*a*)) are frequently encountered. Arabesk is essentially concerned with the plight of the alienated and uprooted migrant, the *garib* or *gariban*, who is separated from the bedrock of village life, without friends and money and completely at the mercy of the unscrupulous. The focus of the drama is the powerlessness of the protagonist to choose his or her own destiny. The only moral resource of the *gariban* is a sense of honour, which is portrayed as inadequate and inapplicable to the situations in which they find themselves.

A number of films focus on the question of legal justice. Official legal justice is seen in many parts of rural Turkey as an alien system of justice: an unwelcome assertion of state power which has little applicability in the context of rural Turkish society. The feud (*dava*) provides an important illustration of this, in which people recognize the existence and operation of two distinct systems of order, each with its own mode of punishment and control. As Güneş-Ayata has recently illustrated, this situation is particularly fraught amongst Black Sea migrants in Istanbul,[16] for whom elopement (*kaçırma*) is an accepted 'alternative' system of marriage. When elopement takes place involving Black Sea and non-Black Sea communities in the city, the injured party has recourse to both the 'traditional' *dava* and the state legal system. The latter, as a result of the disruption which frequently follows, regards elopement as an extremely serious offence punishable by a heavy gaol sentence. It is recognized then that there are many ways of interpreting the 'legality' of a set of actions, such as an elopement or feud. Arabesk films make a feature of the conflict of systems of control. The audience is asked to sympathize with, if not actually condone, the resort to violence to eradicate the sources of injustice, or violators of personal honour (see films (*b*) and (*c*)). Loud cheering in the cinemas as vengeance is exacted seems to indicate that this is the case. But this positive action is short-lived. The final victory of fate is represented by the heavy hand of official legal justice, and the incarceration of the protagonist of the drama. Imprisonment represents a final state of social dislocation, a kind of death. It is therefore quite striking that arabesk songs dwelling on the theme of imprisonment, such as Ferdi Tayfur's famous song 'Mapushane' ('The Prison'), do not question the issue of justice, but focus on themes of loneliness and isolation.

This may make more sense if we compare the arabesk 'Gaol' song with those in the halk-music repertoire, which are so numerous that Öztelli dedicates an entire section of folk-song lyrics in his collection to *Mapushane Türküleri*, giving by way of illustration some eleven individual songs.[17] The language and imagery of the arabesk gaol song clearly owes a great deal to the folk genre. The *Mapushane Türküleri* employ stylized references to natural life existing within the prison walls (the fig tree, the birds), and focus on the figure of the singer himself, his loneliness, the hours of confinement playing the *bağlama* and longing for the company of family and friends. No reference at all is made to the circumstances under which the protagonist is imprisoned, or even the injustice (we assume) which has resulted in his being there. For here, as in arabesk, the principal enemy is not the machinations of social and official legal justice, but fate itself. As Öztelli points out in the introduction to these songs:

16 Güneş-Ayata 1988. 17 Öztelli 1983, 623–33.

The 'companions' (*ihvan*, i.e. those in gaol) look out from behind the iron bars, and in the evening the iron doors are closed. In a deep state of loneliness, emotions are brought to tongue, in great sorrow (*yürekte yağ kalmaz erir*, literally 'the fat does not remain in the heart, it melts'). Whatever happens, fate is thus, the writing has been written.[18]

To illustrate the point, he quotes one of the recurring refrains from the *Mapushane Türküleri*:

Düştüm ben bir zindana
Yanar döner ağlarım
Demir parmaklıklardan
Boyun büker ağlarım

I have ended up in a gaol | I burn, I turn, I weep | I hang my head | Through the iron bars and weep.[19]

The conflict of two systems of control and punishment, and the ultimate fall of the protagonist of the arabesk film is not portrayed as an issue of justice *per se*, but as a statement about powerlessness. The drama states that, whatever happens, we will find ourselves in situations where we are forced through powerlessness to act in ways which we might find morally wrong and for which we will eventually suffer. The penalty is isolation, alienation, and loneliness, but the actions which lead us to this state are our only alternatives, and we cannot be blamed:

Ben bu garip yer yüzünde
Garibansam suç benim mi?
Gece gündüz dertli dertli
Geziyorsam suç benim mi?
Kimsesizsem çaresizsem
Ümitsizsem suç benim mi?

If I am a stranger (*gariban*) in this strange place | am I at fault? | If I wander in turmoil night and day | am I at fault? | If I have nobody, am helpless | and without hope, am I at fault? ('Gariban', Dündar Yeşiltoprak)

The lack of focus upon issues of justice may perhaps be attributed to the fact that official justice is a dramatic mechanism and a metaphor, but not an issue in its own right. What matters is not that the protagonist is in prison, but that his very attempt to organize his life meaningfully is what finally condemns him. Fate decrees isolation and alienation, and this fact of life cannot be escaped. So arabesk

[18] Ibid. 624. [19] Ibid. 624.

presents a quite explicit form of social critique, in which the bad characters systematically exploit the powerlessness of the central character for their own sexual gratification and material gain, in which the lot of the poor but honest man and woman is a poverty-stricken and anomic existence on the periphery of the city, and in which official justice and legality are seen to conspire against the integrity of fundamentally honest and honourable people. In spite of this, arabesk has never become the focus of explicit political protest.

Critics of arabesk interpret this in terms of its message of passivity. For them arabesk not only numbs the critical faculties but deadens a sense of political awareness and responsibility by blaming everything on fate. It might be argued, on the contrary, that arabesk lyrics do in fact constitute a form of political commentary, but one which is expressed through an aesthetic of indirectness, metaphor, and circumlocution. One of the threats posed by arabesk to successive Turkish governments has been the fact that it has indirectly addressed class issues, raising an intense awareness of the migration problem and social issues connected with this on a national scale. However, state-cultivated regionalism, which finds one of its modes of expression in the TRT halk-music department's policy of constructing and controlling representations of regional identity, has meant that for the majority of urban Turks, the problems of their society are seen in terms of regional and not class divisions. Whilst arabesk does contain a repertoire of metaphors which might be used in an explicitly 'political' commentary, this repertoire has remained muted.

A more likely reason for the fact that arabesk has never become a music of political protest is the cultural orientation of rightist and leftist ideologies in Turkey today. Since the 1960s, when Bülent Ecevit took over as the leader of Atatürk's political party, the CHP, the Turkish left, has seen itself as a progressive and Westernizing force in Turkish political life. On the model of Western protest rock, certain genres of popular music in Turkey have become a focus of an explicit political commentary. Arabesk, however, is not only seen by the Turkish left as an aspect of the oriental past which has to be shed along the road to progress, but interprets the tacit support of the Özal government as an acknowledgement of the truly reactionary nature of the music.[20] The need of the Turkish left for a musical symbol of their aspirations has been answered since the mid-1980s

[20] See Ch. 4, s. 3.

by a genre known as özgün ('free') music. Developed by Ahmet Kaya, and achieving wide popularity in 1990 with Fatih Kısaparmak, özgün is a genre which makes extensive use of Western guitar-based harmony, Western rock music instruments, and, very prominently, the *bağlama* to accompany the work of well-known radical poets (including the Turkish communist, Nazım Hikmet, who died in exile in Moscow) and lyrics by the musicians themselves. In the terminology of cantometrics, the songs are 'wordy' and carry a dense information load, as opposed to arabesk which is characterized by a high level of textual repetition and musical elaboration of the textual phrases.[21] The texts of özgün music celebrate revolt ('Başkaldırıyorum', 'I am in Revolt', a 1988 song by Ahmet Kaya) and freedom ('Denizin Ardı Özgürlük' 'Freedom beyond the Sea', from the same cassette). The most that arabesk lyrics provide is not a call for political action but a curse:

Zalimler, kötülere haram
Sevmek nedir bilmeyene
Sevilip de sevmeyene
Kıymet nedir bilmiyene
Haram olsun, haram olsun
Haram, haram, haram
Tüm söyleyen yalanlara
kara diyen tapanlara
İnsanlığı satanlara
Haram, haram, haram
Haram olsun bu dünya
Zehir olsun bu dünya
Seviyorken aldatana
Gülüyorken ağlatana
Bizi büyüle yakanlara
Haram olsun, haram olsun
Haram, haram, haram, haram
Tüm vicdansız zalimlere
Bu insafsız yüreklere
Garipleri ezenlere
Haram, haram, haram
Haram olsun bu dünya
Haram, haram, haram
Zehir olsun bu dünya

[21] Lomax 1968, 128.

A curse[22] on the oppressors, the wicked | What is love to those who don't know | To those who are loved but do not love? | What is value to those who don't know? | May they be cursed, may they be cursed | A curse, a curse, a curse | To all the lies that have ever been told | Those who worship anything evil | To all those who swindle humanity | A curse, a curse, a curse | May this world be cursed | May this world be poison | To those who deceive whilst loving | To those who make others weep whilst they laugh | To those who bewitch us and set us aflame | May they be cursed, may they be cursed | A curse, a curse, a curse, a curse | To all those soulless oppressors | To these hearts without justice | To those who crush the poor | A curse, a curse, a curse | May this world be poison | A curse, a curse, a curse | May this world be poison ('Haram', Uğur Bayar)

5.5. Fate, Love, and Self

The arabesk drama describes a situation in which the real enemy is fate, for whom the human actors are just playthings. Fate, described variously as *baht* and *talih*, but most commonly as *felek* and *kader*, is cursed in the most forceful rhetoric available to Turkish speakers:

Bu genç yaşımda beni dertlere attın felek
Acımadan sen benim bağrımı yaktın felek
Hayınsın, zalimsin, sen felek felek

You have immersed me in torments, fate, in this my youth | You have burnt my heart without mercy, fate, | Fate, fate, you are treacherous, you are tyrannical ('Bağrı Yanık', Müslüm Gürses)

Ben feleğin neylemişem bana böyle zulüm eder?

What am I to fate that it should oppress me so? ('Ben Feleğin Neylemişem', Emrah)

İsyan ettim, haykırdım yaşantıma bahtıma

I rebelled and cried out at my life, my fate ('Hasret Akşamları', Hüseyin Altın)

The religious objection to this cannot be overemphasized, and it is probably as a result of this that those arabesk songs which are cast in the form of a prayer, imploring God to change fate, tend to use the old Turkish word for God, *Tanrı*, rather than *Allah*:

[22] *Haram olsun* literally means 'let it be canonically forbidden'.

Görüyorsun Tanrım beni
Değiştir bu kaderimi
Açtım sana ellerimi
Yalvarırım dertli dertli

You see me my God | Change this fate of mine | I open my hands to you | I plead in anguish ('Dertli Dertli', İbrahim Tatlıses)

In this context it is also important to note the complex language of gestures used by urban singers, whether they are performing arabesk, halk, or sanat music. The most common gesture employed whilst singing is one in which the hands are spread open on either side of the body, between waist and chest height, in a gesture of prayer and supplication.

It would be a mistake to see in the arabesk text a monolithic statement of a single message. Listeners and musicians define sub-genres within arabesk and define themselves in relation to these sub-genres. Musicians trying to distance themselves in particular contexts from the negative image of arabesk assert that the subject-matter of their music reflects a wider range of issues and emotions. Gökhan Güney, associated by many with the most *koy* ('heavy') arabesk that there is, stated at a concert in Gülhane Park in 1990 that the much publicized *Acısız arabesk* had misled people into thinking that arabesk was all about doom and gloom. Arabesk had always reflected the whole of life, he asserted, adding, 'arabesk has got everything in it. Happiness, Joy . . .' ('arabesk'te her şey var. Neşe, sevinç . . .'). Many songs have complex inner voices in the text, entering into a dialogue with the central proposition that we are fated to isolation and outsidership. A song by Orhan Gencebay from a cassette which appeared in 1987 appeared to make a striking claim that fate should not be blamed when things go wrong:

Artık kızmıyorum kaderime
Bıraktı beni kendime
Bahtın açık olsun
Yolun açık olsun
Bırak beni halime

I no longer blame fate | It has left me to myself | May your fate be open [i.e. uncomplicated, easy on you] | May your road be open | Leave me to my state (*hal*) ('Dünya Dönüyor', Orhan Gencebay)

Discussing this song in an interview with *Müzik Magazin*, Orhan Gencebay explained that

> As far as I can see around me, human beings love one another and come together. So far so good, but after they split up, they get themselves into a state (*hal*) in which they render the world unliveable for themselves ... I think this is very wrong, because life goes on. Even if a person splits up with their loved one, they must recognize that they have to go on living. In the light of these feelings (*duygu*) I composed 'Dünya Dönüyor'.[23]

But even in these lines it is possible to see that a radically different argument is not being suggested. In spite of an inner dialogue in which the singer may not be blaming fate unequivocally, may have nothing but good wishes for the departed lover, and may have reconciled himself to the fact that he has to go on living, he still invites pity for the state (*hal*) in which he has been left by events.

These are events of love (*sevgi, aşk*). The *aşık* (lover-musicians) of Turkish folk poetry are condemned by their vocation to a life of unfulfilment and wandering. Similarly, in arabesk films, the object of love is the fatal prime mover. Without the emotion of love, the dramatic machinery of the narrative cannot be set into motion. The protagonist is portrayed as a passive victim of his emotions, which define the true, inner self as opposed to the social, outer self. The dictates of love override all others, powering the drama through to its inexorable conclusion. Love and fate are thematically intertwined. Without love, the protagonist has no fate. Put another way, the fate of the protagonist is to love, and this love is the cause of self-destruction. The focus of arabesk drama is not the actual conclusion but the progressive state of the protagonist's decline, a state which is metaphorically represented by the social and spatial peripherality of the lover. Arabesk lyrics are almost entirely concerned with a description of this 'state' (*hal*) afflicting the individual. This is both a symptom and a cause of the malaise affecting that with which it is most often linked, the *gönül*, the inner being, the soul. The relation of the two is in a sense circular. The *gönül* was described to me as being like a glass of water, ready to overflow, in a state of complete sensitivity to 'outside' influences. The reaction of the *gönül* may be responsible for the initiation of the *hal*.

The *gönül* might be described as the inner and secret self as opposed to the outer, public self. Frustratingly vague, Redhouse gives us both 'heart' and 'mind' as a translation of the term. The concept of *gönül* does not fit easily with theological constructions of the self. Islam provides us with the duality of the rationally reflective

23 *Müzik Magazin*, 25 Jan. 1988.

and materialistic *nefs*, and the spiritually oriented *ruh*. *Ruh* is occasionally cited in arabesk as the seat of the emotions, that which is 'affected', suggesting that the popular notion of *gönül* has some points of similarity with the spiritual aspect of the *nefs/ruh* duality:

Ruhumu yakmazdı böyle şarkılar

These kind of songs didn't inflame [burn] my soul ... ('Sevseydin Beni', Gülden Karaböcek)

References to the *yürek* or *kalb* (heart), the *can* (the soul, or individual), the *dil* (a Persian poetic term for 'soul'), and the *bağrı* (breast) occur in roughly equal measure. But the term *gönül* contains and transcends all of these, defining an inner (*iç*) domain of concealed, secret emotion, in opposition to the outer (*dış*) and social self. The following lyric makes this clear:

İçim yanar, kan ağlarım
Halimden anlayan yok

My insides burn, I weep blood | Nobody understands my state ('Güzelin Talihi Yok', Ferdi Özbeğen)

The reaction of the *gönül* is the 'state' or *hal*, which is in arabesk a fated condition of alienation, dishonour and decline. Outside of its religious meaning (to be discussed in Chapter 7), the term *hal* generally has the negative sense, as in English, of 'being in a state'. The expressions 'sana bir hal olmuş' (literally, 'a *hal* has happened to you') and 'bu ne hal?' ('What *hal* is this?', 'what's come over you?') imply that the inner state of agitation and turmoil has been sufficiently powerful to disrupt the smooth functioning of the outer social persona. I was often greeted in these terms on my return from the *yayla* (mountain pastures) to my host's restaurant in Trabzon, dirty, unshaven, ill, and seemingly unable to talk—i.e. dispense my social obligations—until I had been given a large *kebab* and several glasses of tea. Whilst the *hal* is primarily the result of the reaction (*tepki*) of the *gönül*, the condition of the *hal* also provides an outside stimulus to the *gönül*. The progress of the *hal* in arabesk can only be, it seems, a vertiginous downward spiral.

5.6. *Hal* and Urban Space

So although the *hal* is essentially a passive state in arabesk, with fate as the prime mover, it is by no means stationary. In fact, it is of its very essence in a state of motion, but motion that is circular and undirected. The *hal* of the arabesk hero results in the individual never being able to come to rest but still having nowhere to go. It is important to note that the social ideal for the male adult in Turkey is to be in a state of repose: entertainment, business, food, pleasure, and guests are all brought to him; he is never required to go and get them. My relationship with my informants nearly always expressed an asymmetry in which I was always the party expected to travel and be entertained. My first *bağlama* teacher expressly forbade me to take notes during our loosely structured lessons, telling me that whenever I wanted to know something I simply had to go and visit him, committing me to long and tiring journeys across the city. In this way, the flow of knowledge, information, and status expressed in spatial movement were immutably linked. Even when meetings were arranged in neutral space, informants who had left their apartments in order to see me would invariably indicate that their trips coincided with other (often unspecified) visits, establishing between us that I was the most inconvenienced party in terms of the journey that had been made.

These relationships between myself and my informants involved whole networks of hierarchies and levels. An interview with an informant in a café in the commercial centre of the city, to which both of us might have travelled some distance, would involve a supplementary visit to a certain Necat *hoca* or Dursun *amca*. The use of the honorific titles *hoca* ('teacher') and *amca* ('maternal uncle') put the matter beyond argument. Ostensibly these were arranged with the intention of providing me with assistance in my research. Indeed, they often happened to have this effect. Tacitly, however, they aligned me with chains of musical and musicological authority, in which, amongst other things, my relationship with the original interviewee would achieve a greater clarity. Through having done Necat *hoca* or Dursun *amca* the double honour of a visit in the company of a prestigious foreigner, the original interviewee had turned a neutral meeting into an opportunity to define our status, and subsequent transactions between us, to his advantage. Not only would I have clearly been dependent upon him as the recipient of a favour generally connected with my overt intentions, but I would have demonstrated my willingness to travel across Istanbul in order to accord with his higher (but concealed) plan. Thus a certain hierarchy of spatial movement was delineated in which I was the most mobile, in the orbit of my original interviewee, who was in turn in the even less mobile orbit of an 'uncle', 'elder brother', or 'teacher'. One could, it would seem, rank Turkish society according to the spatial distance covered by each individual in the course of their day-to-day existence, ranging from the perpetually mobile to the utterly inert. All movement in space is ideally limited to the directed and essential. The freedom with which children move around at concerts, dancing and playing around the seated adult audience and even on the stage itself, illustrates the extent to which social maturity is expressed in spatial stability. Having attained social maturity, a man has nowhere to go—what he needs is brought to him. The backs of his shoes are carefully trodden down, stating unequivocally that he is not at anybody's beck and call, and that if he has to go anywhere, he will do so at his own speed.

The state into which the arabesk protagonist is plunged is necessarily the antithesis of this; it is not only indirect, but circular and pointless. Turkish musician figures have always been portrayed in these terms. The *aşık* musician-lovers are shown a picture of a woman by a wandering dervish or *pir*. They fall in love with this image and never cease their wandering until they find their lover—which they may never do. In the medieval stories, such as those of Aşık Garip, Aşık Kerem, Cemşit and Hurşit, Güllühan and Melikşah, Ferhat and Şirin, and the Turkish versions of the story of Leyla and Mecnun, the *hal* is induced by the sight of the picture of the beloved (*ma'şuka*), and the lover is eventually found, whether the conclusion is happy or not. Another account of the *hal* experienced by the *aşık* is that a glass of wine (*bade*) is drunk and the *aşık* goes into a trance in which he either meets the lover, or has the lover described to him by his *pir*; the quest for this lover in 'real life' occupies the rest of his days. The story of the famous Aşık Sümmani, who died this century, relates that at 14 years of age he was out duck-hunting when he fell into a trance, only to be discovered by the villagers when he was missed several days later. Aşık Sümmani was given in his trance a new name, and the knowledge of Arabic, Persian, and Hebrew (*İmran*).[24]

It is also acknowledged that the *aşık* may be forced to travel as a result of war, feud, or poverty. The *aşık* resembles in many ways the protagonist of the arabesk drama; they are both engaged in a terminal conflict with fate. As Şahin points out: 'anyone who begins

[24] Şahin n.d., 58.

to revolt against their fate has attained the spirit of the *ozan (ozanlık ruhune gelişmiştir)*'.[25] Both are obliged to leave the security of their homes and villages in order to travel; the *aşık* on a quest for the *ma'şuka*, and the arabeskçi to Istanbul, where he finds himself engaged in that occupation which perfectly symbolizes his state of unrest, driving a *dolmuş*. The *dolmuş* follows circular routes through and around the city, coming to rest only temporarily in that most liminal of places, the Topkapı garage. Movement in the *hal* is always depicted as being circular. Even in the gaol song cited above, the only motion possible is circular:

Düştüm ben bir zindana
Yanar döner ağlarım

I have ended up in a gaol | I burn, I turn, I weep.[26]

We can perhaps argue the existence of a continuum between repose and music expressed in the arabesk film and song text, which draws upon deeply rooted metaphors relating to space, movement and outsidership.

5.7. Emotions and Secrets

Let us now return to the metaphor of burning with which this chapter began. We have already noted that a parallel explanation of the state of *hal* is the 'burning' of the *gönül*:

Yanardağ misali yanıyor gönlüm

My soul burns like a volcano ('Çaresizim', Ferdi Tayfur)

But the verbs *yanmak* and *yakmak* refer not to the passive experience of affliction, but to the attempt to communicate something which by its very nature cannot be communicated. This incommunicability is not a result of any romantic conception of the inability of verbal and musical language to convey a vision or experience. It is rather that nobody wants to hear, due to the socially marginalized state of the *gariban*:

Kulak veren yok garibin sesine

Nobody listens to the voice of the *garib* ('Kullarına Kul Yapmış', Müslüm Gürses)

[25] Ibid. 21. [26] Öztelli 1983, 624.

Popular lyrics gain much of their tension from this situation and image it in a variety of ways. Deeming himself to be unfit or unacceptable to speak out, the singer may call in the text upon the services of a go-between, or representative (*vekil*). He may also make a rhetorical call to the instrument to do the job for him; the *bağlama* may be exhorted to weep, or speak out ('*ağla sazım*!'—'Cry, my *saz*!').

We may infer when the instrument speaks by itself, in the instrumental *taksim* of art music, or the free instrumental forms of folk music (for example, the *açış* introducing *uzun hava*), that it is telling a story shadowing that which the muted singer would have told or is about to tell. The principal function of music is to tell stories. A tale from Kastamonu, collected from a certain İsmail Yıldırım by the musicologist Süleyman Şenel, and related to me as a mixture of the original story and his own commentary, illustrates the point in an interesting way:

Bir vezirin iki hizmetçisi varmış; bunlardan birini öldürüp bir kuyuya atıyorlar. Öteki hizmetçiye 'sen bunu hiç kimseye anlatma, yoksa seni öldürüp kuyuya atarlar'. Hizmetçi bu olayı uzun süre sırrı olarak saklıyamıyor ve bir kuyuya bağrıyor. Kuyuda bulunan kamış denen bir bitki kammazlık yapıyor, ot dile geliyor: 'Vezir filan kuyuya birisini attı' diye duyuruyor. Ve ceset kuyudan çıkartılıyor. Kamış kammazlık yaptığı için, kamış çalmak günahtır. Kamış kammazlık yaparak kalabalık topluyor.

(A *vezir* has two servants; one of these they kill and throw down a well. He says to the other: 'Don't tell anybody about this or you will be killed and thrown down the well.' The servant cannot keep it a secret for a long time and shouts it [his secret] down a well. The reeds from this well (used by local musicians for their instruments) tell tales, the plants begin to speak: '*Vezir* so-and-so threw someone down a well', they exclaim. And the corpse is taken out of the well. Because the reeds tell tales, it is a sin to play them. When the reeds tell tales, it attracts a crowd.)

The point of this story (one of many) that I wish to draw out is not that music plays a role in righting social wrongs: nothing actually happens to the *vezir*, and the story ends up with the narrator explaining that the story provides a reason for music being a sinful activity. Indeed, this story was offered to me along with several others providing rationalizations for the sinfulness of music. What is of more importance is the simple fact that music was speaking the unspeakable truth, bridging the gap between the secret inner world (the world of the solitary servant) and the public outer world (the world of the crowds who gather to hear the tale). Nothing is achieved by this. We assume that the *vezir* is left to continue with his tyranny unchecked. But his secret is revealed when the corpse is brought out of the well.

Music is often described in terms of an emptying or ejaculation (*boşaltma*), or of a 'bringing-out' (*çıkartma*). When a musician is experiencing difficulty in working out the notes of a song, he will describe his difficulty in terms of this bringing-out. The full aesthetic weight of this metaphor of burning only makes sense in terms of the process of bringing out, or converting the inner realm of unsayable secrets into the light of day. The association of flame and combustion with music lies in their shared transformatory role, as well as in the metaphorical connection with pain and suffering. But music does not 'do' or 'achieve', in the Jungian sense of uniting the battling elements of the psyche, the masculine and the feminine, into a sound and healthy whole. Arabesk describes the ultimate failure of the attempt to reconcile individual and public experience, emotions and the dictates of social life.

The prominence of the metaphor of burning suggests that what is important is not just what the story is about but the way in which it is told. Arabesk is communicated through the medium of music, a fact of the utmost significance to which we shall turn in the next chapter.

6
The Musical Organization of Arabesk

6.1. Inspiration

For arabesk musicians, the prime mover in the musical organization of arabesk is inspiration, *ilham*. Explanations of *ilham* focus on metaphorical expressions of the emotional states described in the previous chapter. Just as the central figure in the arabesk drama is imaged as a passive victim of fate, so too is the musician powerless before the remote, manipulative, and unpredictable force of *ilham*. *İlham*, as lyricists and composers informed me on a number of occasions, is not something which can be trained or cultivated. They could set up the situation most likely to inspire them, but might remain devoid of inspiration for days. Inspiration could strike when least expected, forcing the musician to stop what he is doing and get the words and notes down on paper at the first opportunity. The circumstances in which inspiration strikes are essential proof of the power of *ilham* and its expression in words and music. Each song therefore has 'a story', relating the private and specific circumstances in which inspiration struck.

For songwriters, these stories are an essential element in the explanation of each song. The following account is typical in its localization of the generalized expressions of the texts in a specific narrative which describes a chance encounter on public transport with a mysterious and beautiful girl:

Sıcak bir yaz günüydu. Yapacak bir iş bulamıyordum. İçimden gelen bir dürtüyle vapur yolculuğu yaparak adaya kadar gidip üstümdeki ağırlığı atmak istedim. Oturduğum sıranın karşısında sarışın mavi gözlü bir kız oturuyordu. Güzel bir kızdı ancak fazla ilgimi çekmemişti. Bakışlarını yüzümde hissetiğim zaman ben de ona baktım. Bu kez onun çekindiğini ve bakışlarını kaçırdığını gördüm. Öyle mahsun, duygulu bir hali vardı ki, onun bu halinin beni çok etkilediğini farkettim. Karmakarışık duygularla düşünmeye çalışırken, karşıma baktığımda onun yerini boş olduğunu gördüm. Aramama çevreme bakınmama rağmen bir daha da göremedim. Bu yoğunluğumu da şarkı sözü haline getirdim.

It was a hot summer's day. I couldn't find anything to do. Following some inner impulse I decided to go as far as the islands on a boat trip and throw off the heaviness that weighed on me. A blonde, blue-eyed girl was sitting opposite the bench on which I was sitting. She was a beautiful girl, but I didn't take much notice of her. When I felt her eyes on my face, I too looked at her. This time I saw that she pulled back and averted her gaze. She was in such an innocent and beautiful state that I realized that this state of hers had affected me highly. When I looked across, whilst trying to think with my utterly disordered emotions, I saw that her place was empty. In spite of looking all around me I never saw her again. And I made this stupidity [lit. 'denseness'] of mine into the words of a song.[1]

This narrative owes much to the conventions of arabesk. We assume that the girl is from a higher social class, perhaps a wealthy islander, since her hair is uncovered and she is apparently travelling alone. The poet casts himself in the role of the typical *gariban*, wandering about the city with nothing to do.[2] The girl disappears, leaving the poet in a state of turmoil. The narrative emphasizes the sexual power of the man as well as his social powerlessness to make anything of the encounter. In this, *ilham* is closely identified with all of the major themes of the arabesk drama described above: the anomic urban existence of the *gariban*, the remote and unattainable object of desire, states of loneliness, and disordered emotion.

The power of the image of the musician in the arabesk drama is such that many composers and lyricists can only compose if they themselves replicate the state of dislocated outsidership described in films and song texts. Solitude is considered essential, as is a bottle of *rakı*. In the context of the metaphors of movement described in the previous chapter, the fact that musicians are susceptible to *ilham* whilst travelling is of some significance. Malatyalı İbrahim once mentioned to me that he could induce a state in which he could think up tunes and texts by driving around in his car. For this purpose, he always carried a small 'Walkman'-type cassette recorder with an inbuilt microphone wherever he went, enabling him to record whenever inspiration struck. He would then use the tape to work out a full version upon the *bağlama*.

[1] Yıldırım Caner on the words of 'Sarışınım', *Müzik Magazin*, 24 Aug. 1987, 17.

[2] *Gariban* and *flaneur*, in Benjamin's study of Baudelaire and 19th-cent. Paris (1976), share an identity as solitary characters observing the crowds and perambulating the public space of cities in the grip of radical processes of transformation. The symbolic domain of both converts the outer public space of shopping arcades and public transport into an interior in which the dramas of their lives are played out.

Musicians' accounts of the process of creating arabesk evoke images of spontaneity and individuality which relate closely to the portrayal of the musician figure discussed in the previous chapter. Musicians are, however, active participants in a highly organized music industry with an annual turnover of about 7,000 million TL a year, which shapes, controls, and packages their product. Some 170 out of the 200 million cassettes which are produced every year by this industry are the work of five large companies, Raks, Foneks, Nora, Plaksan, and Üzelli.[3] Major arabesk stars such as Ferdi Tayfur and Orhan Gencebay have their own recording studios (Ferdifon and Kervan) dedicated largely to the production of their own music, but also rear younger singers who aspire to run their own studios. Unkapanı, the centre of this industry in Istanbul, is thus a mixture of companies run by recognized stars, smaller companies run by lesser-known singers and entrepreneurs, and the five large companies which deal with smaller stars, the rank and file of arabesk.

The principal aim of recording companies and musicians is to survive in a highly competitive market. It is in the interests of both to produce a distinctive sound, but one which is immediately assimilable in terms of its basic patterns and techniques, as mass-culture theorists from Adorno onwards have demonstrated. These patterns and techniques are for the most part supplied by halk and sanat music. Arabesk is different, therefore, not so much in its deviation from established genres, but in the techniques it combines. Arabesk is also a studio-produced music. The patterns, techniques, and structures of arabesk are very much those of the recording studio and the social organization of the producers, musicians, arrangers, lyricists, and composers whose work depends upon the studio and the recording company. Arabesk is thus the result of a highly organized industry serving the business interests of those who work in it, through musical products which resemble one another to a high degree.

How should we interpret the fact that musicians explain the production of the music in terms of *ilham*, and that those who listen to arabesk perceive in it the very essence of disorder and disorganization? It is possible to argue that a romantic myth of individuality and inspiration is propagated by the recording industry to mystify its mode of production and to generate choice.[4] It is also possible to argue that this ideology relates to myths of music-making which

[3] Güngör 1990. [4] See Stratton 1983.

exist in Turkey outside the context of arabesk and the commercial market, which continue to articulate the way the music is created by its musicians and is perceived by its audience. Certainly, the recording industry has no need to generate its own myths if pre-existing myths can be made to serve its purposes. In either case, they have to be communicated in terms of recognizable symbols and metaphors. To a large extent these myths are conveyed through the verbal metaphors discussed in the previous chapter. They are also encoded in the musical organization at a non-textual level. In the remainder of this chapter I will discuss the way in which the musical organization of arabesk is affected by the social and technological organization of the recording studio, and the musical training and experience of the musicians who produce arabesk. This will then enable us to examine the way in which metaphors of disorder are encoded in the musical vocabulary of arabesk.

6.2. The Recording Studio

Many commentators suggest that the disruption of the recording industry by rampant cassette piracy has created a situation in which arabesk has thrived. In fact, the legal recording industry has for the most part been able to establish a *modus vivendi* with cassette piracy. The enforcement of law 3257 in 1989 has rendered cassette piracy more difficult in that every cassette is now required to display a stamp (*bandırole*) indicating that tax has been paid. Since the early 1980s the recording industry has also dealt exclusively in cassettes and not records, which can be reproduced on to blank cassettes at a high quality in large quantities outside their control. Directors of recording companies at Unkapanı with whom I spoke in 1990 saw wider economic trends such as inflation as more of a threat to their livelihood than cassette piracy.

Cassette production processes are of course highly organized. After signing a contract with a singer, the studio appoints a director (*yönetmen*) who is responsible for assembling musicians and music, contacting the recording studio, establishing a timetable and a budget, and overseeing the final mix of the cassette. Decisions about the number of musicians and the quality of the recording studio depend on commercial decisions made by the recording company. In 1990, calculations were based roughly on profits of 1,000 TL per cassette. The amount that the company is prepared to pay depends upon their estimates of how many cassettes they can sell. An arabesk cassette can be made with a capital outlay of about 25 million TL. Up to 100 million will be spent for a well-known singer, but the average that a recording company is prepared to spend is about 50 million. Sales of only about 50,000 are therefore required to break even, and even less well-known arabesk singers such as Malatyalı İbrahim can reckon on sales of over 200,000 cassettes.

The decision of which recording studio to use is critical. In 1990, the cost of hiring a well-appointed twenty-four-track studio in the centre of Istanbul was 100,000 TL per hour, whilst a cheaper sixteen-track studio would cost only 50,000 TL. The amount of time taken is relatively inflexible, varying, in the estimation of Ali Osman Erbaşı, between 100 and 150 hours. Costs in studio time alone, then, might vary between 5 and 15 million TL. A bigger studio makes the employment of more musicians possible, but greatly increases the overall expense. Musicians, songwriters, and lyricists are paid by the song. The string section and rhythm instruments, the essential elements of arabesk, are employed for the duration of the production of the cassette, which usually includes between ten and fifteen individual songs. Often the singer writes his or her own songs, and it is in the interests of both the singer and recording company to include as many of these in the recording as possible. Many singers are aware that this might become monotonous. Often a few songs are commissioned from friends, for the sake of *renk*, 'colour'. Most composition and lyric writing in a cassette is done by musicians directly involved with other aspects of the cassette production process. Composition and lyric writing as separate professional activities are therefore not lucrative or regular sources of employment, commanding sums of around 200,000 TL for a composition or lyric. There is a certain tension between the company, which wants good production but as few extra costs as possible, and the directors, for whom their prestige is reflected in the sizes of the orchestras and variety of material that they can assemble. The dream of all directors at Unkapanı, and certainly a favoured topic of conversation, is a ten-piece string section with violas, cellos, and double basses.

The economics and social organization of the recording studio have important ramifications for the structure of the music it produces. The composer provides a single melody line, which is sung first, usually with a *bağlama*, as a 'pilot' track. Everything else is added cumulatively to this skeleton as and when the musicians are available. Musicians are hired in groups who normally operate together in the commercial market. The most important is a group of strings, whose director can add or shed instrumentalists according to the requirements of the cassette director and recording company. Since each track can be doubled, often a group of only four instrumentalists (including a cello) suffices to create the sound of a full string section. Rhythm sections again often operate as a team in recording studio and live performance work, consisting of a group of *darbuka*, *def*, and *hollo*. These work out the rhythmic patterns that will be used in the piece according to rhythmic modal cycles (*usul*) peculiar to arabesk, and known for the most part only by the rhythm players themselves. The director indicates what he wants, and the musicians organize the sequence of rhythmic cycles amongst themselves. Similarly an electric bass and keyboard player work together to write out the chordal accompaniment of the song independently. So the director works with largely autonomous instrumental groups, who have no idea of what the final sound is going to be like. This depends entirely upon the mixing process.

Arabesk is conceived as contrasting blocks of instrumental and vocal sound, balanced on a multitrack recording system. Since the volume of each track is controlled by the director and recording engineer (*tonmayster*), solo sounds can be balanced in regular antiphonic alternation with the string chorus. The size of this chorus is important to arabesk producers, since a large and full sound will provide the greatest contrast to a solo voice or instrument. The model for this is clearly provided by Arab music. Salwa es-Shawan has pointed out that one of the features of the 'revived' traditional style of Egyptian music in the 1960s was the use of a large chorus of violins where a group of three or four would previously have sufficed.[5] The *Fiqrat al-Musika al-Arabiyyah*, founded in 1967 with the aim of resuscitating the classical film style of the 1940s, had for example a chorus of 15 violins. The regular antiphonic alternation of this group with a solo voice is a consistent feature of Egyptian popular music which has been adapted to the demands of arabesk. The various musical functions of the string chorus can be exemplified with reference to 'Dünya Dönüyor':[6] metrically

[5] El-Shawan 1984.

[6] See s. 4 below for a transcription and detailed analysis of this song.

Ex. 17

balanced 'echo' antiphony (Ex. 17), metrically balanced runs to connect last note of vocal phrases with first note of the next (Ex. 18), and brief runs punctuating breaks between two bar phrases (Ex. 19).

Ex. 18

Ex. 19

The possibilities of the recording studio mean that the director can extend this antiphonic alternation to contrasting blocks of instrumental sound. These textures organize contrasting motifs and musical 'rhymes' at phrase endings in instrumental introductions in a way which is highly characteristic of arabesk and quite untypical of Turkish sanat and halk music. This can be illustrated by the patterns of alternation between solo instruments (principally the *bağlama* and *kaval*) with the string group in the opening passage of Mahsun Kırmızıgül and Yıldırım Caner's 'Sarışınım' (see Ex. 20).

Ex. 20 'Sarışınım'

Speed ♩ = 141, transposed up a major sixth (voice up an octave plus a major sixth) from the version recorded by İbrahim Tatlıses.

The distribution of these instruments across the sixteen or twenty-four tracks of a recording studio enable textures to be mixed and balanced at will, usually with the guidance and advice of the singer or composer. The organization of instruments for a sixteen-track studio provides a spatial referent for the musical organization of arabesk, with the string chorus on one side, the vocalist in the middle, and the rhythmic and chordal accompaniment on the other. Solo instruments are grouped asymmetrically around the central voice. The following example is taken from a recording in Stüdyo Marşandiz of a cassette by a young arabesk star, Canan Nergis, in August 1990: (1) blank, (2) string chorus (three violins and one cello), (3) string chorus, (4) synthesizer, brass, flute, bells, guitar, (5) *elektrobağlama*, (6) *kanun*, (7) vocal chorus, (8) vocalist, (9) vocal chorus, (10) *bağlama*, *zurna*, *kaval*, (11) *darbuka*, (12) *hollo*, (13) *def*, (14) Rhodes keyboard, (15) bass, (16) blank.

The live performance of arabesk replicates this spatial organization in every possible way. When a large band is used at a *Halk Konseri*, or in a large *gazino*, the organization of musicians across the stage reflects the musical principle of antiphony in arabesk, with solo instruments in the middle, the string chorus on the left, and the rhythm section on the right. The relationship between the distribution of the musicians across the stage and the organization of the musical material are thus clearly visible. Smaller groups maintain this structure in live performance, using the resources available (see Fig. 6).

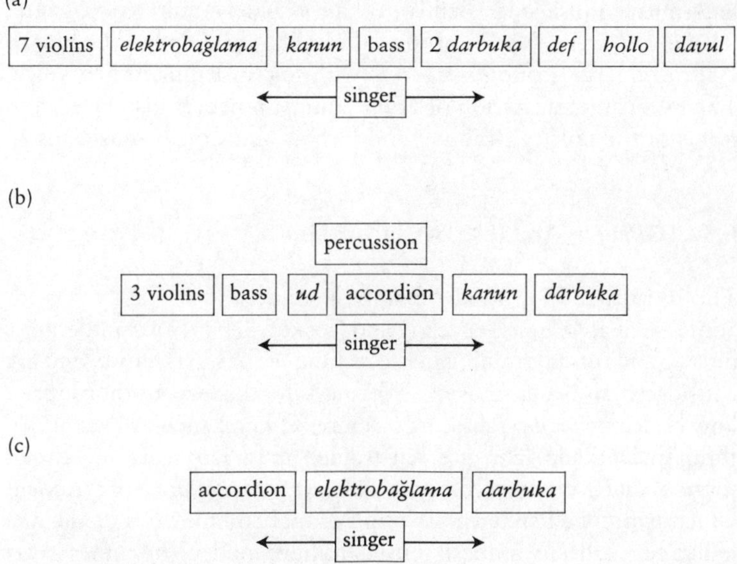

Fig. 6. Spatial organization of arabesk orchestras
(*a*) Müslüm Gürses, *Halk Konseri* at Gülhane Park, September 1990
(*b*) Ayşe Mine, Fenerbahce Ordu Evi, November 1986
(*c*) Unknown young girl, small *düğün salonu* at Fenerbahce Ordu Evi, September 1990

The *elektrobağlama* on its own is a highly versatile instrument in the context of arabesk. Since it is often played in Kara *düzen* with a cadential tone on the middle string G, the instrumentalist has recourse to an antiphonic alternation of passages played on the middle string course and the 'bottom' string course which often has an octave double. This alternation produces quite distinct textures eminently suitable to the musical organization of arabesk. I watched the singer Ahmet Yiğitses entertain a small crowd at a beer-garden in Gülhane Park, accompanying himself on the '*elektro*', backed only by a rhythm section consisting of a *darbuka*, a *zilli def*, and a *davul*.

Arabesk is therefore rendered distinct as a musical genre by techniques which were developed and explored in the context of commercial recording studios. It is only relatively recently that producers of halk and sanat music have attempted to exploit these antiphonal techniques in their own commercial recording activities. Amongst halk-music musicians, Belkis Akkale's widely imitated cassette, *Türkü Türkü Türkiyem*, produced in 1985, was one of the first to contrast a large group of *bağlama* with solo instruments and voice. The musical organization of arabesk must however also be seen in terms of the musical training and backgrounds of its musicians.

6.3. *Makam* in Arabesk: 'Sevda Gözlüm'

The musical background of arabesk musicians is highly varied. Some, such as Orhan Gencebay and Coşkun Sabah, have undergone intense and formal training in the techniques of sanat music, and are considered by sanat-music performers to possess as thorough a knowledge of *makam* and *usul* as any. Others, such as 'Malatyalı' İbrahim Dulkadıroğlu, are self-trained musicians with no knowledge of *makam*, who compose upon the *bağlama*, an instrument which is not well suited to the microtonal complexities of the art-music genre. Many arabesk musicians have made their names in art or folk music and move with some flexibility between genres. İbrahim Tatlıses began as a singer of halk music before moving into arabesk. His vocal skills still command a great deal of respect amongst singers and programmers in the TRT halk-music section. His prestige in these circles is such that on Şeker Bayramı in 1990 he was invited to sing an *uzun hava* to *bağlama* accompaniment on a TRT halk-music programme as a guest artist. Bülent Ersoy, Zeki Müren, Muazzez Abacı, and, in some circles, Orhan Gencebay, continue to be the most highly respected musicians in sanat-music circles, even though all have moved in and out of arabesk with great frequency. The career of Orhan Gencebay has spanned professional employment in halk and sanat music. Bülent Ersoy's *Süskün Dünyam*, released in 1987, was her first cassette in an unambiguous arabesk idiom. Of this she is alleged to have claimed that the feeling of homesickness (*sıla hasreti*) experienced in exile in West Germany led her to arabesk. This was followed by a recording released later that year of a concert of *fasıl* (suites) performed in the most austere classical style of monophonic art music. Undoubtedly this was a calculated move to fuel an intense political debate over censorship. The wide sales of the first cassette would have reminded the government of the political capital to be gained by repealing the laws which forbade her performing in Turkey, and the second would have added the weight of centre-left critics of the government's cultural policies. Musicians who have made a name for themselves are able to manipulate their identities to maximize their popularity and respectability in official circles by making calculated moves in and out of arabesk. This makes it impossible to see arabesk as a clearly defined urban sub-culture with its own rules and norms.

Arabesk is perceived by many of its listeners to be divided into a section consisting of musicians who have moved into arabesk from halk music and another consisting of musicians who have moved from sanat music. Some people claimed to like arabesk but dislike that sung by Zeki Müren and Bülent Ersoy. Others dismissed 'folk' musicians such as İbrahim Tatlıses and Mahmut Tunçer. Within the general field of arabesk, listeners create highly idiosyncratic taxonomies, defining themselves in terms of the perceived sophistication of the art-music side of arabesk, or in terms of the charismatic figures and life stories of folk-music arabesk singers.

This distinction is hard to sustain when we look at the training and musical experience of the majority of musicians, singers, and composers, as well as studio technicians and directors involved in arabesk. A firm distinction between halk and sanat music is sustained only by particular institutions and individuals associated with official government and media music circles and is the result of specific historical and political circumstances. Contrary to the Gökalpian ideology maintained by these institutions, rural musicians have never existed in a hermetically sealed village culture. Art-music techniques, particularly in Southern and Eastern Anatolia, had been widely disseminated from urban centres long before the media and recording industry made them even more readily available. Many arabesk singers came from a rural town background, such as Mustafa Keser from the *kaza* of Maden, near Harput in Malatya, in which they were able to develop a thorough knowledge of the *makam* as well as maintain their fluency in rural styles. Their early professional experience in regional cities in the mid-1960s required of them an ability to perform regional songs in a *bağlama*-orientated style as well as urban classics. This experience has enabled musicians such as Orhan Gencebay and Mustafa Keser to pursue a professional existence at the highest levels in both halk- and sanat-music genres. Most musicians of this generation involved in arabesk thus have familarity with the *makam* system and knowledge of rural styles and *bağlama* technique. When my sanat-music teachers dismissed most arabesk composers as knowing nothing of the complexities of the *makam* system, my first reaction was to agree, assuming that it was simply sub-culture with a different kind of music to which the terminology of art music was inapplicable. Ethnomusicological literature is full of examples of musicians borrowing terminology from higher status musical forms in order to upgrade their musical practice.[7] In fact, most composers and musicians had at least as much understanding and experience of the *makam* system in sanat-music contexts as my teachers. When composers claim to be composing 'in' a *makam*, invariably they are doing just this. There are, however, complications.

The *bağlama* is the instrument upon which most musicians compose, since it allows the composer to sing and establish the pitch of the notes as he does so. As Mustafa Keser pointed out to me, 'Tek çalıp söylemeye uygun saz bağlamadır', 'The only instrument which is suitable for playing and singing to is the *bağlama*', which allows the musician to play tunes, chords (*armoni*), and drones (*dem sesler*) when required. As I pointed out above, theoretically the fretting of this instrument does not allow for a full rendition of many of the microtonal intervals required by art music. In particular, sanat-music theory requires a single-comma flattened B, whilst the *bağlama*, according to halk-music theory, can only provide a two- or three-comma flattened B. In practice this discrepancy is not so important. When playing with fully fretted art-music instruments, a *bağlama* player is able to adjust the precise positioning of the fret in order to be in tune with the other instruments. Many musicians have an extra fret added. They can thus produce the different shades of B

[7] See Baily 1981.

required for common *makam* such as Rast (specifying a one-comma flat) and Uşşak (in which theoretical texts specify a one-comma flat in the notation, but instruct the musician to play a note somewhat lower than this, between two and three commas flat) without having to fiddle with the movable frets on the instrument. There is a limit to the amount of extra frets that can be attached, since the *bağlama* does not have a sufficiently long neck to include all of the extra frets required and remain playable. This is probably the final point of a process described in detail by Picken, in which frets were being progressively added to the instrument in order to allow it to replicate the tonal complexities of urban music.[8]

Without doubt, the precise details of the tonal structure of the *makam* are not as important as the typical melodic shapes and configurations which take place within it. The size and structure of the instrument does however have ergonomic implications. Arabesk is usually played on the *bağlama* in a manner which uses all three string courses at the 'top' of the fretboard, in other words, a 'vertical' rather than linear technique, resembling the performance technique associated with the *ud*. Since it is a long-necked rather than a short-necked lute, the performance of a piece of music in this manner is highly idiosyncratic. The rapid leaps of tessitura and melodic line which can be achieved with ease on the *ud* are not feasible upon the *bağlama*. Composition is thus more restricted, and will be determined by the kind of configurations of notes which fall under the fingers. These will *de facto* bear a certain resemblance to the melodic tropes of halk music. For the most part, this does not interfere with the ability of the musician to perform *makam* upon the *bağlama*.

In spite of this, the concept of *makam* is used with very little deviation from the prescriptions laid down in sanat-music textbooks. Ex. 21 is a transcription of the original notation of the song 'Sevda Gözlüm'. This song was written by Yılmaz Tatlıses with words by Hamza Dekeli, and recorded by a number of (mainly female) arabeskçi, including Tüdanya, Küçük Ceylan, Gülden Karaböcek, Ali Seven, Esin Engin, Erol Ulupınar, and the group Şen Kızlar. Yılmaz Tatlıses described the composition of 'Sevda Gözlüm' in the following terms:

> Hamza Dekeli'nin sözlerini elime aldıktan sonra bir süre okudum. Ardından yavaş yavaş notalar gelmeye başladı kulağıma ... Elimdeki bağlamayla melodiyi oluşturmaya başladım. Uşşak makamı hem piyasada beğeni top-

[8] Picken 1975, 225.

Ex. 21 'Sevda Gözlüm'

Speed ♩ = 102, transposed up a minor sixth from the version recorded by Tüdanya.

ARASAZ
gül sev - da göz - lüm
tr
3
Top - ra - ğa can ve - ren
yay
yağ - mur gi - bi - sin
kır - lar - da do - la - şan
1.
yay
2.
yay
ba - har gi - bi - sin
ba - har gi - bi - sin
sen in - san de - ğil - sin
ben - ce me - lek - sin
yay
hep ay - nı de - ğer - de
kal sev - da göz - lüm
D.C.
hep ay - nı de - ğer - de
kal sev - da göz - lüm

layan hem de son yıllarda halkın kulağında yer eden bir makam. Bu nedenle Uşşak makamındaki ezgiyle sözler uyum sağladı. Şarkının ana melodisi ortaya çıktıktan bir süre sonra da yeni düzenlemelerle son haline geldi.

After getting hold of Hamza Dekeli's words, I read them for a bit. Shortly after, the notes slowly began to come to my ear . . . I began to create the melody with the *bağlama* in my hands. Uşşak *makamı* is a *makam* which is approved on the market and also in recent years one which has established itself on the people's ear. A little while after the main melodies of the tune emerged, it assumed its final form with new arrangements.[9]

In order to compare the use of Uşşak *makamı* in 'Sevda Gözlüm', it will be useful to outline the concept of *makam* in Turkish art-music theory. The classical *makam* consists of a series of named notes, three of which have a specific function. These are a finalis (*durak*), a 'leading note' (*yeden*), and a 'dominant' (*güçlü*), although the rules applying to these terms in Western art-music theory, in which the leading note always rises and the dominant has a harmonic function, obviously do not apply in the context of Turkish music. Strictly speaking, the *yeden*, the note immediately below the *finalis*, is included in the *makam* performance because of its cadential role, even though it lies outside the gamut of the *makam*. The *güçlü* is of structural importance because it marks the division of the *makam* into a tetrachord and pentachord and, somewhat in the manner of the dominant in Western theory, is the note towards which melodic movement progresses and upon which it comes to an initial cadence. Unlike the dominant, however, it lacks a harmonic function (since the music is not polyphonic) and generally falls upon the fourth or fifth degree of the scale. The *makam* is also constituted by the concept of *seyir* (literally 'path', 'way'), that is, predominant melodic direction. This may be either ascending (*çıkıcı*), descending (*inici*), or a combination of both (*inici-çıkıcı*). Uşşak *makamı* is thus built up out of the notes shown in Ex. 22.

Ex. 22

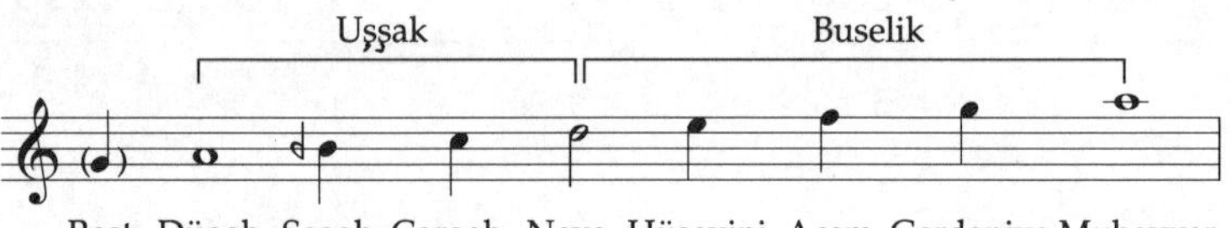

[9] *Müzik Magazin*, 22 June (1987), 20.

Each *makam* is made up, as indicated, of a tetrachord (*dörtlü*) and a pentachord (*beşli*). Uşşak is constructed from the Uşşak *dörtlüsü* and the Buselik *beşlisi* transposed up to the note on which the tetrachord finishes. The note upon which the structure of the *makam*, and hence the improvised or composed performance hinges is Neva, the *güçlü* of the mode. The importance of this note is that in improvisation the opening statement, which begins with a characteristic device peculiar to each mode, is required to come to a half-close (*yarım karar*) on the *güçlü*. The bottom tetrachord is thus delineated, lending its distinctive identity to the improvisation that follows. Improvisation in the classical tradition has the function of revealing the mode in which the following piece is to be if it begins a performance. Half-way through, an improvisation has the function of modulating between two different *makam*. So it is essential that improvisations are clear, and are not muddled by instrumental pyrotechnics. *Makam* are taught by reference to a form (*kalıp*) which is more detailed than the three basic outlines specified by *seyir*. I was expected to memorize the opening sequences of improvisations in each *makam*, which were taught to me note by note, not just so that I should perform good *taksim*, but so that I should thoroughly internalize the *seyir* and *kalıp* of the *makam* for the purposes of recognizing it in composed pieces. So the structural principles of the *makam* underpin not just improvisation but notated composition.

The opening sequences of *taksim* are performed in more or less the same way, although a number of variants are known and permitted. My own teacher's instructions for Uşşak conformed closely to the prescription laid down in the model *seyir* illustrated in one of the standard textbooks[10] (see Ex. 23). The salient features of this opening consist of a cluster of notes adjacent to and coming to rest initially on the *durak* (A). They are followed by an ascent and then stepwise descent coming to rest on the *güçlü* (D), emphasized by approach from the note lying immediately underneath it.

Ex. 23

[10] Yılmaz 1977, 76.

Ex. 24

If we turn back to the opening of 'Sevda Gözlüm', it will be possible to see how the first two bars of the song encapsulate this schema with terse precision (see Ex. 24). The play of notes around the *durak* is reduced to a stark reiteration of the opening note. The downward approach to the *güçlü* is reduced to a three-note figure (e–d–c), which is prepared by the last two crotchets of the first bar. The next two bars which make up the first phrase of the instrumental section repeat this with some melodic elaboration, but with a descent to the *durak*. 'Sevda Gözlüm' states from the outset that it is clearly and unambiguously in Uşşak *makamı*.

The question of *seyir* is slightly more complex. That specified for Uşşak is *çıkıcı* (ascending). It will be clear from the textbook that an 'ascending' mode contains a high degree of descending motion. The *makam* begins and ends on A. An ascending mode can best be characterized as a mode in which ascending movement takes place at the beginning of the phrase, following pauses in the improvisation or piece. The attention is thus focused clearly on the ascending aspect of the totality. The rest of the model Uşşak *seyri* notated by Yılmaz illustrates this clearly (see Ex. 25).

Ex. 25

Yılmaz stresses that Uşşak is a *makam* of 'solid build' (*ağır yapılı*),[11] indicating that it is not suitable for virtuoso demonstrations of compositional or instrumental technique, unlike

[11] Ibid. 76.

Nihavent or the Hicaz group. In the classical repertory, Uşşak is characterized by a predominance of stepwise melodic movement, and a tendency to gravitate towards the lower end of the scale. Karadeniz indicates that some musicians descend as far as Yegah (D),[12] and Yılmaz acknowledges that an entire Rast pentachord may be added in practice to the bottom of the mode.[13] It will be noticed in 'Sevda Gözlüm' that the composer does not descend below the note G, but the piece in general stays predominantly within the bottom tetrachord of the mode.

In every respect, then, 'Sevda Gözlüm' is a model of Uşşak *makamı*. The issue is not confused by the mixes used in most recordings of the song. Those of Ceylan and Tüdanya favour a clear monophonic sound, in which the electric bass and keyboard instruments are scarcely audible, following the contours of the melody rather than indicating a functional pattern of harmonic movement. In general, the musicians providing the bass and harmony in recording studios are trained in Western techniques, and work independently of the composers, singers, and studio directors, few of whom have any understanding of the techniques of Western functional harmony. They simply apply a chordal backing to an already existing melody which is composed according to the strictly monophonic principles embodied in the *makam* system.

6.4. Structure and Modality in *Fantezi*: 'Dünya Dönüyor'

So far we have dealt with the application of the modal principle of art music in arabesk by illustrating the conformity of a simple piece in the classical model. There are, however, a number of problems involved in the analysis of pieces which are recognized to be more complex. As I have already noted, those of Orhan Gencebay are widely considered to be particularly intricate. This intricate style is often described as *fantezi*, differing from 'real' arabesk only in its compositional technique and not its essential content. It is still instantly identifiable as arabesk to its listeners by virtue of the subject-matter of its texts, the style of vocal delivery, and the recording-studio musical organization of the orchestration. Let us turn to a recent example, 'Dünya Dönüyor' (see Ex. 26).

The first problem to deal with is the question of the modality of the

[12] Karadeniz 1965, 94. [13] Yılmaz 1977, 75.

Ex. 26 'Dünya Dönüyor'

Speed ♩ = 84 at opening, ♩ = 116 at drums entry, transposed up a minor seventh (voice up an octave plus a minor seventh) from the version recorded by Orhan Gencebay.

elektro
tr.
yay
orch.
yay
yay
rhythm
2
Sen ne der - sen de
orch.
sen ne der - sen de
piano
Dün - ya dö - nü - yor dö - ne - cek

piano
Ha - yat sen - siz de sü - re - cek
Bi - te - cek a - cı - lar bu gün - ler geç - e - cek
kanun
Sen ne der - sen de
yay
Ya - lan de - ğil
yay
Ya - lan de - ğil
orch.
se - ni sev - di - ğim ya - lan de - ğil
orch.
Kah - rol - du - ğum ya - lan de - ğil
Du - yar - sın bir gün bas - ka sev - gi - li bul - du - ğu - mu
orch.
FINE
Ya - lan de - ğil

orch.
3
(MEYAN)
Ar - tik kız - mı - yo - rum ka - der - i - me
orch.
tr
Bı - rak - tı be - ni hal - i - me
Bah - tın a - çık ol - sun yol - un a - çık ol - sun
orch.
Bı - rak be - ni hal - i - me
Dün - ya dö - nü - yor dö - ne - cek
orch.
Ha - yat sen - siz de sü - re - cek
orch.
Bi - te - cek a - cı - lar Bu gün - ler ge - çe - cek
tr.
sen ne der - sen de

kanun
electro
sen ne der - sen de
yay
yay
piano
yay
yay
trumpet
5
3
5
3
kanun
orch.

song. The notation of Uşşak *makamı* in 'Sevda Gözlüm' rendered the B as $B\flat^{2}$ in conformity with the notational conventions associated with the *bağlama* and halk music and not sanat music. Here, the situation is reversed. The notation of the key signature (*donanım*) conforms with some exactitude to the conventions of sanat music, consisting of a B♭, indicating that it should be flattened by four commas to render the note Dik Kürdi in the lower octave and Dik Sünbüle in the upper. This on its own is unproblematic, since it would indicate an approximation of the classical *makam* Kürdi if the B were lowered by just one comma to B♭. But this is contradicted two bars later by the comma-flattened D (Dik Hicaz). This note does not exist in the context of any known *makam*. But in recorded performance this is somewhat overblown by the *ney* player who is on his own at that point. The result is at first a sound closer to a full four-comma flat (i.e. D♭). If we were determined to interpret this in terms of a classical *makam*, as my *kanun* teacher immediately did, this would bring us close to the sound of Saba *makamı*, which is a *birleşik* (combinatory) *makam* constructed from a combination of the Saba tetrachord, with a transposition of the entire Hicaz Zirgüle *makamı* to the note Çargah (C) (see Ex. 27).

Ex. 27

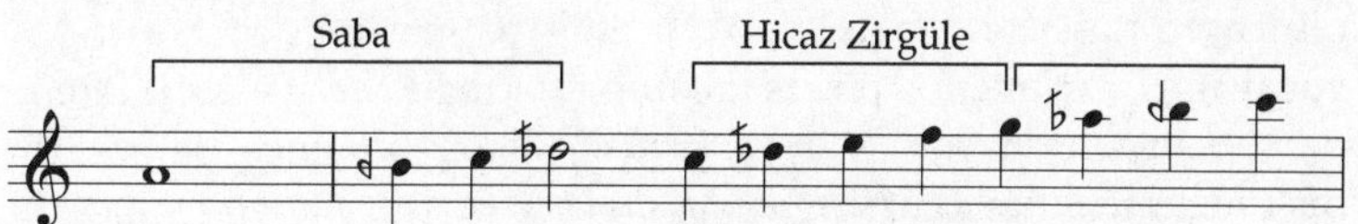

However, this would contradict the four-comma flattened B of the key signature, since the B in Saba is flattened by only one comma. So my *kanun* teacher could only interpret this in terms of either Kürdi or Saba. According to the theoretical canons, it could not be both at the same time. His conclusion was that musicians such as Orhan Gencebay could do as they pleased, unlike himself; their only responsibilities were their audiences. In the context of *fantezi* it would of course be legitimate to interpret the modality of the piece as one in which phrases in Saba were alternated with phrases in Kürdi. This modal 'dialogism', reflected in the alternation of the D and D♭, is turned into a major organizing principle in the piece, which is emphasized by the orchestration. The Saba scale in the introduction (including the D𝄳) is performed upon the *ney*, a sound intimately associated with Mevlevi mysticism. This contrasts with the D♮ of the Kürdi scale in the seventh bar, emphasized by the 'military' sound of the trumpet. This musical dialogism complements an inner dialogue taking place within the text, in which the singer declares on one hand a determination not to blame fate for his situation and on the other invites pity for his loneliness and suffering. The alternation of the D and D𝄳 has its textual correlate at the end of the song in the contrast of 'Kader, kader' ('Fate, fate', line 24) with 'Kader değil, kader değil' ('It is not fate, it is not fate', line 27).

Alternatively, the modality of the piece could be interpreted in terms of the Bozlak *ayağı* of rural folk music. The fourth note of this scale, which cadences on A, is not fixed, but can fluctuate between D and D♭, even though folk-music theorists are reluctant to acknowledge the existence of these fluctuating (*oynak*) notes.[14] So even though the song is subtly complex when analysed in terms of *makam* theory, the end result is instantly assimilable as a modal construct familiar in halk music, and the desired contrast between 'mystical' *ney* and military trumpet is registered at the level of orchestration and studio arrangement as well as modal structure.

It would be possible to look at this piece as a complex play on well-established conventions of modal theory in Turkish art music. The overall formal organization of the piece also deviates from but returns to classical principles. According to sanat-music theorists, all vocal and instrumental pieces fall into four major sections: (i) *zemin*, (ii) *zaman*, (iii) *meyan*, and (iv) *karar*.[15] The *zemin* incorporates the opening melodies (*baslangıç nağmeleri*) of the *makam*, and the *zaman* the closing melodies (*karar nağmeleri*). The *meyan* presents either a modulation to another *makam*, or the same *makam* played in a higher octave. At any rate, all *meyan* take place in a higher register. Modulation is preferred on account of the fact that it is held to add a different 'lustre' (*parlaklık*) to the work. Often the final section (*karar*) is a repeat of the *zaman*, but it may well contain different music in the same style (*tavır*) as the *zaman*. This fourfold structure underpins the composition of most pieces in the classical tradition.

Arabesk songs are described as *şarkı* rather than *türkü*, referring them to the conventions of art rather than folk music. *Şarkı* is a generic term for 'song'. Technically, it is also a variation of the basic

[14] See Yener 1987, 344. [15] Karadeniz 1965, 158.

fourfold structure outlined above. Typically, the *şarkı* contains four lines (*mısra*), each of which conforms to one of the four musical divisions. The principal difference is that in the *şarkı* the second line of music, corresponding to the *zaman* of the basic schema, is repeated in the fourth line (whether the words are repeated or not), and is referred to as *nakarat*. The overall structure is thus:

Words	Music
line 1	*zemin*
line 2	*nakarat (zaman)*
line 3	*meyan*
line 2 or 4	*nakarat (karar)*

Şarkı with more lines exist. In these, Karadeniz states that the number of lines in the *meyan* section is initially increased, and then the length of the *nakarat* is developed.[16] Generally speaking, there is only one verse, but since the *şarkı* is typically composed in shorter *usul*, the *şarkı* is normally a short piece, and an extra verse may be added. This means that the *meyan* section may be repeated.

Turning back to 'Dünya Dönüyor', the vocal section before the *meyan* falls into two subsections, but these do not correspond closely to the definition of *zemin* and *zaman* given by Karadeniz. The second subsection repeats the music of the first to different words, which itself consists of two melodic devices. One is constructed of the descending tetrachord using the D♭ of Saba, followed by its sequential transposition to a higher note in the scale (figure 2 plus two bars). The second is a sequential descending passage of two bars in 'Kürdi' beginning on a top A and repeated on G. This is underpinned by a harmonic movement spelt out by the piano arpeggios that are inserted in the interstices of the vocal line. The sequence continues, but in the phrase it is shortened to a one-bar unit, which is played on F and reiterated on E. The last two bars reintroduce the 'Saba' motif. If we label 'Saba' and 'Kürdi' as X and Y respectively, the diminishment of X and Y as x and y, and the sequential transposition of a phrase by a dash (i.e. X′ or y′), then the initial passage of 'Dünya Dönüyor' combining *zemin* and *zaman* can be clarified in the following terms:

Bar	1	2	3	4	5	6	7	8	9	10	11	12
	X		X′		Y		Y′		y	y′	X	

[16] Karadeniz 1965, 174.

The *meyan* does not modulate to another mode, retaining the tonality of the opening. But it conforms exactly to Karadeniz's definition in that it takes place in the upper octave. The *meyan* is followed by the return of the melodic motif defined as Y, which is extended by two bars through the addition of fragment y′. This then continues as if from bar 5 in the schema above.

The vocal section is surrounded by a long instrumental introduction which consists of an instrumental realization of the first twelve bars of the vocal part, performed once in a free rhythm (as if in a *taksim*) and once with the entry of the drums in strict rhythm. The final instrumental section, marked in the original score as 'Aranağme 2', is as if freely composed, although closer examination reveals it to be based on the melodic fragments of X and Y. The *arasaz* (instrumental interlude) between the first section and the *meyan* is a freely composed passage of four bars length based on the lower tetrachord of the *makams*. This conforms to the position of the *aranağme* in the classical model of the *şarkı*.

'Dünya Dönüyor' has two verses. The chorus coincides with the *meyan* at the words 'artık kızmıyorum kaderime'. It is followed by the second *aranağme* which ends with a cadenza-like run for the *kanun* and leads back to the rhythmic 'motif' which precedes the initial vocal entry (a common compositional technique in arabesk). The chorus text returns with the *meyan*. This momentarily disturbs the classical formula by introducing a textual repetition where none would be expected. Precisely because of these deviations, the song is highly dependent upon an underlying proximity to the formal outlines of classical *şarkı* form.

Words	Music
1–5	*zemin* + *zaman*
6–11	*zemin* + *zaman*
	arasaz
12–15	*meyan*
16–19	*karar* (= *zemin* + *zaman*)
	aranagme
20–4	*zemin* + *zaman*
25–30	*zemin* + *zaman*
	arasaz
31–4	*meyan*
35–8	*karar* (= *zemin* + *zaman*)
	aranagme

In theory, classical Ottoman song form was regulated not only by the broad formal outlines of the *şarkı* but by the metrical devices of *aruz* or *vezin*, relating to the rules of Arabic prosody. This determined the rhythmic patterns and metre of the texts. Since the larger part of the lexicon of the Ottoman Turkish language was made up of Arabic words, the adaption of the rules of Arabic prosody to Ottoman texts seldom posed any problems for lyricists. Turkish rural folk poetry, conceived in terms of the grammatical and phonetic peculiarities of the Turkish language, is based on an isosyllabic principle in which each line typically contains eight or eleven syllables. Arabesk texts are often based on neither. A cursory syllable count of the first few lines of 'Dünya Dönüyor' reveals startling irregularity in terms of the metrical length of the lines. The text relies instead upon both the repetition of non-rhymed lines ('Sen ne dersen de', 'Yalan değil'), and sections bound together by their end rhymes (*dönecek, sürecek, geçecek*). Clearly the structure of this song, typical of many written by singer-songwriters, has been conceived primarily in terms of balanced and repetitive musical phrases with the text fitted into the spaces created by the music.

To a great extent, this structural primacy of the musical organization of arabesk songs is maintained even when songwriters and lyricists are working separately. In the production of a cassette a text might often be bought from a particularly celebrated lyricist. The tune is added later, as in the case of 'Sevda Gözlüm' described above. It is undoubtedly the case that lyricists are obliged to write texts with a more homogenized structure, in order to allow the composer of the music as much latitude as possible for the treatment that they deem necessary. However, even the lyricists work with particular tunes of their own creation in mind, working out the lyrics along with the tune on the *bağlama*. Fethi Demir, a poet who has provided lyrics for many well-known arabesk songs, expressed his irritation to me at some settings of his lyrics since they conflicted with the musical organization of the lyrics which he had envisaged.

It will be clear from this necessarily brief discussion of an individual song that there are, strictly speaking, no grounds for describing arabesk as a debased version of sanat or halk music, or indeed anything else. It conforms closely to the organizational principles of both sanat and halk music, which do not, as we have seen, differ radically from one another. Its only originality, at the level of the notes, consists of mixing things which are considered, in the official circles of halk and sanat music, to be mutually exclusive. The well-documented existence of rural halk music employing *makam*, which are systematically ignored in these official discourses,[17] and sanat-music renditions of pieces from the halk-music repertoire suggest that, musically speaking, the combination of techniques with which we have been concerned is by no means unique. Some aspects of this technical musical habitus have, however, assumed a particular significance in the context of the themes of arabesk drama, and have as a result become formalized in ways quite specific to arabesk.

6.5. *Usul* and Disorder

A division of performance into 'strict' and 'free' rhythm is common to every genre of music in Turkey. More precisely, this entails a division of music into that which is governed by *usul* and that which is not. *Usul* refers to a system of rhythmic modes with similar properties in art and rural folk music. These consist of a series of regularly recurring temporal values allied to a binary system of pitches, referred to as *düm* and *tek*, which are performed in a variety of ways. Two drums of differing pitch can be used, as with the *küdüm*, a small pair of kettle drums used in Mevlevi music, or with the bongos often used in arabesk. The large double-headed membranophone known as *davul*, common thoroughout rural Anatolia, combines sounds produced with a short heavy stick held in the right hand (*tokmak*) and with a thin stick held in the left hand (*çubuk*). Perhaps the most common technique in the performance of *usul* is the use of different areas of the skin of the drum to create different timbres. A blow in the middle of the skin will produce a low and resonant sound, and a blow on the edge, where the skin meets the frame, will produce a high sound emphasizing the upper partials of the fundamental tone. Instruments such as the *def* and *zilli def*, used in sanat, halk, and arabesk music, are held in the left hand and struck only with the right. In the case of the *darbuka*, a goblet drum whose use is central in the performance of all urban music, the instrument is held between left thigh and left forearm, and both hands are used in the performance of *usul*. The right hand strikes the middle of the skin to indicate *düm*, establishing the principal

[17] See above, Ch. 3, s. 1.

divisions of the *usul*. The left hand and right hands supply varieties of *tek* sounds on the edge of the instrument.

In the art-music genre, these combinations of *düm* and *tek* are highly elaborated, spelling out *usul* which range from simple combinations of two- and three-beat units, such as Nim Sofyan (*düm-tek*, or 2/4 in today's notation) and Türk Aksağı (*dü-üm te-ek tek*, or 5/8),[18] to composite patterns covering 128 beats. As with *makam* and *ayak*, halk-music ideologues have created their own theoretical space, and recognize only *basıt* ('simple'), *birleşik* ('combinatory', i.e. including *aksak* rhythms), and *karma* ('mixed', in which larger rhythmic units are combined with others). The extent to which rural musicians possess knowledge of either system is of course debatable, but the underlying principles of *usul* in sanat and halk music are identical. The art of rhythm-playing in all urban genres lies in a combination of knowledge of the different rhythmic patterns and an ability to perform ornamentations and variations known as *velveleme* (literally 'clamour', 'hubbub') which subdivide the established values and also, with common patterns, vary the distribution of temporal values over the basic time unit.

Arabesk rhythm players possess highly specialized skills, and constitute a recognizable group within urban musical circles. Rhythm players certainly regard their profession as an esoteric art within arabesk. Reyhan Dinlettir, bongo player for Ferdi Tayfur, defines his cultural horizons by reference to Egyptian rhythm players and Indian *tabla* virtuosi quite unknown to other musicians in Turkey. The cursus of the professional rhythm player is seen as a process of enriching the technical vocabulary of *usul* in arabesk, through, for example, adapting the bongo or congas to Turkish rhythmic principles, or applying the techniques of *tabla* playing, studied carefully on video, to the *darbuka*. The separate musical world inhabited by arabesk rhythm players is often underlined by the assertion that most are gypsies (*çingene* or *romen*, an ethnonym which most do not accept and find offensive) from Tarlabaşı and Kağıthane, today somewhat run-down districts close to the old European quarters of Beyoğlu and Taksim. It is true that a number of well-known *darbuka* players are from these districts, although this has less to do with the dexterity and artistry that the urban myth would credit them with

[18] *Dü-üm* and *te-ek* indicate a double length *düm* and *tek* respectively. This is an elaboration of *usul* specified in art-music theory.

than their proximity to the *gazino* and *pavyon* of the Taksim and Beyoğlu areas and their establishment of an economic niche on the periphery of urban nightlife, as musicians, *işkembeci*, pimps, and prostitutes. The dependence of other musicians and recording-studio producers upon these skills is maintained by a system of *usul* peculiar to arabesk rhythm players. The rhythm section usually works on its own in constructing a sequence of rhythmic cycles for each song, whether in live performance or studio conditions. The more elaborate arrangements contain up to five combinations, although many might consist of only one or two throughout (see Fig. 7).

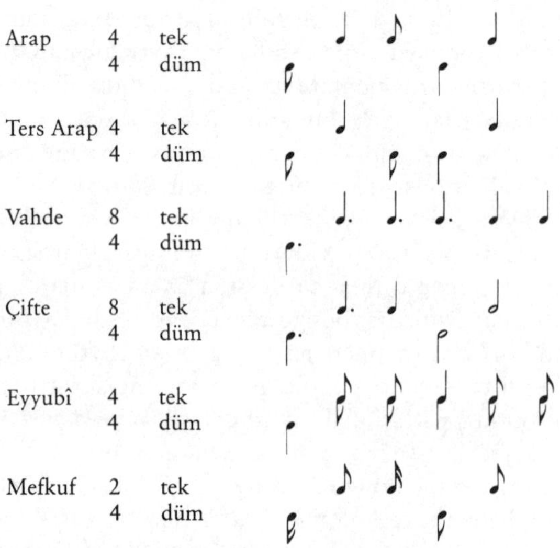

Fig. 7. *Usul* in arabesk. The note values give an indication of their relative speeds. (Right and left hands are used together in Eyyubî)

The *darbuka* is held to lie at the heart of arabesk. To a great extent this is due to the prominent skills of the *darbuka* player in recordings and live performances. The notion of *usul*, the framework around which the *darbuka* player performs, does however have a wider significance, which may also contribute to our understanding of the significant role played by the *darbuka* player. Outside of the musical context, the semantic range covered by this term is wide, implying method, system, and order, that which is fixed, comfortable, and in place. Many of the metaphors of disorder and disintegration discussed in the previous chapter make sense in terms of this play on the wider connotations of *usul* in the musical performance of arabesk.

Arabesk makes a significant distinction between music governed by *usul* and that which is not. This technique, in which solo passages in free rhythm contrast with passages in strict *usul* resembles the distinction in sanat music between free rhythm improvisations on *makam*, such as the instrumental *taksim* and the vocal *gazel*, and strict rhythm compositions such as the *şarkı* or *peşrev*. Halk music also distinguishes the instrumental *açış* or *gezinti* and the vocal *uzun* ('long') *hava* from the strict tempo of the *kırık* ('broken') *hava*. Passages without *usul* in arabesk songs use a melodic vocabulary which is similar both to the free rhythm tropes of the rural *uzun hava* and to the instrumental figurations of the art-music *taksim*, but integrate them into the body of the song in a different way. A useful example of this is provided by a live performance of a song by İbrahim Tatlıses, 'Kadifeden Kesesi' included on a live cassette, *Fosforlu Cevriyem*. The structure of the song can be schematized in the following way:

Vocal *açış*: 'Kadifeden Kesesi'
Full chorus: 'İstanbul'a'
Zurna taksim
Solo verse: 'Kadife yastığım yok'
Full chorus: 'İstanbul'a'

This performance is typical in beginning with a free rhythm statement of the first lines of the song. The inclusion of an instrumental 'break' in the middle is common in performance and studio recorded cassettes, but is confined to a handful of songs in both cases. Perhaps the only unusual feature of this song is its brevity, although singers typically choose short up-tempo songs of this nature to bring a performance to a close.

The opening passage closely resembles the style of rural *uzun hava* in its tonality and vocal delivery. It differs, however, in the close thematic links between the *açış* and what follows. In this case, the opening *açış* is a free rhythm and highly ornamented version of the solo verse music, interspersed by short violin phrases. In other arabesk performances, particularly those of Ferdi Tayfur, every song begins with an *açış* of this nature, with the opening lines of the song performed in a slow and 'free' tempo. This example is unusual only in its length, but the singer, İbrahim Tatlıses, is particularly well known for his performances of rural *uzun hava*, and the extension of these passages in his arabesk performances provides ample scope for the demonstration of his considerable vocal skills. Although in urban performances of rural halk music an *uzun hava* leads straight into a strict tempo song, the two parts were not necessarily conceived as linked pieces of music. In arabesk this distinction is incorporated in the melodic material of the song (see Ex. 28).

The second passage is an instrumental break which has many of the musical characteristics of an *usullü taksim*, an instrumental improvisation accompanied by a rhythmic ostinato passage (see Ex. 29). There are two unusual features of this *taksim*. The first is its positioning within the context of the song. *Taksim* in the art-music genre are positioned at the beginning of a suite (*fasıl*) of songs and pieces in order to introduce the characteristics of the *makam* that will be performed in the fixed rhythm pieces that are to follow, or in the middle in order to effect a modulation between two modes. Even though arabesk is often composed within a modal framework, the sequence of songs is not determined by their modal relationship, as in a classical suite. Instead audience requests are communicated either by shouting or passing pieces of paper, along with flowers, to the singer. Instrumental introductions therefore have no function in specifying *makam* or effecting modulations between *makam*. Secondly, this *taksim* is performed upon the *zurna*, a double-reed aerophone associated primarily with the rural halk-music repertory. The use of this instrument is so closely related to ritual occasions, such as weddings, circumcisions, wrestling and animal fights, that it is scarcely regarded as a 'musical' instrument at all. However, the figurations of this improvised break, up to instrumental variation upon the opening chorus phrase at bar 25, relate closely to the long phrases and arch structure of classical *taksim* form.[19] This is far removed from the more traditional use of this instrument, in which short melodic fragments of narrow melodic range are repeated with small variations.[20] This kind of instrumental break thus employs the melodic vocabulary of the classical *taksim* form on a variety of

[19] See Touma 1971.

[20] See Bartók 1976, 168–9, and Picken 1975, 496, for transcriptions of rural *zurna* performance.

instruments—including *elektrobağlama*, electric guitar, synthesizer, *yaylı tanbur*, *kaval* or *ney*, *kanun*—in a quite different context, devoid of its functional role in the classical suite.

The role of the *taksim* in the classical genre indicates only that the instrumentalist should reveal the *makam* in the most clear and uncluttered way possible. Virtuosity and instrumental pyrotechnics are considered to have no place whatsoever in performance since these would only detract from the prescribed function of the *taksim*. The music is a semantically dead space in the performance, with a simple and unobtrusive job to do. This is quite different in arabesk. The opening *açış* clearly celebrate the vocal skills of the singer, and the instrumental breaks, those of the instrumentalist. They also have the distinct character of an emotional epicentre to the song. In performance, the opening *açış* of a well-known song draws a storm of applause and cries of appreciation. This is true even in the cinema, where such *açış* often accompany the scenes in which the piteous state of the protagonist is portrayed in its most naked and direct way. Audience response to the singer and the song is thus concentrated in the opening free rhythm passages of the song. When particularly well-known singers are performing in the highly charged atmosphere of a *Halk Konseri*, the audience enacts highly formalized representations of distraught emotional states, through tears, fainting, shouting and screaming, and the tearing of clothes. The behaviour that accompanies music without *usul* is thus itself the very definition of the lack of *usul* in its widest sense: excessive noise, a lack of concern for dress codes and decent appearance, an inability to stand straight and still, the unrestrained expression of the inner, emotional self.

The instrumental breaks acquire a similar semantic density. Extended instrumental breaks are common in small *gazino* performances by lesser stars, where the clientele have come to the event to be together, enjoy a meal and a dance, and not specifically to hear a particular person singing. Songs in this case frame quite lengthy instrumental breaks, spinning out the musical material to prolong the dancing when required. In the context of the dance, the instrumental break also provides the opportunity for stylized representations of ecstatic states. At the beginning of a song people get up to the floor in couples or small groups, dancing in a *çifte telli* style with arms at chest or shoulder height, bobbing their weight from one foot to another. As the music moves from song text to instrumental

Ex. 28

Speed ♪ = 134, transposed up a major sixth from performance.

♩ = 99
Is-tan - bul - a İs - tan - bul - a yol - la hay - di
Bey - og - lu - na
yol - la İs - tan - bul - a yol - la yol - la
zurna
yol - la yar yol - la
Solo Verse
3
ka - di - fe yas - tığ - ım yok o - da - ma
mas - tığ - ım yok Ku - ran - 'a el ba - sar - ım Al - lah
sen - den ba - şka sen - den ba - şka
violins
dost - um yok Ku - ran - 'a el
6:5
ba - sa - rım sen - den ba - şka
sen - den ba - şka dos - tum yok

Ex. 29

Speed ♩ = 99, transposed up a minor third from performance.

3
3
3
5:4
3
9:8
5:4
6

taksim, a group forms in which people are called in to the centre of the circle to display their talents as isolated individuals. Whilst this is undoubtedly an expression of pleasure (*zevk*), the vocabulary of dance gestures in this popularized form of the *çifte telli* unambiguously connotes an inner domain of ecstatic and erotic emotion, through the shaking of upper torso and hips, and the turning on one's axis around the circle of dancers, with head upturned and eyes half closed. Even if one has not mastered the dance techniques involved, the emphasis in this style is on isolation (relative to the group), and everybody present is called in turn into the centre of the group.

Whilst this emotional intensity is lacking in the *taksim* of sanat music, the free rhythm style of *uzun hava* in rural halk music acts as a focus for the textual and musical expression of sentiments of grief and inner turmoil occasioned by death and separation. These arabesk *taksim* therefore use the technical vocabulary of sanat music, but the contexts of the songs in film and live performance invests them with the semantic density of free rhythm passages in the rural folk-music genre. This semantic density is a result of the alternation in the individual song form of music with and without *usul*, focusing emotional attention closely on the 'free' passages which present a highly organized simulacra of disorder.

The musical syntax of arabesk, constructed primarily in the recording studio under conditions determined by the recording industry in Turkey, thus provides the clearest possible enactment of the themes of solitude, alienation, and disorder. The themes pervade not just the lyrics and films, but also the narratives of inspiration with which this chapter began. All of these themes have a religious resonance. It is to these that we shall turn in the final chapter.

7
Arabesk and *Sema*

In arabesk, the description of the *hal* revolves around the social dislocation of the protagonist from his family and loved ones, provoking a crisis which is both characterized and reinforced by images of drunkenness, weeping, solitude, and an aimless circular movement which is exhausting but achieves nothing. The expression of this state through music is metaphorically equated with burning. We have also noted that the term *hal* has a meaning in the context of *sema* (religious music and dance in Sufi thought and practice). Religious tropes pervade arabesk texts and films, the gestures of singers in performance evoke prayer and supplication, and the dances with which arabesk is associated employ a vocabulary of ecstasy which has much in common with those of Muslim mystical practice in Turkey. Arabesk, I have argued, is an essentially new music whose creation must be seen primarily in terms of the technology and organization of the recording industry in Turkey, and whose consumption must be understood in the context of a society undergoing rapid urbanization, industrialization, and absorption into world economic systems. However, the language of arabesk is not new. This chapter looks at the ways in which the language of mysticism has been redefined in arabesk.

The issue of the centrality of religious music in a general discourse about Turkish music arose on numerous occasions during my fieldwork, and was invariably the subject of hot dispute. Perhaps the most striking of these occasions took place in 1986, at a tea-break in a TRT recording session at the studios in Harbiye. I was introduced to Yıldırım Gürses, a singer and teacher of music at Boğaziçi University, whose name was then associated with experiments in reconciling Turkish art music and Western compositional techniques in a way which was intended to bridge the gap between highbrow and popular music. He immediately invited me to visit him at the university and attend his courses. In the course of the subsequent conversation I made it clear that I had already devised a structure for the initial period of my research at the TRT, getting used to the music, meeting people, and learning the *bağlama*. He approved my plan, but stressed, with a brief glance to implicate the assembled company of musicians and singers from the folk-music department, that I should move on as soon as possible from the *bağlama* to religious (*dinî*) music. In this he suggested that I would quickly discover the clue, the key, to my research. It was the kind of unambiguous and forthright statement that any field-worker would warm to, suggesting a simple short cut in a confusing new landscape. Much to the intense irritation of my companions, standing around myself and the large, seated figure of the singer, I agreed. His remarks could not have been calculated to irritate or offend in a more inflammatory fashion the rest of his audience, who leapt to the defence of halk music, arguing its logical, historical, and even moral priority in the cultural milieu of Turkey today. The passions that were roused immediately suggested that this topic touched upon matters of significance.

These matters were difficult to pursue. When I put them to Mustafa Keser, he dismissed my suggestion that there was a link between arabesk and *tasavvuf* as 'totally wrong' (*muhakkak yalnıştır*). In spite of what I felt to be close parallels, it was evidently a connection which ran against the grain of Turkish thinking about music in terms of immutable genre. Turkey has no equivalent of the Egyptian *mashayikh*, whose reputation as popular singers had been made as *hafız*, professional reciters of the Koran, and who maintained the belief that the integrity of Egyptian music in its totality is dependent upon the recitation of the sacred text.[1] There were also substantial disparities in the extent of knowledge about religious music amongst both listeners and performers, and of awareness of the theological issues involved. For many, the perception of arabesk as an entirely secular genre meant that links between arabesk and Islam would be inconceivable. Others with more knowledge of *tasavvuf* and its practice in urban *tarikat* were less inclined to condemn the idea. To those of 'orthodox' religious dispositions, with an intellectual readiness to dismiss urban trash culture out of hand, the connection between arabesk and *tasavvuf* had a certain plausibility. For them, tacit religious strictures found themselves in a temporary and unlikely alliance with Kemalist Turkism, suggesting a common theme to the rot working away at Muslim Turkish society. Others who I

[1] See Danielson 1989.

knew to be actively involved in Alevi and Mevlevi groups in the city were receptive to the idea that Sufi concepts of music might underpin the larger part of Turkish musical experience (folk, popular, or otherwise), but none volunteered information on this subject of their own accord. A more vocal perspective was offered by halk-music ideologues, journalists, and academics of the centre-left, for whom the confluence of popular Islam and popular music in arabesk was self-evident, indicating the collapse of the Atatürkian tradition of bureaucratic reform and the 'hegemony of the periphery'. Views about the religious content of arabesk thus depended to a high degree on the ideological position of the speaker, and varied greatly. In spite of this, it is possible to argue from an outsider's perspective that there are clear continuities at the level of a general syntax of the music, dance, and song texts between arabesk and *sema*.

7.1. *Sema*

Sema is an ecstatic technique which is used in ritual gatherings by *tarikat* brotherhoods throughout Turkey. Details of the practice of the technique of *sema* vary substantially amongst these groups, but the ideas which sustain the practices have been developed within a common fund of Sufi thinking in Turkey for at least 800 years. Two of the best-known forms of *sema* are practised today by members of the Mevlevi brotherhood and the Bektaşi-Alevi. In Istanbul, these groups have radically different histories and social orientations. The Mevlevi *tarikatı* was essentially an urban phenomenon, drawing strongly upon a classical Arabic and Persian literary and musical culture. Bektaşı thought took root amongst the heterodox populations of rural Anatolia and the Balkans. Its poetry was expressed to the accompaniment of the *bağlama* in syllabic verse, as opposed to the classical metres known as *aruz*, and in simple Turkish which can still be understood relatively easily today. Apart from their quite separate social constitutions and orientations, a further political opposition was introduced as a result of the close connections between the Bektaşi-Alevi and the Janissaries, and the subsequent attempts of the Ottoman sultans to build up a power base among the Mevlevi in an attempt to counteract the increasing influence of the Janissaries in Ottoman political life from the end of the sixteenth century onwards.[2] In addition, the Bektaşi-Alevi were heterodox, revering Ali and his manifestation in the person of Haci Bektaş Veli as the final revelation and the incarnation of God in a profoundly humanistic philosophy. The Mevlevi remain Sunni, although critically at odds with the orthodoxy of the present-day Sunni community on such issues as music and dance. Whilst the technique of *sema* is recognized by 'conservative' *tarikat* such as the Nakşibendi, its practice is held to be silent and contemplative.[3] The active role of music and dance in *sema* as practised by the Mevlevi is the subject of outright opposition in accordance with orthodox proscriptions.

In spite of the radically different social and historical character of the two groups, a number of Turkish writers have suggested close links between Bektaşi-Alevi and Mevlevi thought. Possibly as a result of a common opposition to the conservative *tarikat* which constitute the vocal majority in Istanbul today,[4] a feeling of affinity between the two *tarikat* have arisen. In 1929, Fuad Köprülüzade pointed out the common roots of Turkish mysticism (*tasavvuf*) in Shamanism, Buddhism, and Zoroastrianism, encountered by the Turks in the course of their migrations through Central Asia, and brought into Anatolia by the wandering mystics who migrated south-westward from Khorasan along with the Turcoman armies and nomads, from the thirteenth century up to the beginning of the fifteenth. For Köprülüzade, this mystical tradition constituted a typically progressive contribution by the Turks to Islamic thought and culture. Köprülüzade provided the means by which later writers connected with both traditions could emphasize the strength of a cultural core which unites the two against what is currently perceived to be the reaction and intolerance of the larger urban *tarikat*.

The relationship of this body of scholarship to the practice of *sema* is more complex. The practice of *sema* in Istanbul amongst the two groups with which I was tangentially connected during my fieldwork has undergone something of a decline. Istanbul was once the site of numerous thriving Mevlevi *tekke*, the most notable being that in Beyoğlu (Galata), close to the now run-down street of dilapidated music shops and brothels known as the 'Yüksek Kaldırım' in Kara-

[2] Lewis 1968, 157. [3] See Molé 1963, 150.

[4] The Nakşibendi, the Nurcu, and the Süleymancı, whose *tekke* and *zaviye* are grouped around the central city mosques, share a political power base in the universities and political parties.

köy. But since the official closure of the dervish lodges by Mustafa Kemal in 1925, the practice of the *mukaabele* ceremony, during which the Mevlevi *sema* is performed, is now carried out in some secrecy. More informal gatherings of Mevlevi musicians take place, in which the Koran is read and music played, somewhat in the manner of a gathering of friends in certain circles in England to play piano duets or chamber music classics.

Much the same could be said about the *sema* of the Bektaşi-Alevi in the context of the ritual known today as the *cem* (or *aynicem*). Although large communities of Alevi migrants from the predominantly Alevi provinces of Sivas, Yozgat, Tunçeli, and Çorum exist in Istanbul, there is little doubt that the practice of the *cem* ceremony has undergone a relatively recent decline. Many of my Alevi informants, male and aged 20–30, could remember having participated in the *cem* as young children, but not since, and it was clear that this could not be pinned down simply to a lack of interest in or commitment to their ethnic and sectarian identity. Being inextricably linked with subversion by centrist political discourse from the Ottoman empire until today, the Bektaşi-Alevi were seen as fifth-column activists in the Ottoman wars against the Shiite Safavid dynasty of Persia, resulting in their ruthless persecution during the seventeenth and eighteenth centuries. The practice of *sema* was forbidden by Vani Mehmet Efendi as early as 1666, in spite of the fact that its practice had been categorically defined as permissible in a *fetva* issued by the Şeyhülislam from 1490 to 1575, Ebussu'ûd Efendi.[5] In 1826 the Alevi *tekke* were closed down entirely because of their close affiliation with the Janissaries. Today Alevis frequently attribute the difficulties that they experience at the hands of Turkish bureaucracy to their leftist political affiliations and to the fact that a significant proportion of Alevis are Kurds. The Alevi in Turkey today have thus had a lengthy experience of the need to conceal their identity ('takiye'), a situation which is not conducive to mass participation in the *cem* rituals. However, since I am only concerned here with perceptions of links between *sema* and arabesk, based on a theoretical rather than participatory knowledge of *sema* for the reasons mentioned above, the complexities of obtaining information about the urban practice of *sema* need not detain us.

If the theory of *sema*, or even the mere existence of music in an Islamic society, appears to flout orthodoxy at every level, this is

[5] Erseven 1990, 119.

because we are inclined to take the totalizing claims of Islamicist discourses at face value. In fact, music has been the subject of intense debate from an early date in the Muslim world to the present day, providing the means by which proponents of *sema* could argue the theological and moral benefits of music in certain contexts. The theological argument is essentially one of terminology, principally concerning the definition of various kinds of music and the legal category to which these should be assigned. The principal five categories of legality are *farz* (obligatory, as enjoined by the Koran), *sünnet* (obligatory, as enjoined by the Hadith), *mübah* (agreeable, but not enjoined by the Koran or the Hadith), *mekruh* (disagreeable, but not explicitly condemned by the Koran or Hadith), and *haram* (canonically forbidden).

The argument over which category music should be assigned to is complicated by several factors. Firstly, the concept of 'music' (*musiki*) as understood today in the Muslim world did not exist at the time of the Prophet. In the opinion of Uludağ, the vocal art of singing was 'natural' (*tabii*) before the development of the *makam* system and cultural influence from Persia centuries later gave rise to the kind of music to which evidence from the Koran and Hadith is subsequently made to refer.[6] Uludağ credits a certain Said b. Miscah and his pupil Ibn Muhriz with the introduction of music into the Arab world, learnt on their travels in Persia and Byzantium. The concept of *makam*, and the 'science of music' (*ilm-i musiki*), began to develop from this point on. The Muslim debate has much in common with the debate over the legitimacy of music in the Christian church during the Reformation and Counter-Reformation. Since the Koran provides no definition of music, it was difficult to separate kinds of music felt to be beneficial from those which everybody knew were not. Those who preferred to err on the side of caution could draw on the *rivayet* traditions of Müslim and Buhari, which claim that there is a category of things which are doubtful or questionable (*müstebihat*), to which the entire category of 'music' should be allocated and condemned accordingly. Those arguing the moral permissibility of music in certain contexts are consequently obliged to construct elaborate taxonomies to differentiate those forms of music which have a claim to legitimacy (including Koranic cantillation, the call to prayer, Pilgrimage songs, praise songs known as *medh*, *nat*, and *tahmid*, songs celebrating the family, work, and

[6] Uludağ 1976, 30.

war) and those intended solely for pleasure (*zevk*) which everyone would recognize to be entirely out of order.[7]

Ayet in the Koran explicitly condemning music therefore do not exist. By definition, an activity can only be condemned as *haram* if it is clearly stated to be so in the Koran. Condemnation of music drawing upon Koranic evidence is thus vague and imprecise in the extreme. Lokmân 6 is cited to condemn music as a distraction, and also as an object of commercial activity: 'There is a man who purchaseth a ludicrous story that he may seduce men from the way of God, without knowledge, and may laugh the same to scorn; these shall suffer a shameful punishment.'[8] The professionalism of musicians remains an issue in many Muslim societies today.[9] The 'voice of Satan' mentioned in Al-Najm 59–61 and al-Isra' 64 are often considered to be references to music itself. Linked with its dangers as a distraction, music was also associated in the mind of scholars critical of music with the worship of the polytheists and idolators at the time of the Prophet. Al-Anfal 35 is held to condemn music in its reference to the whistling and clapping of idolators during worship. The paucity of material in the Koran is amply compensated by a proliferation of stories relating to music in the non-canonical texts of the Hadith, which provide accounts of the line taken by the Prophet on a number of subjects, including the selling of musical slave girls and attendance at weddings at which musical entertainment was provided. The Hadith is an arena of legitimate debate over matters of interpretation and meaning, and condemnation of music expressed in these passages is contradicted by other passages, in which, for example, the Prophet is reported to have permitted his young daughter Ayşe to dance and sing.[10] Whilst this evidence is used by the four principal schools of Islamic jurisprudence to consign music to the legal categories of *mekruh* or *mübah*, this evidence is by no means binding, and allows great scope for alternative positions to be argued legitimately.

The theological dispute over the legitimacy of music gains a particularly sharp focus over the question of the role of music in worship. Two issues in particular are involved: whether the reading of the Koran (*kıraat* or *tilavet*) should be 'musical', and the permissibility of

[7] Al-Faruqi 1985, 8. [8] Sale's transl. (1734).

[9] See Baily 1988 and Nelson 1985 for ethnomusicological accounts of this debate in Afghanistan and Egypt.

[10] This well-known Hadith is cited in Uludağ 1976, 67 n. 10.

non-canonical poetry, music, and dance in the context of worship (*sema* and *zikr*). As Al-Faruqi points out, the ideal form of music, occupying the top position in her hierarchy, is the cantillation of the Koran.[11] But nowhere is it canonically stated exactly how it should be done. Much of the argument over the acceptability of music revolves around the question of how the Koran should be read. Various Hadith point to the specification of seven methods of cantillation, called the 'Seven Letters' in the *rivayet* of Ömer b. el-Hattab.[12] In another frequently cited Hadith from the *rivayet* of Ibn Mace the Prophet is reputed to have said: 'It is beyond doubt that this Koran was revealed with sadness. Weep when you read it . . . He who does not read the Koran with melody (*teğanni*) is not one of us.'[13]

In Turkey most commentators would agree that a 'good voice' is necessary for the recitation of the Koran, but in the opinion of many scholars as well as the *muezzin* themselves, the Koran should under no circumstances be sung with the rules of composition applying to *şarkı*, the *makam* system. Whilst it is common to hear musicians referring to Hicaz or Saba *makamı* as 'the mode' of the *ezan*, this is bluntly rejected by those religious authorities who wish to stress the non-musicality of *kıraat* and the *ezan*. The supposed presence or absence of *makam* is thus a major issue relating to the legitimacy or illegitimacy of music in Islam.

So it is strange that Karaçam, the author of a text on cantillation published by the Theology Faculty of Marmara University in Istanbul should stress that the Koran is to be read 'with *makam*', citing the second-century Hadith example of Ubeydullah b. Ebu Bekri.[14] Karaçam stresses the importance of a harmonious *makam*, and the employment of an appropriately non-secular style. The term '*makam*' would certainly have had no currency at this early date, but it is clear that Karaçam uses the term *makam* in his argument to make a clear case for the role of 'music', as understood today, in religious practice. In fact he goes further, emphasizing the importance of music in the recitation of the Koran: 'chanting and melody endow man's mind (*nefs*) and then his heart with power (*nüfüz*), and its effect is to be seen in a clearer form.'[15] Music is more than mere *sus*—ornament—but endows the *nefs* (the rational, reflective mind)

[11] Al-Faruqi 1985, 8. [12] Karaçam 1976, 20.
[13] Cited in Uludağ 1976, 103–4.
[14] Karaçam 1976, 145. [15] Karaçam 1976, 131.

and then the *kalb* (the 'inner', the heart) with *nüfüz*, power which enables one to see the innermost part of something. It is clear from Karaçam's strictures and comments that it is possible to argue for the recitation of the Koran with *makam* in a way which does not reduce the sacred text to the status of a *şarkı*. Most *muezzin* with whom I discussed the issue in Istanbul were understandably evasive when I asked them about the extent of their musical knowledge, sidestepping the debate neatly by claiming that they recited as they had been taught without being aware whether or not it conformed to any musical theory.

Criticism of the popularity of the *Mevlid-i Şerif* of Süleyman Çelebi rests on this point of musicality. It is admitted that the recitation of the *Mevlid-i Şerif* is not in itself a bad thing—quite the contrary—but the fact that it has assumed the status in 'popular religion' of a second sacred text is regrettable and verges on blasphemy.[16] What is more, the *Mevlid* is recited by a body of professional singers known as Mevlidhan whose recitation of this text explicitly uses *makam*. In fact the rules governing the recitation of the *Mevlid* according to a defined progression or modulation from one *makam* to another are quite clear, and an advanced level of musical training, quite apart from a fine voice, are considered indispensable. Both Belviranlı and Tavaslı point out that familiarity with the famous Rast *Kar-ı Natik* of Dede Efendi is essential if modulation between the relevant *makam* is to be successfully and smoothly achieved.[17] The style of recitation in the *Mevlid* is not markedly different from *kıraat*. What is problematic is the element of 'musicality' acknowledged in the *Mevlid* but denied in *kıraat*, and the fear that music, with all the dangers involved in it, such as listening to the singer and not the text, is always capable of creeping into Koranic recitation. Nelson has described a similar problem in Egypt, where a conventional musical education is considered to be indispensable to particular forms of Koranic recitation. As a result of this, purists are engaged in a continual battle with media treatment and cassette sales, which is seen as turning Koranic recitation into 'music'.[18]

[16] The *Mevlid-i Şerif* is recited at *Mevlut* ceremonies. As N. and R. Tapper (1987) have described, there are two distinct forms of *Mevlut* ceremony in Turkey. One is a public mosque ceremony, often in honour of prominent men in the community shortly after their burial. The other tends to be a domestic occasion when the *Mevlid* is recited for women at private celebrations.

[17] See Belvıranlı 1975 and Tavaslı 1976. [18] Nelson 1985, 136–52.

The principal issue however is musicality, and the extent to which a 'musical' rendition of the Koran is capable of distorting the language and hence potentially interfering with the meaning of the text. Along with Catholic and Protestant critics of music in the Reformation period, notably Erasmus and Cranmer, Islamic orthodoxy has continually objected to a medium of worship which actually interferes with a perception of the message itself, and, even worse, is potentially capable of leading the mind off on other more dangerous paths. It was this that led Archbishop Cranmer to insist on his famous dictum that Anglican liturgical music should be composed in such a way that there would be 'for every syllable a note' and no more. The condemnation of the involved melismatic polyphony of the late renaissance church in Western Europe, and the construction of new forms of liturgical music, was central in the doctrinal debate over the role of 'the word' in the reformed churches. It was also a vital political symbol of the process of reform itself and the manipulability of forms of religious practice, indicating in the aesthetic space of public ritual that a new period of history had been entered.

In sixteenth-century Western Europe, both reformers and counter-reformers went so far as to invite the collaboration of specialists to hammer out a coherent and applicable theory of liturgical music. As regards Koranic cantillation, thinkers and reformers in the Muslim world have not been in the same position. The central terms of the argument have never been bound by musical notation and have undergone long processes of mutation over the centuries. If Karaçam, writing as a representative of the Faculty of Theology at Marmara University, can be held to represent the current state of thinking on this subject in Turkey today, it is clear that the matter is far from resolved. For Karaçam music is not only permissible, but in some sense desirable. However, anything which distorts the text and draws attention to itself (*tasannu*) is to be condemned. Karaçam illustrates this distortion with a ninth-century Hadith from the *rivayet* of Imam Ahmed:

'I do not approve of cantillation with melody. It is non-canonical (*bid'at*)', he [the Prophet] said. To someone who questioned him about melody and cantillation, he asked,

'What is your name?'

And he replied,

'Muhammed.'

And he illustrated his disapproval by saying to him,

'If they called you "Mûhâmmed" [elongating the syllables], how would you like it?'[19]

Indeed the principal objection to the four recognized methods of cantillation (contrasted always with a fifth 'natural' style) is the elongation of the syllables and the drawing out of the *med*.[20] This extends to the insertion of the *med* where there should be none, as in the style known as *Tatrib*, or adding vowel points (*hareke*) to the *med* and silencing the quiescent letters (*sakinler*) in a manner characteristic of the style known as *Terkis*.

So for Karçam the respect due to the Arabic language is of paramount importance, and it can best be observed by reading the Koran in a 'natural' voice (*tabii sesle*). Exactly what a 'natural voice' consists of is seldom specified, except in not being *Ter'id, Tatrib, Terkis*, or *Tahzin*. It is thus possible, according to Karaçam, to read the Koran in a 'natural' way whilst still employing *makam*. Others would deny that anything involving *makam* could ever be 'natural'. In this debate it is clear that the principal cause of conflict is two rival interpretations of the word 'music' itself. One is 'music' as an acoustic medium of communication and expression. The other is *musiki*, inextricably associated with the concept of *makam* in Islamic scholarship and an unambiguously secular frame of reference. The former is essentially value-free whilst the latter is unambiguously condemnable. The theoretical issue lies in the question of whether the subject of debate is 'music' or *musiki*.

The whole argument over the legality of music shifts into a higher gear on the subject of *sema*, which exploits this semantic ambiguity to the full. At one level, the definition of an area of 'legitimate' musical experience, terminologically assigned to a different category from less reputable musical genres, allows Sufi thinkers in Turkey to challenge orthodoxy on its own terms. At another level, the high status accorded to *sema* in the spiritual quest is an example of the deliberate flaunting of orthodoxy as a spiritual technique cultivated in Turkish Sufism. For the Bektaşi-Alevi, this attitude towards the external and internal aspects of the law are imaged in terms of a right–left, outer–inner duality. In a story told of the thirteenth-century founder and saint of their order, Haci Bektaş Veli, it is related that he learnt the Koran with the Prophet Muhammed seated at his right-hand side, explaining the 'outer' or exoteric meanings of the

[19] Cited in Karaçam 1976, 139.

[20] The lengthening of the Arabic letter 'a'.

text, and with Ali (the son-in-law of the Prophet, and according to the Alevi, his rightful successor) seated at his left, explaining the 'inner' or secret, esoteric meaning.[21] To those aware of the inner secrets of Bektaşi-Alevi mysticism, the outer rules are rendered redundant, and in turning the order of the world upside-down, the world is seen as it is. Correctly understood, the ritual celebration of music, dance, and alcohol in *sema* is the path towards understanding and attainment.

7.2. The Language of *Sema*: The Secret and the Feast

We can understand the role of *sema* in Bektaşi-Alevi and Mevlevi thought best in terms of the secret (*sırr*) to which their poetry continually refers. The secret is both the fundamental mystery of the universe and the means of its apprehension. The mystery is the paradox of creation, that God, formerly undifferentiated unity, should have created plurality, interposing a veil between the ultimate Truth (*Hakk*) and the world of illusions. This mystery is expressed in the formula known as the *Küntükenz* to Bektaşi-Alevi and Mevlevi alike. This is an abbreviated form of the Hadith which states: 'I was a hidden treasure, therefore was I fain to be known, and so I created creation in order that I should be known'.[22] As Birge points out, the paradox lies in the fact that understanding can thus only be achieved by means of its opposite. Thus the duality of the world (*ikilik*) prevents the perception of the unity of God (*birlik*) but at the same time is the only means by which this unity can be apprehended. This paradox underpins the most celebrated teaching method of the Bektaşi-Alevi: the joke. In the joke, truth is presented as an apparent absurdity. Most Turkish jokes, traditional (such as the stories of Nasreddin Hoca and the Bektaşi *fikra*) or otherwise (such as the pervasive Laz jokes), have an overt didactic function. Understanding the joke is a matter of seeing beyond the absurdity or contradiction to an inner coherence or resolution. In the same way, experience of the divine Truth can only be achieved in a world of plural appearances. Perception is thus a secret, a key which provides access to the real through the unreal. This process is most frequently described in Bektaşi-Alevi thought in terms of pain (*dert*) and remedy (*derman*). Indeed, Birge claims that: 'there is no more constant refrain in

[21] Birge 1937, 36. [22] Ibid. 109.

Bektaşi poems than the reference to some trouble, *dert*, especially the pain of separation, the disharmony that comes from the realisation of *ikilik*, "duality", the cure of which is to be found in Ali and his descendants'.[23] This view of the universe engenders a series of parallel oppositions; *ikilik–birlik*, outer–inner, *dert–derman*, Muhammed–Ali. To these we might add the 'Lying' or 'Illusory World' (*Yalan* or *Fani Dünya*), also a common trope in the popular poetry of gravestone verse and arabesk, opposed to divine Truth. The secret is then the perception of Truth through the Lie and the point of mediation between two apparently irreconcilable poles.

A theory of *sema* which is held in common by Mevlevi and Bektaşi-Alevi is that of the *Bezm-i Elest*. This term, meaning literally 'the feast of am-I-not', refers to the experience of oneness with God in which the souls of men existed prior to their corporeal creation. This experience resides in man as a distant memory which is subject to recall through the correct perception of a word or sound, often interpreted in terms of the 'beautiful word' mentioned in the Koran.[24] This act of perception is a secret, understandable only to the initiate. The role of music in *sema* is precisely this act of perception. The term *sema* itself strictly speaking means 'audition', and this can refer to the audition of a particular sonic 'key' or to a mode of audition of sounds in general. In the latter case, *sema* refers to the audition and recitation of particular sequences of sounds, framed in the ritual context of the *mukaabele* or *cem*. Amongst other groups, exactly the same spiritual process is considered to take place in the ritual recitation, or 'remembering', of the names of God in *zikr*. In this conception of *sema*, sound has the function of bringing the individual into alignment with the principle of divine unity. According to the literature on *tasavvuf* in Turkey, the ignition of this memory of the pre-human state takes place through the medium of music and dance, although any sound, correctly perceived, can be identified as an utterance of God's name.

Alcohol also plays a vital, though diffuse and polysemic, role in this theory. Alcohol provides a metaphor for ecstatic religious experience, with which anglophone readers are thoroughly familiar from Fitzgerald's translation of Omar Khayyam and Nicholson's translations of Celaleddin Rumi. It also plays a vital ritual role in Alevi *muhabbet* gatherings. Whilst Gölpınarlı and others have identified in this traces of shamanic and Zoroastrian belief, the com-

[23] Ibid. 137 [24] Al-Zumar 18

plex symbolism of alcohol and the grape is interpreted amongst the Mevlevi and Bektaşi-Alevi firmly in the context of the Islamic theory of the *Bezm-i Elest*. The consumption of wine or *rakı* in the *cem* ceremony, which can be seen as an enactment of the pre-creation and spiritual prototype of the earthly gathering, is explained in the Bektaşi-Alevi version of the story of the *miraç* (the Prophet's ascent to heaven), outlined in a number of hymns (*nefes*). Birge collates most of the elements of the Bektaşi-Alevi *miraç* from Ziya Bey and a poem by the early sixteenth-century Bektaşi-Alevi poet Hatayi:

Called by Gabriel to make the ascent, Muhammed took a guide, *rehber*, as he was commanded, then met on the way a lion who greatly frightened him until a voice from God calmed him by saying that the lion simply wanted from him a token. Muhammed gave him his ring, then passed on into the presence of God with whom he discussed the ninety-nine thousand mysteries. Since the conversation took place through a screen Muhammed finally ventured to ask if this screen could not be raised. The screen was raised and behind it he saw Ali. Before leaving, God gave him a bunch of grapes to give to his grandchildren, Hasan and Hüseyin. Selman who was also present asked for a grape and Muhammed gave him one. On the way back he came upon a group who said they were the 'Forty'. Counting them Muhammed found only thirty-nine. But at that moment, Selman arrived and completed the Forty. As they conversed together an invisible hand squeezed the grape in Selman's hand. One of the Forty drinking from the juice thus produced, all became intoxicated. They began to dance, playing the while on instruments, *çalpane*, and reciting the word that stands for God, *Hu, hu*, literally 'He, he'. Ali then, more overflowing with ecstasy than the others, put himself in the middle and took from his mouth the seal ring Muhammed had given the lion. Muhammed then recognised Ali, and understood his true nature, thus attaining by this act of understanding to the Divine Reality.[25]

Birge adds that a poem by Aşık Hasan explains that the owner of the invisible hand, the squeezer of the grape, is none other than Ali/Haci Bektaş Veli himself. In this story, the grape, a present from God to Muhammed's grandchildren, Ali's sons, is intercepted by Selman. At the gathering of the forty saints the grape is transformed into wine by the hand of Ali; the ecstatic communion that follows is the spiritual prototype of the *cem*. It is during this intoxicated ecstasy that Ali reveals himself to Muhammed not only as the lion, the protector of God, but as the figure behind the screen, the inner, esoteric secret of the divine law. The present of God for the holy family thus becomes,

[25] Birge 1937, 137–8.

through Ali, available to all those at the earthly gathering of the forty, the *cem*. Furthermore, it is the means by which the outer perceives the inner, secret dimension of the law. In this ritual context the forbidden ecstasy of alcohol turns the world on its head and in the process 'informs' the otherwise empty structure of orthodox doctrine.

7.3. The Dance

Both Mevlana Celaleddin Rumi and Haci Bektaş Veli are credited by their followers with the invention of the particular form of their ecstatic dances. But it is also accepted that the formalization of these dances, as they are now practised, was left to their successors. For the Mevlevi, the ceremony in which *sema* is practised is known as *mukaabele* and was established by Mevlana's successor, Sultan Veled (1226–1312), also considered to be the founder of the *tarikat*, the 'Second Saint' (*Pir-i Sani*). For the Bektaşi-Alevi, the *Pir-i Sani* was Balım Sultan who lived in the first half of the fifteenth century, and is credited by Bektaşi-Alevi writers as the originator of most present-day Alevi practices and beliefs: the formalization of the *cem*, the initiation ceremony, and the institution of Dedelik, a celibate chain of spiritual leaders (who claimed that Haci Bektaş Veli had no children other than 'children of the way'—in opposition to the Çelebis, who claim direct agnatic descent from Haci Bektaş Veli himself).

The dances associated with *sema* amongst the Bektaşi-Alevi and Mevlevi are strikingly similar; a slow anti-clockwise movement, head tilted gently to the right, arms upstretched with the right hand pointing upwards and the left down, in a posture of complete asymmetry. Explanations of the particular movements and gestures of the dance are extremely rare.[26] Alevi generally maintain that the posture imitates a crane (*turna*), but beyond the fact that the crane is considered a 'sacred creature', little is added by way of explanation. To an outside observer, no readily apparent relationship of imitation exists. The lack of commentary on this subject is striking, when so much else seems to suffer from a prolixity of explanation.

Indigenous explanations of *sema* and *hal* which accompanies it

[26] Erseven (1990) describes the general sequence of movements in the *cem* ceremony, but devotes little attention to details of posture.

tend to stress the altered psychic state produced by the ecstatic dance and music. The descriptions of the earliest *sema* practised by Turkish mystics are generally concerned with *irade dışında haller* (uncontrolled states), in which the force of the 'discovering' (*vecd* or *keşf*) that accompanies audition is so strong that the individual is unable to control himself. Neglect of safety results in accidents, and in extreme cases *vecd* ends in mutilation and death. These explanations of *sema* interpret the effects of music in terms of the division of the human psyche into *nefs* and *ruh*. Uludağ provides an explanation which suggests the masculinity of *ruh* and the femininity of *nefs*. Just as God created Eve out of Adam for his pleasure and satisfaction in the material world, as described in the Koran,[27] so in the spiritual world (*mânâ âleminde*), *nefs* was created from *ruh*. Between them exists a relationship of flirtation, love, and correspondence (*mektuplaşma*). Like all lovers, both *ruh* and *nefs* love music, but each responds to it in different ways. *Ruh* is directly exalted by the music, whilst the feminine *nefs* takes its cue from the heart, loses control of itself, and is ultimately only capable of enjoying the pleasure of the masculine *ruh*. *Ruh*, on the other hand, is capable of enjoying music directly and on its own. This explanation of *sema* and the nature of the state of attainment makes a certain sense in terms of Turkish gender relations, although, as Uludağ points out, it is not the explicit belief of any one particular group of people. But the relationship that this expresses between *ruh* and *nefs* in the attainment of *vecd* is of a more general significance. The suppression of the materialistic *nefs* results in the acquisition of a certain perception or state of knowledge (*bilgi*), but also a concomitant loss of control or will (*irade*). This explains the extreme states of inspired 'idiocy' into which the participants of *sema* are plunged in the saintly biographies.

As Rouget points out, this does not adequately account for the austere and highly disciplined manifestations of 'trance' in the *sema* practised by the Mevlevi.[28] The *mukaabele* ceremony is a quiet and measured affair which does not sit easily with these images of passion and violence. 'Trance' is invariably a culturally organized and coded phenomenon and not simply a manifestation of an uncontrolled state. The literature on *zikr* and *sema* emphasizes the order main-

27 Al-A'raf 189.

28 Rouget 1985, 270. Rouget's critique of Neher's thesis concerning the role of particular frequencies in stimulating ecstatic states draws its evidence from the literature on groups such as the Mevlevi, whose severely disciplined ecstatic states are triggered by highly formalized musical messages.

tained in the ritual context. Birge points out, with reference to the Bektaşi-Alevi *cem*, notable amongst other things in that women participate in the dancing, that a *gözcü* ('watchman') is appointed in order to 'interfere if there is the slightest impropriety'.[29] We might also note in passing that the function of the *nuqaba'* of the Hamidiya Shadhiliya in Egypt is 'to restrain any one of the worshippers who loses, or appears to lose, his self control'.[30] There is more to *sema* than simply 'losing control', and a clue to the more general significance of *sema* might be sought in the symbolization of movement in the dances associated with Mevlevi and Bektaşi-Alevi ritual practice.

The explanations of the Mevlevi *mukaabele* by Western and Turkish commentators have invariably stressed that the circular motion of the dancers in the dance-hall (*semahane*) symbolizes a Platonic revolving of the spheres; the dancers align themselves, as they achieve *vecd*, to cosmic principles of order and balance: 'The dance of the Mevlevi Dervishes, in particular, is said to symbolize the movements of the planetary spheres as they circle in perfect order and love for their Lord.'[31]

There is thus a temptation to interpret the circular motion of the Mevlevi and Bektaşi-Alevi *sema* in terms of the spatial representation of the perfection of attainment, or the completeness of unity. All symbolic activity is, however, capable of absorbing conflicting and even contradictory interpretations, even though particular members of a society might be in a position to determine public readings of these symbols and effectively to exclude others. Alternative readings of the symbolization of space in *sema* are certainly possible. The Mevlevi mystic Divâne Mehmet Çelebi observed that in *sema* the right-hand side of the wall in which the *mukaabele* ceremony is held represents the 'visible world' (*sahadet, nasût alemi*, or *halk*), whilst the left is the invisible world (*gayb, melekût*, or *emr alemi*).[32] The circling of *sema* is thus not static, but can be seen as a dialectic between an awareness of unity in the invisible world and the dancer's perception of the visible world of plurality. Secondly, Uludağ cites Ebu Sehl es-Sulûki, who claimed that in performing *sema* he found himself in a liminal state between *istitar* (unity being hidden), in

[29] Birge 1937, 199. [30] Gilsenan 1973, 170.

[31] Godwin 1987, 88. See also Rouget 1985, 270: 'everything about it is extremely controlled, restrained, ordered, in the image of that great celestial mechanism which, as we know, it symbolizes by imitating the spinning motion of the planets'.

[32] Gölpınarlı 1963, 106–7.

which he 'burns', and *tecelli* (unity being manifest), in which he is at peace.[33] The circularity of movement in *sema* can thus be seen as a performance of a state of imbalance, a dialectic alternation between unity and duality, between being in this world and being at one with God. This sheds some light on the statement that the movement and posture of the dancer in the Bektaşi-Alevi *sema* imitates a crane. The crane is a migratory bird, considered auspicious throughout Turkey as an indicator of seasonal change. To the Bektaşi-Alevi, the cyclical appearance and disappearance of the crane suggests the relationship of the soul to the divine Truth, resident at one moment in the visible world and in the next the invisible, one moment here and the next there. In short, the symbolization of the circular movement of the dancers in *sema* does not so much represent an achieved attainment as an active dialectical process of attaining.

7.4. *Tasavvuf* and the Music of the Spheres

Christian mysticism relating to music is based largely on the Platonic conception of the Music of the Spheres, which sees in music an earthly reflection of cosmic principles. This conception of music, developed by Plato but given fuller exposition in the work of later Roman philosophers, notably Cicero's 'Dream of Scipio', Plutarch's 'The Vision of Timarchus', and Plotinus' 'Universal Harmony', was grafted on to Western Christian theology in the late fifth century by Martianus Capella and the Neoplatonist Boethius. As a constant theme in European theology and science throughout the Middle Ages and Renaissance, the concept of the Music of the Spheres surfaced in the physics and astronomy of Kepler and later in the speculations of the twentieth-century avant-garde in, to cite two strikingly different examples, the work of Paul Hindemith and Karlheinz Stockhausen. The foundation of much of the work of the post-war avant-garde on specific mathematical, geometrical, or architectural principles (notably the work of Boulez, Xenakis, and Varèse) can be seen as less obvious products of a Platonic musical cosmology which continues to provide a bedrock for our way of thinking about music.

Islamic mysticism, whose chief classical input was Aristotelian and hence critical of the Platonic tradition, lacked this totalizing concept which placed music at the centre of an entire cosmological

[33] Uludağ 1976, 264.

system. It is interesting to note that the description of the ascent of the Prophet into heaven in the *Miraç Bahrı* of the *Mevlid-i Şerif* of Süleyman Çelebi clearly draws on the dream-journeys to the heavens described by Cicero, Plutarch, and Plotinus, but the exegesis on the Music of the Spheres which constituted the theoretical focus of the classical narratives is entirely absent. Indeed, the entire concept of music in *tasavvuf* differs radically from our own tradition of musical mysticism. From this perspective it constitutes something of a puzzle. If *sema* is audition, aural perception of the unity of God, why then does music occupy such a negative domain of expression in mystical thought? This problem is compounded by the fact that musical instruments play such an important and central role amongst the Mevlevi and Bektaşi-Alevi as symbols of sectarian integrity, and such a visible role in their central rituals. The Mevlevi instrument is the *ney*, the long, end-blown reed flute. The symbolic value of the *ney* and its music in Mevlevi thought is made quite clear in the opening passage of the *Mathnawi* of Mevlana Celaleddin Rumi, known as the 'Song of the *Ney*':

Listen to the Ney, how it tells its tale, complaining of separations—
Saying, ever since I was parted from the reed-bed my lament has caused man and woman to moan.
I want a bosom torn by severance, that I may unfold [to such a one] the pain of love-desire.
Everyone who is left far from his source wishes back the time when he was united with it . . .[34]

These verses provide a commentary on the inner symbolism of the *ney*. Cut from the reed-bed and turned into an instrument, the sound of the *ney* expresses its longing to return to the reed-bed. In a similar way the human soul laments its alienation and separation from God. Furthermore, the sound of the *ney* 'hath caused man and woman to moan'. Man is, in a sense, played by the *ney* just as the *ney* is played by man. To borrow Rouget's term, man is 'musicated' into a state of awareness of duality. This is a doctrine of affect far removed from the Platonic model of harmony and unity. We should understand *sema*, then, in terms of the attention it draws to man's alienated state.

The association of this process with symbols of fire, flame, and combustion is intense: the prototype *sema* for the Bektaşi-Alevi were

[34] Nicholson's trans., Rumi 1930, 8.

the dances conducted around fires by Haci Bektaş Veli, a part of the 'fire-cult' embedded in early Turkish mysticism.[35] In Bektaşi-Alevi ritual practice the candle plays an important role. In its poetry, the dervish is the moth (*pervane*) fluttering round the flame. Music and flame are closely identified with each other. The ninth verse of the *Mathnawi* expresses this clearly:

> This noise of the Nay is fire, it is not wind:
> Whoso hath this fire, may he be naught![36]

We have already noted that burning is a property of being in this world, in which the unity of God is hidden (*istitâr*). The principle of *sema* and music in particular becomes clear as the expression of separation, in which the awareness of separation provides the real foundation for the longing for unity. Here, as elsewhere, understanding can only proceed through the medium of its opposite.

7.5. Conclusion

Before putting these somewhat speculative observations back into an ethnographic context, let me elucidate the parallels that I wish to draw between arabesk and *sema*. These exist at a variety of levels, many of which will have become clear in this discussion of *sema*. Firstly, there is a level of textual correspondence between the poetry of *sema* and that of arabesk. Most specifically, the references to *dert* and *derman* in *sema* are echoed in a number of arabesk texts. More generally, utterances of frustration in *sema* and arabesk share an identical rhetoric. The separation of man from God in *sema* and the lover from the beloved in arabesk is expressed in similar poetic tropes. In particular, the depiction of the burning soul is, as I have noted, an aspect of a general aesthetic of Turkish music which assumes a particular intensity both in the mystical poetry of *sema* and in arabesk. Secondly, I have related the textual and iconographic expression of the 'state' (*hal*) in arabesk to a concept existing in a theological discourse upon *sema*, but not in the poetic texts of *sema*. Whilst the term *hal* is one of wide applicability in the Turkish language, in both arabesk and *sema* it describes the separation of the lover from the beloved and a disintegration of social and psychic order.

[35] Ocak 1983, 187–8. [36] Rumi 1930, 8.

Thirdly, there is a level of musical correspondence transcending the political perspective outlined above, in which arabesk and popular Islam are implicated together in the 'hegemony of the periphery'. The sounds associated with the public expression of Islam are intensely familiar: the *ezan*, *kıraat*, the recitation of the *Mevlid-i Şerif*. In most parts of Turkey the *ezan* is recited into the ear of a baby immediately upon being born. It is the first sound a human being hears, and one that will follow them, five times a day, to the grave. Koranic cantillation is considered to be essentially 'non-musical', in that it does not employ the concept of *makam* to organize the progression of pitch levels in recitation. We have seen that this has resulted from a need to maintain a firm distinction between the sacred text and the profane activities associated with *şarkı*. When *muezzin* claim that there is nothing musical about their recitation it is because of concern about the pollution of the most sacred object of the Islamic faith, the Koran, but not necessarily because the basic process of organizing sounds, its music in the widest sense, is fundamentally different. When musicians identify *makam* in the *ezan* or *kıraat*, they are not simply foisting an entirely irrelevant analytical framework upon the sounds, but perceiving a common logic to the organization of pitches in the recitation of a text. I would suggest that this shared musical vocabulary is the appropriate vehicle for the expression of the common condition which underpins Koranic cantillation, *sema*, and arabesk, one of suffering and alienation. As the Hadith cited above relates, the Koran 'was revealed with sadness. Weep when you read it . . .'.

Fourthly, the slow circular movement of the dancers in the Mevlevi *mukaabele* and the Bektaşi-Alevi *cem* ceremony bears a certain resemblance to the kind of circular dance that invariably accompanies all kinds of secular music, but particularly arabesk, the *çifte telli*. Unlike rural Anatolian chain dances, but like *sema*, the focus in the *çifte telli* is upon the individual. The 'musication' of ecstatic moments in this popular dance has been discussed above. Within the highly coded language of dance, the more the ecstasy and isolation are accentuated, the greater the approval of those watching. On many occasions, at concerts or evenings in a *gazino*, I watched a single man, usually slightly more drunk than his companions, rise to his feet, raise his arms, and dance in full public view, to a storm of laughter, applause, and cries of 'Helal olsun!'—'May it be permitted!'—a vital expression sanctioning behaviour where a line is perceived to have been crossed, but no harm has been done. The person in question would be described as having 'surpassed himself' (*kendinden geçmiş*), an expression which is also used to indicate entering the *hal* in the context of *sema*. In both *sema* and the *cifte telli*, this liminal, ecstatic state is represented by a wheeling motion, in which the individual dancer moves about his or her own axis.

Fifthly, I have pursued this idea of liminality in more abstract terms. In explanations of *sema*, the saint, musician, and dancer are in a state of liminality between an intense awareness of the plurality of the world of appearances and the unity of the 'real' world. In this the values of the world of appearances are inverted. As nonsense becomes sense, music speaks with the precision of words and the loss of *irade* (individual self-control) results in the acquisition of an individual power to apprehend the truth. The world of arabesk is at first sight a world similarly inverted. The musician figure in the arabesk film loses his or her social self, defined by appropriate gender stereotypes and models of honourable behaviour, and ends in a state of abasement.

This state of abasement is encapsulated by the notion of *rezalet*. To translate this term as 'shame' or 'dishonour' would imply the oversimplistic dualism of 'honour and shame' which has often been criticized in the context of Mediterranean ethnography. Herzfeld has pointed out that this blurs semantic distinctions of vital importance in the societies studied.[37] The Glendiots and Pefkiots distinguish two categories of dishonourable behaviour. One, *atimia*, is a mode of behaviour which is considered to lie entirely outside the domain of predictable behaviour, applicable to the activities of wolves, Turks, and so on. The other, *grousouzia*, interprets the behaviour of insiders who deviate from an expected norm.[38] Meeker has discussed at length the concepts of honour amongst the Black Sea Turks, distinguishing *şeref*, *namus*, and *ırz*.[39] The notion of shame in Turkey, which has only been discussed by anthropologists under the category of *ayıp*,[40] requires similar attention. A distinction between *ayıp* and *rezalet* could be made on the lines of Herzfeld's distinction between *grousouzia* and *atimia*. *Ayıp* covers temporary infractions of rules recognized by everybody, including the offender. *Rezalet* describes a situation which is beyond the pale, a terminal

[37] Herzfeld 1980. [38] Ibid. 345. [39] Meeker 1976.
[40] See Stirling 1965, 217.

aspect of character or appearance about which nothing can be done. When I asked, I was told that the term *rezalet* is simply 'more serious' than *ayıp*. I first understood this to mean that the distinction was one of scale in which at a certain point a disorder ceases to be *ayıp* and become *rezil*. In fact, the terms relate to entirely different categories of disorder. An *ayıp* is something about which one should have known better. *Rezalet* is something about which nothing can be done. The description of the traffic system in Istanbul as a *rezalet* was perhaps less of a joke than I had first assumed. Arabesk presents a situation of terminal disgrace in precisely these terms.

Thus, the notion of *hal*, as it pertains to arabesk, is a state of *rezalet*. This moral liminality is emphasized by the metaphor of movement around the city presented by the *dolmuş* driver. Just as the circling of the dancer in *sema* represents a circling around truth which will never (in this life) penetrate the veil of appearances and get to the centre, the movement of the *dolmuş* driver around the city can be viewed as the inability of the individual to find a position, a point of repose, in society. It is further emphasized by the issue of gender markers in Turkish music, and, more particularly, by the ambiguous sexuality of the singers themselves. Turner points out that the liminal status of neophytes in Ndembu initiation rituals are not only considered to be neither living nor dead, but that they are 'sometimes treated or symbolically represented as being neither male nor female'.[41] In both *sema* and arabesk the performers are in effect reduced to a common humanity which lies beyond the socially constructed duality of male and female. As we have seen, in arabesk this is achieved in a variety of ways. Men look like men, but sound like women, or may sound like a man and look like a woman. Alternatively, the ideal medium of arabesk is the prepubescent child, who has not yet attained the age at which mature masculinity and feminity have been conferred by society. As amongst the Ndembu, sexlessness is a fact of spiritual and social liminality.

The existence of a common fund of symbols and metaphors provides grounds for linking arabesk and *sema* closely. However, symbols and metaphors are interpreted and used by different social groups in different ways. When interpretations conflict, those with the power at their disposal can attempt to control rival interpretations and claim a monopoly on symbolic meaning. From a certain ideological perspective of musicians and others associated with

[41] Turner 1967, 98.

secular, centre-left critics of the Anavatan Party and arabesk, this common symbolic core is seen as evidence of the pernicious and negative effects of popular Islam and arabesk upon the social body. Those with a closer involvement with 'popular Islam', a respect for the mysteries of *sema* and an awareness of the proscription of secular music could argue the same material in the other direction. One singer stated the difference between arabesk and *sema* lay in the fact that the former cursed the world, and that a curse against creation could never be accepted in a spiritual context. *Sema*, he argued, was a kind of flirtation (*naz*), or like a child wailing for its mother or father when left alone. One could extend this argument by describing *sema* as an 'upwardly mobile' state of liminality in which perfection is possible by embracing its opposite, and arabesk as one which is decidedly downwardly mobile, in which perfection can never be possible. Whilst *sema* is performative, being the means by which man elevates himself, arabesk does not touch the world it describes. The sexlessness of *sema* is one of transcendent humanity, in which mundane society, constituted on the fundamental premise of the division of male and female, is left far behind. In arabesk the sexlessness of the musician is a form of social castration which denies the possibility of that meaningful union between male and female through which a person becomes a participating unit in the social entity.

Arabesk does, however, share with *sema* the property of expressing and enacting a confrontation with official discourses about the self and the social. In both cases this fact is of significance. Apologists for *sema* have argued its legitimacy according to the terms and procedures laid down by Islamic orthodoxy. At the same time, as we have seen, the power of *sema* is held in many cases to derive precisely from the fact that it inverts the order of the world. Arabesk also confronts 'the world' and its rationality. It does so by drawing on a vocabulary of text, music, and dance that has a long history in Turkish society. The use of these tropes is very different and refers to a specific situation, a theodicy in which natural justice is perceived to have withered, and man's lot in life is a state of powerlessness and alienation. Arabesk provides a multifaceted resource of symbols and metaphors which can be drawn upon to make sense of this state. To a large extent, this resource has been controlled and shaped by the recording industry, but this industry has not had a completely free hand. Arabesk is something which is used, not passively consumed, at a concert, or whenever a cassette is put in a cassette player, or whenever a group of friends gather to have a drink, sing, and talk about themselves and the past. Whilst the existence of this resource implies a perception of powerlessness, the use of it does not entail the despair and moral decline with which the genre is credited by its critics.

In the case of *muhabbet* gatherings, arabesk is used as a resource to make a statement about solidarity in a world in which moral and cultural perfection is simply not for real people. To cite Herzfeld's eloquent phrase, arabesk celebrates the 'essential imperfections of sociality'.[42] It is precisely this fact which has attracted the censorship of a state which cannot tolerate the existence of representations of the self and the social body which undermine the claims it has made for a society extracting itself from an 'oriental' past and moving towards an ideal. Censorship, overt and otherwise, has not however been able to begin to affect the innumerable and intimate performative contexts in which arabesk is used. In these, arabesk provides a focus for the despair of an urban society on the periphery of world economic systems, in which nearly everybody is faced with social and economic forces over which they have no control. Where this despair can be rendered meaningful and shared in song and ecstatic dance, some form of transcendence is always possible.

[42] Herzfeld 1987, 46.

APPENDIX A
Makam and *Ayak*

The notational conventions of this chart of modal similarities are taken from Yener 1987. In the modal subgroups, the direction of notes indicates predominant melodic direction. In the case of the *makam*, this is indicated by whether a mode is ascending, descending or a mixture of both. The halk music *ayak* does not formulate predominant melodic direction in such a specific way, but Yener notates them as either ascending or descending to indicate a more general *seyir*. Relative note values indicate structurally important notes in the mode. In *ayak* longer note values indicate cadential tones. In *makam* they indicate the dominant note (*güçlü*) which divides the lower pentachord or tetrachord from the upper, and acts as a pivotal cadential note in compositions and improvisations.

Kerem Ayağı
Yanık Kerem Ayağı
Kesik Kerem Ayağı
Kandilli Kerem Ayağı
Yahyalı Kerem Ayağı
Hüseyinî Makamı
Muhayyer Makamı
Neva Makamı
Tahir Makamı
Uşşak Makamı
Bayati Makamı
Karçığar Makamı
Garip Ayağı
Hicaz Makamı
Hümayun Makamı
Uzzal Makamı
Zirgüle Makamı
Müstezat Ayağı a (transposed to G and F)
Müstezat Ayağı b (transposed to G)

Çargâh Makamı
Rast Makamı
Mahur Makamı
Nikriz Makamı
Zavil Makamı
Acemaşıran Makamı
Misket Ayağı (transposed to B and E)
Segâh Makamı
Hüzzam Makamı
Eviç Makamı
Irak Makamı
Bozlak Ayağı
Kürdî Makamı
Derbeder (Kalenderi) Ayağı
Saba Makamı

APPENDIX B
Şarkı and *Türkü* Texts

'Acı Gerçekler' (Orhan Gencebay)

Yolum düşer meyhaneler üstüne
İçtikçe aklıma sevgilim gelir
Silsem gözlerimi kurusun diye
Bahar seli gibi boşanır gelir
Nerde sevdiklerim hani sevenler
Ağlatıyor beni acı gerçekler
Bitmiyor isyanlar bitmiyor suçlar
İhtiyar olmadan ağardı saçlar
Kar beyaz saçımı yolasım gelir
Görüpte bilmeyen deli sanıyor
Bilmezler melhemsiz yaram kanıyor
Ben mazimi mazim beni arıyor
Ölmeden mezara giresim gelir
Nerde sevdiklerim hani sevenler
Ağlatıyor beni acı gerçekler.

'Painful Truths'

I end up in the *meyhane*,
the more I drink, the more my lover comes to mind.
If I wipe my eyes to dry them,
they empty like a spring flood.
Where are those I have loved, where are those that love me?
Painful truths make me weep.
Defiance does not end, the guilt does not end
My hair went white without me being old.
I feel like tearing out my snow-white hair.
Those that see me but don't know think I am mad.
They do not know that without balm my wound bleeds.
I am seeking my past, my past seeks me.
I feel as though I should enter the grave before I am dead.
Where are those I have loved, where are those that love me?
Painful truths make me weep.

'Ağlıyorsam Yaşıyorum' (Gülden Karaböçek: words, A. Selçuk İlhan, music, Osman Baysu)

Bakarsan anlarsın gözlerime sen
Eğer ağlıyorsam yaşıyorum ben
Bu benim kaderim doğduğum günden

'If I am Weeping, I am Living'

If you look into my eyes, you will understand;
if I am weeping, I am living.
This is my fate from the day I was born;

Bil ki ağlıyorsam yaşıyorum ben
Dertlerim inleyen bir keman gibi
Mutluluk gönlüme bir düşman gibi
Hayatım ağlatan bir roman gibi
Eğer ağlıyorsam yaşıyorum ben
En acı dertleri attım içime
Ümitsiz aşkımı gömdüm kalbime
Çaresiz ağlarım kendi halime
Bil ki ağlıyorsam yaşıyorum ben.

know that if I am weeping, I am living.
My anguish is like a moaning violin,
happiness is like an enemy to my soul,
my life is like a tearful novel;
If I am weeping, I am living.
I have thrown the most painful troubles inside me,
I have buried my hopeless love in my heart,
I weep helplessly at my state;
know that if I am weeping, I am living.

'Atmacayı Vurdular' (**İbrahim Can**)

Atmacayı vurdular
Bir avuç kanı için
Gel edelim sevdalık
Babanın canı için
Kadırga yok diyular
Nereye gidiyular
Benim ufak gülümü
Ellere veriyular

Kadırga'nın yolunu
Gidemiyum karadan
Sevdalık edenleri
Ayırmasın sevdadan
Hadi gidelim Sis'e
Sis'in yolları çise
Ne dedim de darıldım
Niye gelmiyon bize

Burası derin orman
Görülmiyelim aman
Senin gibi güzele
Canım yoluna gurban
Kadırga'nın başına
Dolu yağiyu dolu
Seni gavurun kızı
Dursak bile ne olur

'They Shot the Hawk'

They shot the hawk
for a handful of blood.
Let's be lovers
for the sake of your father.
They say they are not at Kadirga.
Where are they going?
They are taking my little rose away.

I cannot travel the road to Kadirga
because of the dark.
May those in love
not leave their lovers.
Come on, let's go to Sis,
Sis' roads go up into the mist.
Whatever I said, I was angry.
Why don't you come with us?

This is deep forest,
let's not be seen, *aman*.
For a beauty like you
my soul is a sacrifice to you.
It is hailing on top of Kadirga.
You infidel's girl!
Even if we stop,
what will happen?

'Bağrı Yanık' (**Müslüm Gürses**)

Bu genç yaşımda dertlere attın felek
Acımadan sen benim bağrımı yaktın felek
Hayinsin, zalimsin sen felek felek
Bir gün daha geçti ömrümden
Böyle garip kaldım bağrı yanık
Kader eksik olmaz gönlümden
Gören bana diyor bağrı yanık
Bütün ümitlerim bitmiş
Bütün sevdiklerim gitmiş
Yaşamak hevesim bitmiş
Olmuşum bir bağrı yanık
Off, off, off, bağrı yanık
Şimdi bir şey gelmez elimden
Giden gitti beni benden alıp
Yaşlar akar iki gözümden
Bir başıma kaldım bağrı yanık

'Burnt Heart'

You have immersed me in torments, fate, in this my youth,
without mercy, you have burnt my heart, fate.
Fate, fate, you are treacherous, you are tyrannical.
One more day has passed from my life.
I remain forlorn, burnt heart.
Fate dominates my soul.
Those who see me say, burnt heart.
All my hopes are ended,
all my loved ones gone,
my desire to live has ended,
I have become a burnt heart.
Oh, oh, oh, burnt heart.
Now I can do nothing.
She is gone forever, taking me from myself.
Tears flow from my two eyes,
I am left on my own, burnt heart.

'Beni Hatırla' (**Samime Şanay: words, İlhan Şan, music, Erdoğan Berker**)

Bir şarkı duyarsan sevdadan yana
Bir şiir okursan gözyaşı dolu
Ve hüsran olursa her aşkın sonu
Hatırla sevgilim beni hatırla
Bir çiçek görürsen boynunu bükmüş
Bir ağaç görürsen yaprağını dökmüş
Birine rastlarsan genç yaşta çökmüş
Hatırla beni sevgilim beni hatırla
Gözlerin yollara dalarsa bir gün
Kalbın için için kanarsa bir gün
Ve mazi kapını çalarsa bir gün
Hatırla sevgilim beni hatırla.

'Remember Me'

If you hear a song about love,
if you read a tearful poem,
and if disappointment should be the end of every love,
remember, my love, remember me.
If you see a flower with its head hung low,
if you see a tree with its leaves shed,
if you meet someone young doubled up with age,
remember, my love, remember me.
If your eyes should linger along the way,
if your heart bleeds inwardly one day,
if the past calls at your door one day,
remember, my love, remember me.

'Benim Hayatım' (İbrahim Tatlıses)

Uzaktan gören mesut sanıyor
Bilmezler gözlerim her gün ağlıyor
İçimde dinmeyen yaram kanıyor
Bir meçhule döndü benim hayatım
Geceyi yaşarım doğmaz güneşim
Zamansız küllendi yanan ateşim
Yarıma çikarmı bilmemki dişi
Mevsimsiz sarardı benim hayatım
Zamansız sarardı benim hayatım
Işıklar altında sönmüş gibiyim
Dostlar içinde yalnız biriyim
Bilinmez yollara girmiş gibiyim
Nerede bitecek benim hayatım
Yorgunum dertliyim yürek dayanmaz
Mutsuzum desem de kimse inanmaz
Maziyi ararım böyle yaşanmaz
Çekilmez çiledir benim hayatım.

'My Life'

Those who see me from afar think I am happy,
they do not know that I weep every day.
My incurable wound bleeds inside me,
my life has turned into something unknown.
I live the night, my sun does not rise,
my burning fire smouldered before its time.
Will she turn out to be my lover? I've no idea.
My life went yellow like a leaf out of season,
my life went pale before its time.
I seem to be extinguished under the lights,
I am a loner amongst friends.
I seem to have set out along unknown paths,
where will my life end?
I am tired, I am troubled, the heart cannot bear it,
and if I said I was happy, nobody would believe me.
I search for the past, one can't live like this.
My life is an ordeal which cannot be endured.

'Bir Teselli Ver' (Orhan Gencebay)

Bir teselli ver
Yarattığın mecnuna
Sevenin halinden sevenler anlar
Gel gör şu halimi
Bir teselli ver
Aramızda başka biri var ise
Tertemiz aşkımı bana geri ver

'Console Me'

Console the lover,
whom you have driven crazy.
Only lovers understand the lover's state.
Come and see my pitiful state,
console me.
If there is someone else between us

Ben zaten her acının tiryakisi
olmuşum
Ömür boyu bitmeyen derdimle
sarhoşum
Gülemem sevdiğim
Ben sensiz yaşıyamam.
Bana ne gerek
Senin aşkından başka
Bana ne gerek
Aşkın zehir olsa
Yine içerim
Yolun ecel olsa
Korkmam geçerim
Yeter ki sevdim de
Ben bu aşk ile
Dünyanın kahrına
Gülüp geçerim.

give me back my purest love.
I am already an addict of every grief,
I am drunk with my life-long endless
torment.
I cannot smile my love,
I cannot live without you,
what do I need but your love,
What do I need?
Even if your love was poison
I would still drink it.
Even if you lead me to my death
I wouldn't be afraid, to follow.
If only you said 'I love you',
with this love
I would laugh at all the troubles of
this world.

'Çaresizim' (**Ferdi Tayfur**)

Bir hıçkırık tutar gülmek istesem
Çıkmaz olur yolum gitmek istesem
Kaderim bırakmaz ölmek istesem
İşte böylesine çaresizim ben
Yanardağ misali yanıyor gönlüm
Dermansız yarası kanıyor gönlüm
Hep boşu boşuna geçiyor gönlüm
İşte böylesine çaresizim
İçimden geliyor gülüp eğlenmek
Dünya gözlerimde yıkılmış gibi
Aklıma takılır bir anda ölmek
Yaşamak bitmeyen ızdırap gibi.

'I am Helpless'

If I wish to smile I am seized by a
sob,
if I wish to go my way is blocked,
if I wish to die my fate will not allow
me.
This is the way I am helpless.
My soul burns like a volcano,
the wound of my soul bleeds
without cure,
my soul expires in vain.
This is the way I am helpless.
I feel I want to smile and be happy,
I see the world in ruins.
The idea of dying instantly obsesses
me.
Living is like endless torture.

'Dertli Dertli' (İbrahim Tatlıses)	*'In Anguish'*
Görüyorsün Tanrım beni Değiştir bu kaderimi Açtım sana ellerimi Yalvarırım dertli dertli Bu canımın sahibisin Sığınacak güçüm sensin Derman bana senden gelsin Bekliyorum dertli dertli Ezdiler hep taş misali Gözlerimde çile seli Yaşadığım nereden belli Gecem dertli günüm dertli Dertlerimle yalnız kaldım Bir çıkar yol bulamadım Çilelere adım adım Yürüyorum dertli dertli Çilelere adım adım Gidiyorum dertli dertli Özlediğim güneş doğsun Yarâbbim tek umudumsun Dualarım kabul olsun Yaşanmıyor dertli dertli.	You see me my God, change this fate of mine. I opened my hands to you [in prayer], I plead in anguish. You are the lord of my soul, you are the strength that will shelter me. May the cure come from you to me. I wait in anguish. They crushed me like stones, in my eyes the flood of torment, how do I know I am alive? My nights are troubled, my days are troubled. I remained alone with my troubles, I couldn't find a way out, I am walking step by step, in anguish towards torments. May the sun I yearn for rise. O Lord, you are my only hope. May my prayers be accepted; one cannot live in anguish.

'Domdom Kurşunu' (**İbrahim Tatlıses: words and music, Mahzuni Şerif**)	*'The Dumdum Bullet'*
Kaşların arasına Domdom kurşunu değdi Bir avcı vurdu beni Bin avcı beni yedi	A dumdum bullet pierced me between the eyebrows. A hunter shot me, a thousand hunters devoured me.
Ah dedim ağladım Yaremi bağladım Eğdi yar boynunu eğdi Allah kerimsin dedi	I sighed, I wept. I bound my wound. She submitted, the lover submitted. She said, O God, you are generous.
Hançer yarası değil Domdom kurşunu değdi Gel gel gümle gel Domdom kurşunu	It was not a dagger wound but a dumdum bullet that pierced me. Come, come, thunder, come the dumdum bullet.

Bugünüm harap oldu
Dünden iyimidir ki
Doktor hasta ben hasta
Benden iyimidir ki

Mahzuni yâr benim
Halimi anlasaydı
Butün dertliler gibi
İnleyip dinleseydi.

My day is ruined,
but is it better than yesterday?
The healer is ill, so am I,
but is he better off than me?

If only my love Mahzuni
had known how I felt.
Like all those in anguish,
if only he would have sighed and
listened.

'Dünya Dönüyor' (**Orhan Gercebay**)

Sen ne dersen de, sen ne dersen de
Dünya dönüyor dönecek
Hayat sensiz de sürecek
Bitecek acılar, bu günler geçecek
Sen ne dersen de
Yalan değil, Yalan değil
Seni sevdiğim yalan değil
Kahrolduğum yalan değil
Duyarsın bir gün başka
Sevgili bulduğumu
Yalan değil, Yalan değil
Artık kızmıyorum kaderime
Bıraktı beni halime
Bahtın açık olsun, yolun açık olsun
Bırak beni halime
Dünya dönüyor dönecek
Hayat sensiz de sürecek
Bitecek acılar, bu günler geçecek
Sen ne dersen de
Unutacağım, unutacağım
Gözlerin rengini
Acı veren sevgini
Karar verdim artık senin her şeyini
Unutacağım, kader kader
İçimdeki duygular
Kaybettiğim umutlar
Zalimce imzalanan o acı hatıralar
Kader değil, kader değil
Artık kızmıyorum kaderime

'The World is Turning'

Say what you want, say what you
want,
the world is turning and will go on
turning.
Life will go on without you.
The troubles will end, these days
will pass;
Say what you want.
It is not a lie, it is not a lie,
it is not a lie that I love you.
it is not a lie that I am cursed.
If you hear that I have
found another lover,
it is not a lie, it is not a lie.
At last I do not blame my fate
it left me to my state.
May your fortune be open, may
your road be open;
leave me to my state.
Life will go on without you.
The troubles will end, these days
will pass;
say what you want.
I will forget, I will forget
the colour of your eyes
and your pain giving love.
I have decided, I will forget
everything about you.
Fate, fate;

Bıraktı beni kendine
Bahtın açık olsun, şansın açık olsun
Bıraktı beni halime

the feelings inside me,
the hopes I have abandoned,
those painful memories which have been tyrannically signed;
it is not fate, it is not fate.

'Esmer' (**Ümit Besen**)

Bana öyle naz yapma biliyorum güzelsin
Neden benden kaçarak beni her gün üzersin
Ah esmer ah esmer bakışın ne güzel
Gözlerin gülünce beni sarhoş eder
Tutkunum delice sözüme gücenme
Kim olsa şaşırır böyle yar sevince
O gülüşün yok mu gönlümü deli eder
Bana her bakışında aklım başımdan gider.

'Dark Haired One'

Do not be coy with me like that, I know you are beautiful.
Why do you hurt my feelings every day by running away?
Ah dark haired one, ah dark-haired one, your glances are so beautiful.
When your eyes smile they make me drunk.
I am madly in love, do not be offended by my words.
Anyone would be befuddled loving such a one.
Ah that smile of yours, it makes my heart go mad.
Each time you look at me, reason leaves my head.

'Gönül Yarasindan Acı Duyanlar' (**Alaaddin Şensoy: words, Mustafa Nafız Irmak, music, Selahattin Pınar**)

Gönül yarasından acı duyanlar
Feleğin kahrına boyun eğermiş
Kara bahtın cilvesine uyanlar
Bir gün olur muradına erermiş
Ben de çile çektim gözyaşı döktüm
Canana yalvardım nice diz çöktüm
Şifasız yaramı dağlayıp söktüm
Ağlayanlar bir gün olur gülermiş.

'Those who Feel Pain from a Wound in the Heart'

Those who feel pain from a wound in the heart,
their necks bent to the curse of fate,
those who submit to the blows of fate,
a day comes when they attain their wishes.
I too have suffered torment and wept tears.

I pleaded with the beloved, how many times did I fall to my knees?
I branded and plucked out my unhealable wound.
A day comes when those that weep smile.

'Gülüm Benim' (İbrahim Tatlıses: words and music, Burhan Bayar)	*'My Rose'*
Kalbimdeki tatlı sızı Sensiz bu gönlün yazı Bakışların öyle güzel Öldürüyor beni nazı Kalbe açan çiçek gibi Çölde yağan yağmur gibi Sevincimsin mutluluksun Sana öyle hasretim ki Gülüm benim, gülüm benim Derdim aşkım canım benim Ayırmasın tanrım bizi Budur inan tek dileğim Bir yürürsen bahar yürür Çiçek yürür peşin sıra Gülüşlerin ömre bedel Can katıyor bu canıma Ufkumdaki güneş gibi İçimdeki nefes gibi Ne bir heves ne bir tutku Kara sevda benimki.	The sweet ache in my heart, is the spring of this soul without you. Your glances are so beautiful, her coyness will kill me. Like a flower which opens up the heart, like rain in the desert, you are my joy, you are my happiness. I miss you so much . . . My rose, my rose, my affliction, my love, my own soul, may God not divide us. Believe me, this is my only wish. If you would walk, spring would follow, and the flowers would come out in their turn. Your smiles are worth life. They add life to this soul of mine, like the sun on my horizon, like the breath inside me. Mine is melancholy, neither whim nor passion.

Güvercinim' (Belkis Akkale: words and music, Emel Demiryürek)	*'My Dove'*
Güvercinim süt beyaz Gine geldi bahar yaz Kurban olam Allahım Seveni sevene yaz Ninnayi	My dove is milk white. Spring and summer have come again. My dear God decree love for the one who loves. (Ninnayi)
Yük altında bulgurum Oğlan sana vurgunum Çek elini koynumdan Arpa yoldum yorgunum Ninnayi	I am pounded wheat under its load. Boy, I am in love with you. Take your hand from my breast, I have been reaping barley, I am tired. (Ninnayi)
Teste koydum teleme Kaşın benzer kaleme Uğrun uğrun severdim de Sen duyurdun aleme Ninnayi	I kneaded dough. Your eyebrow resembles a pen. I would have loved you secretly but you told the world (Ninnayi)
Ah ninnayi ninnayi Gel oynayi oynayi Aslan gibi yarım var Satın alır dünyayı.	Oh ninnayi ninnayi come and dance. I have a lover like a lion, he could buy the world (Ninnayi).

'Güzelin Talihi Yok' (Ferdi Özbeğen)	*'Beauty has No Luck'*
Acı haber tez duyulur Bağrıma hançer vurulur Yârın üstüne yâr sevmiş İnşallah Allah'tan bulur Güzelin talihi yok Çirkine sevgili çok İçim yanar kan ağlarım Halimden anlayan yok Türkü söyledim eyledim Balla kaymakla besledim Kimselere yüz vermedim Gelir diye yol gözledim.	Painful news is heard quickly; a dagger is thrust into my breast. She has another lover. If God wills, she will find her punishment from God. Beauty has no fortune, but the ugly have many lovers. My heart burns, I weep blood. Nobody understands my state. I sang her *türkü*, I fed her on honey and cream I did not look at anyone else. I watched her way, hoping she'd come.

'Hasret Akşamları' (Hüseyin Altın)

Dün gece meyhanede içerken dertlerime
Bir pınar gibi yaşlar dolunca gözlerime
Gezdim sabaha kadar gurbet sokaklarını
Son ümitle bekledim hasret akşamlarını
Artık güneş doğmuştu gecemin sabahına
İsyan ettim haykırdım yaşantıma bahtıma
Gezdim sabaha kadar gurbet sokaklarını
Son ümitle bekledim hasret akşamlarını.

'Evenings of Longing'

Whilst drinking away my sorrows last night in the *meyhane*,
tears filling my eyes like a fountain,
I wandered around the strange streets,
I awaited with a last hope the evenings of longing.
At last the sun had risen to the morning of my night.
I rebelled, I cried out at my life, my fate,
I wandered around the strange streets,
I awaited with a last hope the evenings of sorrow.

'Hüzünlü Günler' (Müslüm Gürses)

İki ay oldu ayrılalı hüzün mü doldu
Gözlerime yaş yerine hep kanlar doldu
Mazideki güzel günler demek yalandı
Bir köşeye atılan resmim bez oldu
Çile çektirdin çile
Dile düşürdün dile
Yıllardır arıyorum onu
Göz yaşım döndü sele
Gittin artık uzaklara duyamaz oldum
Gönlüm şimdi teselliyi şarapta buldu.

'Sad Days'

It has been two months since we separated, have they not been filled with sadness?
In place of tears, blood filled my eyes.
So the beautiful days of the past were a lie,
My picture thrown into the corner has turned into parchment.
Torment you made me suffer, torment,
You made us the subject of common gossip.
I have been searching for her for years.
My tears turned into a flood.
You went in the end, far away, I do not hear about you anymore.
Now my soul has found its consolation in wine.

'Kaderimin Oyunu' (Orhan Gencebay)

Ne sevenim var, ne soranım var
Öyle yalnızım ki . . .
Çilesiz günüm yok, dert ararsan çok
Öyle dertliyim ki . . .
Bana kaderimin oyunu mu bu?
Aldı sevdiğimi verdi zulümü
Dünyaya doymadan geçip gideceğim
Yoksa yaşamanın kanunu mu bu?
Bıktım artık yaşamaktan
Çekmekle biter mi bu hayat yolu?
Bu yalnızlık, bu dert ile
Bekleyeceğim, bekleyeceğim
Geri dönmese bile
Alıştım kaderin zulmüne artık
Bana gülmese bile
Geri dönmez artık, giden sevgililer
Her ümit ufkunda ağlıyor gözler
Bitmeyen çilenin, derdin sarhoşuyum
Kahredip geçiyor, en güzel günler.

'The Trick of My Fate'

I have no lover, nor anybody interested.
I am so lonely . . .
Not a day passes for me without torment.
If it is affliction you want, I have plenty.
I am so troubled . . .
Is this fate's trick on me?
It took away my beloved and gave me tyranny.
I am going to pass by and leave this world
without having had my fill.
Or is this the law of life?
I am fed up with living now.
Does this life come to an end with suffering
with this loneliness and hardship?
I will wait, I will wait,
even if she does not return.
I have got used to fate's tyranny at last
even though it does not smile on me.
The loved ones that have gone will not return now.
On every horizon of hope, eyes are weeping.
I am a drunkard of endless affliction and torment.
The most beautiful days pass by in torment.

'Kadifeden Kesesi' (**İbrahim Tatlıses**)

Kadifeden kesesi
Kahveden gelir sesi
Oturmuş kullar oynar
Ah çiğerimin köşesi
İstanbul'a / Beyoğluna yolla
Haydi yolla İstanbul'a yolla
Yar yolla
Kadife yastiğım yok
Odama mastığım yok
Kuran'a el basarım
Senden başka dostum yok

'Her Velvet Purse'

Her velvet purse . . .
His voice comes from the café;
the seated slaves [i.e. slaves of God] play [cards].
Ah my love
Send the beloved, come on, send her to Istanbul / Beyoğlu.
I have no velvet pillow,
I have no ribbons in my room;
I swear on the Koran
I have no lover apart from you.

'Kullarına Kul Yapmış' (**Müslüm Gürses**)

Bu nasıl dünya her şey tersine
Kulak veren yok garibin sesine
Zaten karalardan kara bahtımız içimiz
Çeşme gibi akar göz yaşlarım
Kullarına kul yaratmış yaratan
Bir yar için beni gurbet elinde
Doğruluk misali kendisi olmuş
Kulunu yalancı yapmış yaratan
Sevginin kaynağı kendisi olmuş
Yarımı taş kalblı yapmış yaratan
Güldü mü zannettin zalim kulunu
Kimine şaşırtmış doğru yolunu
Kiminin bağlamış elin kolunu
Benimse çıkmaz etti yolumu
Bir yar için beni gurbet elinde
Kullarına kul yaratmış yaratan.

'He Made Me a Slave for His Slaves'

What kind of world is this, everything upside-down?
Nobody listens to the voice of the *garib*.
Our fate and our inner state are already blacker than black.
My tears flow like a fountain,
The creator has made me a slave for His slaves,
for the sake of a lover when I'm in *gurbet*.
the creator has become the exemplar of truth
but has made His slave a liar
The creator has become the fount of love
but has made my beloved with a heart of stone.
Did you think your tyrannical slave smiled?
Some, He made them go astray,
He has bound the hands and arms of some.
As for me, He made my road lead nowhere,
For the sake of a lover when I'm in *gurbet*.
The creator has made me a slave for His slaves.

'Mavi Mavi' (**İbrahim Tatlıses: words and music, Burhan Bayar**)	*'Deep Blue'*
Yıllardır bir özlemdi Yanıp durdu bağrımda Tam ümidi kesmişken Onu gördüm karşımda Mavi mavi masmavi Gözleri boncuk mavi Bir gördüm aşık oldum Bu gelen kimin yarı Hayat denen bu yolda Yürürken adım adım Mutluluğu ararken Bir de onu rastladım.	There was a yearning for years which burnt continually in my breast. Just when I had given up all hope I saw her before me. Blue, blue, deep blue, her eyes are blue like beads. As soon as I saw her I fell in love Whose beloved is this? Whilst walking step by step Along this road called life Whilst searching for happiness All of a sudden I met her.

'Seni Sevmeyen Ölsün' (**Küçük Ceylan: words, Şakir Aşkan, music, Yılmaz Tatlıses**)	*'May He Who Doesn't Love You Die'*
Saçlarını dağıtırsın Rüzgarlara bırakırsın Sen sevmeye yakışırsın Seni sevmeyen ölsün Her şey yalan gerçek sensin Gelir senden senden gelsin Bence aşkın kendisisin Seni sevmeyen ölsün.	You scatter your hair and leave it to the winds. You deserve to be loved. May he who doesn't love you die. Everything is a lie, you are the truth. It comes from you, let it come from you to me, you are love itself. May he who doesn't love you die

'Seni Seviyorum' (**Ümit Besen**)	*'I Love You'*
O güzel gözlerini gördükten sonra Aşık oldum birden tutuldum sana Seviyorum seni sanki deli gibi Öldürecek beni bu kara sevda Senden başkasını düşünmez oldum Eridim mum gibi sararıp soldum Ümitsiz aşkının esiri oldum	After seeing those beautiful eyes of yours, I fell in love, I suddenly became obsessed by you. I love you, as if I were mad. This melancholy will kill me. I can't think of anybody but you.

Öldürecek beni bu kara sevda
Günlerce bir ümit bekledim senden
Kararsızım dedin hep kaçtın benden
Gülmedin yüzüme bir kere olsun
Öldürecek beni bu kara sevda.

I've melted like wax, I've gone pale and faded,
I've become a slave of a hopeless love for you.
This melancholy will kill me.
I waited for days for a sign of hope from you.
You said you couldn't make up your mind, you always ran away from me.
You never smiled once to my face.
This melancholy will kill me.

'Sevda Gözlüm' (**words, Hamza Dekeli' music, Yılmaz Tatlıses**)

'My Love Eyes'

Göz değmesin sakin mutluluğuna
Dilerim hep böyle kal sevda gözlüm
Mutsuzluk yakışmaz güzelliğine
Dilerim her zaman gül sevda gözlüm

Toprağa can veren yağmur gibisin
Kırlarda dolaşan bahar gibisin
Sen insan değilsin bence meleksin
Hep aynı değerde kal sevda gözlüm

Mutsuz geçen bir tek günün olmasın
Gönlünce sevilip sev sevda gözlüm
Gönlünde kalmasın hiçbir muradın
Ömrünce bahtıyar ol sevda gözlüm

Let the eye not touch your happiness,
I wish that you will always stay like this my love eyes.
Unhappiness does not suit your beauty.
I wish that you will always smile my love eyes.

You are like the rain giving life to the earth
you are like the spring strolling around the plains
you are not a person, to me you are an angel.
Stay just as you are my love eyes.

May you not have one unhappy day.
Love and be loved as much as you want my love eyes.
May you not have one unanswered desire;
be happy for life my love eyes.

'Seviyorum Diyebilsem' (**Muazzaz Abacı: words, Aslan Tunçata, music, Mustafa Erertez**)	*'If Only I Could Say I Love You'*
Gece gündüz düşündüğüm Düşlerini bölüştüğüm İlmek ilmek, düğüm düğüm Seviyorum diyebilsem Tutabilsem ellerinden Aşkı içsem gözlerinden Bir gün sana ta derinden Seviyorum diyebilsem Güne hasret yaprak gibi Suya hasret toprak gibi Şırıl şırıl ırmak gibi Seviyorum diyebilsem.	You whom I think of night and day, you whose dreams I share Loop by loop, knot by knot, if only I could say I love you, if only I could hold you by the hand, if I could drink love from your eyes, if only I could say one day to you I love you right from my innermost self. Like the leaf longing for the sun, like the earth longing for water, like a gurgling river, if only I could say I love you.

'Yağdır Mevlam Su' (**Emel Sayın: words, Erol Martal, music, Mahmut Oğul**)	*'Make it Rain My Lord'*
Çatlayan dudaklara Sararan yapraklara Kuruyan topraklara Yağdır Mevlam su Alev sanacak kadar Yandım yanacak kadar Suya kanacak kadar Yağdır Mevlam su Toz duman savrulurken Gül çimen kavrulurken Can tenden ayrılırken Yağdır Mevlam su. Suya hasret güllere Sana açık ellere Yağdır Mevlam su.	For cracked lips, for yellowed leaves, for parched earth, make it rain my Lord. I am burnt as much as I could be to the point of flames. Make it rain my Lord, until I shall have had my fill of water. When clouds of dust are everywhere, when the rose and the grass are shrivelled up, when life leaves the skin, make it rain my Lord. For the roses longing for water, for the hands open to you in prayer, for the souls inflamed with love, make it rain my Lord.

'Yanımda Olmayınca' (**Zeki Müren: words, A. Selçuk İhan, music, Selami Şahin**)

Hayatın ne anlamı var
Yanımda sen olmayınca
Yaşamanın ne tadı var
Yanımda sen olmayınca
Aşkın, hasret çölüyüm ben
Bir gözyaşı gölüyüm ben
Yaşan bir ölüyüm ben
Yanımda sen olmayınca
Nasıl çekmem kadere ah
Yazan yazsın bana günah
Gecelerim olmaz sabah
Yanımda sen olmayınca
Bence ölüm ayrılıktır
Sensizliktir, yalnızlıktır
Her kahkaham hıçkırıktır
Yanımda sen olmayınca.

'When You are Not by My Side'

What meaning does life have
when you are not by my side?
What taste does life have
when you are not by my side?
I am the longing desert of love,
I am a lake of tears,
I am a living corpse,
when you are not by my side.
How can I not say 'ah' to fate?
May God write it down as my sin.
My nights do not become morning
when you are not by my side.
I think separation is death,
It is being without you, it is loneliness.
My every laugh is a sob
when you are not by my side.

'Zoruma Gidiyor' (**Küçük Ceylan: words and music, Şeyfi Doğanay**)

Seni kırdığımı biliyorum
Şimdi özür diliyorum
Aklıma geldikçe bazan
Kendime çok kızıyorum
Bakıp durma bana öyle
İki könüş iki söyle
Bir acı gönlüme yeter
Derman olsun dertlerime
Kavuştuk yar geç olsada
Yaşım artık son olsada
Sen baksan yar bak yanıma

'I am Finding it Difficult'

I know I have hurt you,
now I apologize.
Sometimes, when I remember,
I am very angry with myself.
Do not keep staring at me like that!
Talk to me, say something!
One pain is enough for my soul.
May there be a cure for my afflictions.
Even if it be late, we have met up my love.
Even if my life is at an end,
look, my love, look to me.

BIBLIOGRAPHY

Abu-Lughod, L. (1986), *Veiled Sentiments: Honor and Poetry in a Bedouin Society* (Berkeley, Calif., Univ. of Calif. Press).

Adorno, T. W. (1941), 'On Popular Music', *Zeitschrift für Sozialforschung*, 9: 17–49.

—— (1976), Introduction to the Sociology of Music (New York, Continuum).

Akin, E., and Karasapan, Ö. (1988), 'The Rabita Affair', *Middle East Report*, 153: 15.

Alderson, A., and İz, F. (1959), *The Concise Oxford Turkish Dictionary* (Oxford, Clarendon Press).

Al-Faruqi, L. I. (1985), 'Music, Musicians and Muslim Law', *Asian Music*, 17 1: 3–36.

And, M. (1959), *Karagöz: The Turkish Shadow Theatre* (Istanbul, Dost Yayınları).

Ardener, E. W. (1972), 'Belief and the Problem of Women', in J. La Fontaine (ed.), *The Interpretation of Ritual* (London, Tavistock).

Arel, H. S. (1969), *Türk Musikisi Kimindir?* (Istanbul, Milli Eğitim Basımevi).

Armstrong, H. C. (1940), *Grey Wolf* (Harmondsworth, Penguin Books).

Arseven, V. (1958), 'Halk Müziğinde Tonal-Modal Bünye', *Türk Folklor Araştırmaları*, 5: 1739, 1761.

—— (1959), 'Halk Müziğinde Çokseslilik (Armoni)', *Türk Folklor Araştırmaları*, 5: 2027.

Baily, J. (1977), 'Movements in Playing the Herati Dutar', in J. Blacking (ed.), *The Anthropology of the Body* (London, Tavistock).

—— (1981), 'A System of Modes used in the Urban Music of Afghanistan', *Ethnomusicology*, 25 1: 1–40.

—— (1988), *Music of Afghanistan: Professional Musicians in the City of Herat* (Cambridge, Cambridge UP).

Banarlı, N. S. (1972), *Türkçenin Sırları* (Istanbul, Istanbul Fetih Cemiyeti).

Bartók, B. (1976), *Turkish Folk Music from Asia Minor*, ed. B. Suchoff with an afterword by K. Reinhard (Princeton, NJ, Princeton UP).

Başbakanlık Devlet İstatistik Enstitüsü (1988), *Türkiye İstatistik Cep Yıllığı* (Ankara, Devlet İstatistik Enstitüsü Matbaası).

Beeley, B. W. (1983), *Migration: The Turkish Case* (Milton Keynes, Open UP).

Behar, C. (1987), *Klasik Türk Musikisi Üzerine Denemeler* (Istanbul, Bağlam Yayıncılık).

Belaiev, V. (1963), 'The Formation of Folk Modal Systems', *Journal of the International Folk Music Council*, 15: 4–9.

Belge, M. (1990), 'Toplumsal Değişme ve "Arabesk"', *Birikim*, 17: 16–23.

Belvıranlı, A. K. (1975), *Mûsikî Rehberi: Dînî Mûsikî* (Konya, Nedve Yayınları).

Benedict, P., Tümertekin, E., and Mansur, F. (eds.) (1974), *Turkey: Geographical and Social Perspectives* (Leiden, E. J. Brill).

Benjamin, W. (1976), *Charles Baudelaire: A Lyric Poet in the Era of High Capitalism* (London, Verso).

Berkes, N. (1964), *The Development of Secularism in Turkey* (Montreal, McGill UP).

Birdoğan, N. (1988), *Notalarıyla Türkülerimiz* (Istanbul, Özgür Yayın Dağıtım).

Birge, J. K. (1937), *The Bektashi Order of Dervishes* (London, Luzac).

Blacking, J. (1982), 'The Structure of Musical Discourse: The Problem of the Song Text', *Yearbook for Traditional Music*, 14: 15–23.

—— (1987), *A Common Sense View of All Music* (Cambridge, Cambridge UP).

Bourdieu, P. (1977), *Outline of a Theory of Practice* (Cambridge, Cambridge UP).

Brown, K. (1976), *People of Salé: Tradition and Change in a Moroccan City 1830–1930* (Manchester, Manchester UP).

Cachia, P. (1973), 'A Nineteenth Century Arab's Observations on European Music', *Ethnomusicology*, 27 1: 441–51.

Clifford, J., and Marcus G. E., (1986), *Writing Culture: The Poetics and Politics of Ethnography* (Berkeley, Calif., Univ. of Calif. Press).

Danielson, V. (1988), 'The Arab Middle East', in P. Manuel (ed.), *Popular Music of the Non-Western World* (Oxford, Oxford UP).

—— (1989), 'Cultural Authenticity in Egyptian Musical Expression: The Repertory of the Māshayikh', *Pacific Review of Ethnomusicology*, 5: 51–61.

Dorsay, A. (1989), 'An Overview of Turkish Cinema from its Origins to the Present Day', in C. Woodhead (ed.), *Turkish Cinema: An Introduction* (London, School of Oriental and African Studies).

Dubetsky, A. (1977), 'Class and Community in Urban Turkey', in C. O. van Niewenhuijze (ed.), *Commoners, Climbers and Notables: A Sampler of Studies in Social Ranking in the Middle East* (Leiden, E. J. Brill).

Duffield, M. (1981), *Maiurno: A Study of Rural Capitalism in the Sudan* (London, Ithaca Press).

Durrell, L. (1959), *The Bitter Lemons of Cyprus* (London, Faber and Faber).

Eckmann, J. (1962), 'A Contest in Verse Between Stringed Instruments from the Chagatay Literature of the 15th Century', in D. Sinor (ed.), *Aspects of Altaic Civilization* (Bloomington, Ind., Indiana Univ. Publications).

Eğribel, A. (1984), *Niçin Arabesk Değil?* (Istanbul, Süreç).

El-Shawan, S. (1984), 'Traditional Arab Music Ensembles in Egypt since 1967', *Ethnomusicology*, 28 1: 271–88.

Erseven, İ. C. (1990), *Aleviler'de Semah* (Ankara, Ekin Yayınları).

Farhat, H. (1990), *The Dastgāh Concept in Persian Music* (Cambridge, Cambridge UP).

Feld, S. (1982), *Sound and Sentiment: Birds, Weeping, Poetics, and Song in Kaluli Expression* (Philadelphia, Univ. of Pa. Press).

Finnegan, R. (1989), *The Hidden Musicians: Music Making in an English Town* (Cambridge, Cambridge UP).

Foucault, M. (1984), 'Truth and Power', in P. Rabinow (ed.), *The Foucault Reader* (Harmondsworth, Penguin Books).

Frith, S. (1983), *Sound Effects: Youth, Leisure, and the Politics of Rock'n'Roll* (London, Constable).

Gilsenan, M. (1973), *Saint and Sufi in Modern Egypt: An Essay in the Sociology of Religion* (Oxford, Clarendon Press).

—— (1983), *Recognizing Islam* (London, Croom Helm).

—— (1990), 'Word of Honour', in R. Grillo (ed.), *Social Anthropology and the Politics of Language* (London, Routledge).

Godwin, J. (1986), *Music, Mysticism and Magic: A Sourcebook* (New York, Arkana).

Gökalp, Z. (1923), *Türkçülüğün Esasları* (Ankara, Milli İçtimiyat Kitabhanesi).

Gölpınarlı, A. (1963), *Mevlevî Adâb ve Erkânı* (Istanbul, Yeni Matbaa).

—— (1983), *Mevlânâ'dan Sonra Mevlevîlik* (Istanbul, İnkilap ve Akâ)

Görmüş, A., and Baştürk, A.(1987), 'Bülent Ersoy Sahneye . . . ', *Nokta*, 20: 13–19.

Grillo, R. (1980), *'Nation' and 'State' in Europe* (London, Academic Press).

Güneş-Ayata, A. (1987), 'Migrants and Natives: Urban Bases of Social Conflict', in J. Eades (ed.), *Migrants, Workers and the Social Order* (London, Tavistock Publications).

Güngör, N. (1990), *Arabesk: Sosyokültürel Açıdan Arabesk Müzik* (Ankara, Bilgi Yayınevi).

Hale, W. (1981), *The Political and Economic Development of Modern Turkey* (London, Croom Helm).

Hann, C. M. (1990), *Tea and the Domestication of the Turkish State* (Huntingdon, Eothen Press).

Hennion, A. (1983), 'The Production of Success: An Anti-Musicology of the Pop Song', *Popular Music*, 3: 159–93.

Heper, M. (1985), *The State Tradition in Turkey* (Beverley, Eothen Press).

Herzfeld, M. (1980), 'Honour and Shame: Problems in Comparative Analysis of Moral Systems', *Man,* NS 15/2: 339–51.

—— (1982), *Ours Once More: Folklore, Ideology, and the Making of Modern Greece* (Austin, Tex., Univ. of Tex. Press).

—— (1987), *Anthropology Through the Looking Glass: Critical Ethnography in the Margins of Europe* (Cambridge, Cambridge UP).

Hobsbawm, E., and Ranger, T. (eds.) (1983), *The Invention of Tradition* (Cambridge, Cambridge UP).

Hornbostel, E. M. von, and Abraham, O. (1922), 'Phonographierte Türkische Melodien', *Samelbande für Vergleichende Musikwissenschaft*, 1: 251–90.

İhsanoğlu, E. (1987), '19. YY. Başında Kültür Hayatı ve Beşiktaş Cemiyet-i İlmiyesi', *Belleten*, 51 cc, 801–28.

Jefferson, A. (1986), 'Russian Formalism', in A. Jefferson and D. Robey (eds.), *Modern Literary Theory: A Comparative Introduction* (London, B. T. Batsford).

Karaçam, İ. (1976), *Kur'ân-i Kerîm'in Fazîletleri ve Okunma Kâideleri* (Istanbul, Marmara Univ. Publications).

Karadeniz, M. E. (1965), *Türk Mûsikisinin Nazariye ve Esasları* (Ankara, Türkiye İş Bankasi Kültür Yayınları).

Karpat, K. M. (1963), 'The People's Houses in Turkey: Establishment and Growth', *Middle East Journal*, 17: 55–67.

—— (1976), *The Gecekondu: Rural Migration and Urbanisation* (Cambridge, Cambridge UP).

Keleş, R. (1990), *Kentleşme Politikası* (Ankara, İmge Kitabevi).

Keyder, Ç. (1987), *State and Class in Turkey: A Study in Capitalist Development* (London, Verso).

—— (1988), 'Class and State in the Transformation of Modern Turkey', in F. Halliday and H. Alavi (eds.), *State and Ideology in the Middle East and Pakistan* (London, Macmillan Education).

Kiel, C. (1966), *Urban Blues* (Chicago, Univ. of Chicago Press).

Kinross, Lord (1964), *Atatürk: The Rebirth of a Nation* (London, Weidenfeld and Nicolson).

Kongar, E. (1976), 'A Survey of Familial Change in Two Turkish Gecekondu Areas', in J. G. Peristiany (ed.), *Mediterranean Family Structures* (Cambridge, Cambridge UP).

Kunst, J. (1959), *Ethnomusicology: A Study of its Nature, its Problems and Representative Personalities*, 3rd edn. (The Hague, Martinus Nijhoff).

Kurt, İ. (1989), *Bağlamada Düzen ve Pozisiyon* (Istanbul, Pan Yayıncılık).

Lane, E. W. (1836), *An Account of the Manners and Customs of the Modern Egyptians* (London, Charles Knight).

Lewis, B. (1968), *The Emergence of Modern Turkey* (Oxford, Oxford UP).

Lewis, G. (1965), *Turkey* (London, Ernest Benn).

Lomax, A. (1968), *Folk Song Style and Culture* (New Brunswick, NJ, Transaction Books).

Lutz, C. A. (1988), *Unnatural Emotions: Everyday Sentiments on a Micronesian Atoll and Their Challenge to Western Theory* (Chicago, Univ. of Chicago Press).

Lyotard, J.-F. (1984), *The Postmodern Condition: A Report on Knowledge* (Minneapolis, Univ. of Minn. Press).

Marcus, S. (1989), 'The Periodization of Modern Arab Music Theory: Continuity and Change in the Definition of the Maqāmāt', *Pacific Review of Ethnomusicology*, 5: 35–49.

Mardin, Ş. (1969), 'Power, Civil Society and Culture in the Ottoman Empire', *Comparative Studies in Society and History*, 11: 258–81.

—— (1989), *Religion and Social Change in Modern Turkey: The Case of Bediüzzaman Said Nursi* (Albany, NY, State Univ. of NY Press).

Markoff, I. J. (1986), 'Musical Theory: Performance and the Contemporary Bağlama Specialist in Turkey', Ph.D. thesis, Univ. of Washington.

Meeker, M. (1976), 'Meaning and Society in the Near East: Examples from the Black Sea Turks and the Levantine Arabs (I)', *International Journal of Middle Eastern Studies*, 7 2: 243–70.

Memmedov, M. (1981), 'Azerbaycan Mugamları', in E. Eldarova (ed.), *Azerbaycan Halq Musiqisi* (Baku, ELM).

Middleton, R. (1990), *Studying Popular Music* (Milton Keynes, Open UP).

Molé, M. (1963), 'La Danse extatique en Islam', in *Les Danses Sacrées* (Sources Orientales, 6; Paris, Editions du Seuil).

Nelson, K. (1982), 'Reciter and Listener: Some Factors Shaping the Mujawwad Style of Qur'anic Reciting', *Ethnomusicology*, 26/1: 41–8.

—— (1985), *The Art of Reciting the Qur'an* (Austin, Tex., Univ. of Tex. Press).

Nesin, A. (1977), *Istanbul Boy (Part One)* (Austin, Tex., Univ. of Tex. Press).

Nettl, B. (1956), *Music in Primitive Culture* (Cambridge, Mass., Harvard UP).

Neubauer, E. (1971), 'Drei "Makamen" des Aşık Divani', *Orbis Musicae*, 1/1: 39–56.

Ocak, A. Y. (1983), *Bektaşî Menâkıbnamelerinde İslam Öncesi İnanç Motifleri* (Istanbul, Enderun Kitabevi).

Ögel, B. (1987), *Türk Kültür Tarihine Giriş 9: Türk Halk Musikisi Aletleri* (Ankara, Kültür ve Turizm Bakanlığı Yayınları).

Olson, E. A. (1985), 'Muslim Identity and Secularism in Contemporary Turkey: The Headscarf Dispute', *Anthropological Quarterly*, 58/4: 161–6.

Oransay, G. (1985), *Atatürk ile Küğ: Belgeler ve Veriler* (Izmir, Küğ Yayını).

Özgüven, F. (1989), 'Male and Female in Yeşilçam: Archetypes Endorsed by Mutual Agreement of Audience and Player', in C. Woodhead (ed.), *Turkish Cinema: An Introduction* (London, School of Oriental and African Studies).

Özkan, İ. H. (1984), *Türk Mûsikîsi Nazariyatı ve Usülleri Kudüm Velveleri* (Istanbul, Otuken Neşriyatı).

Öztelli, C. (1983), *Halk Türküleri: Evlerinin Önü* (Istanbul, Özgür Yayın Dağıtım).

—— (1985), *Bektaşi Gülleri* (Istanbul, Özgür Yayın Dağıtım).

Öztuna, Y. (1987), *Türk Müsikîsi: Teknik ve Tarihi* (Istanbul, Türk Petrol Vakfı Lâle Mecmuası Neşriyatı).

Pena, M. (1985), *The Texas-Mexican Conjunto: History of a Working-Class Music* (Austin, Tex., Univ. of Tex. Press).

Peristiany, J. G. (ed.) (1965), *Honour and Shame: The Values of Mediterranean Society* (London, Weidenfeld and Nicolson).

Petropoulos, E. (1986), 'Rebetika', *Proceedings of Akdeniz Müzik Festivalı* (Antalya).

Picken, L. E. R. (1953), 'Instrumental Polyphonic Folk Music from Asia Minor', *Proceedings of the Royal Musical Association*, 80: 73–86.

—— (1962), Review of Reinhard (1962), *Ethnomusicology*, 8S2: 186.

—— (1975), *Folk Musical Instruments of Turkey* (Oxford, Oxford UP).

Pitharas, L. (1988), *Music of the Outsiders* (London, Channel Four Television).

Redhouse, J. (1976), *Redhouse Yeni Türkçe- İngilizce Sözlük* (Istanbul, Redhouse).

Reinhard, K. (1962), *Türkische Musik* (Berlin, Museum für Völkerkunde).

Rosaldo, M. Z. (1980), *Knowledge and Passion: Ilongot Notions of Self and Social Life* (Cambridge, Cambridge UP).

Rouget, G. (1985), *Music and Trance: A Theory of the Relations between Music and Possession* (Chicago, Chicago UP).

Rumi, J. (1930), *The Mathnawi*, ed. and tr. R. A. Nicholson (Cambridge, Cambridge UP).

Şahin, S. (n.d.), *Ozanlık Gelenekleri ve Doğulu Saz Şairleri* (Ankara, Yorum Matbaacılık).

Said, E. (1978), *Orientalism* (Harmondsworth, Penguin Books).

Sale, G. (1734), *The Koran: Commonly Called the Alkoran of Mohammed* (London, Frederick Warne).

Saran, N. (1976), 'Squatter Settlement (Gecekondu) Problems in Istanbul' in P. Benedict, E. Tümertekin, and F. Mansur (eds.), *Turkey: Geographic and Social Perspectives* (Leiden, E. J. Brill).

Sarısözen, M. (1962), *Türk Halk Musikisi Usulleri* (Ankara, Resimli Posta Matbaası).

Saygun, A. A. (1975), *Bela Bartok's Folk Music Research in Turkey* (Budapest, Akademie Kiado).

Scognamillo, G. (1987), *Türk Sinema Tarihi, 1896–1959* (Istanbul, Metis Yayınları).

Şenel, S. (1988), 'Dârü'l-Elhân Heyeti Tarafından "Fonoğraf" la Derlenen İlk Türkü', *Türk Folkloru Belleten*, 1/2: 121–39.

Shaw, S. J., and Shaw, E. K. (1977), *History of the Ottoman Empire and Modern Turkey*, ii. *Reform, Revolution and Republic: The Rise of Modern Turkey, 1808–1975* (Cambridge, Cambridge UP).

Shiloah, A., and Cohen, E. (1983), 'The Dynamics of Change in Jewish Oriental Music in Israel', *Ethnomusicology*, 27/2: 227–37.

Signell, K. L. (1974), 'The Modernization Process in Two Oriental Music Cultures: Turkish and Japanese', *Asian Music*, 7: 72–102.

—— (1977), *Makam: Modal Practice in Turkish Art Music* (Washington, DC, Asian Music Publications).

Skelton, G. (1977), *Paul Hindemith: The Man Behind the Music* (London, Gollancz).

Slobin, M. (1969), 'Conversations in Tashkent', *Asian Music*, 2: 7–13.

Stirling, P. (1965), *Turkish Village* (London, Weidenfeld and Nicolson).

Stokes, M. H. (1989), 'Music, Fate and State: Turkey's Arabesk Debate', *Middle East Report*, 160: 27–30.

—— (1991), 'Hazelnuts and Lutes: Change in a Black Sea Valley', in P. Stirling (ed.), *Culture and the Economy: Change in Turkish Villages* (forthcoming).

Stratton, J. (1983), 'Capitalism and Romantic Ideology in the Record Business', *Popular Music* 3: 143–56.

Szyliowicz, J. S. (1966), *Political Change in Rural Turkey* (The Hague, Mouton).

Tapper, N., and Tapper, R. (1987), 'The Birth of the Prophet: Ritual and Gender in Turkish Islam', *Man*, NS 22/1: 69–92.

Tapper, R., and Tapper, N. (1987), '"Thank God We're Secular!": Aspects of Fundamentalism in a Turkish Town', in L. Caplan (ed.), *Studies in Religious Fundamentalism* (London, Macmillan).

Taptık, G. (1977), *Notaları ve Tavırları ile Türküler* (Ankara, Çaba Matbaası).

Tavaslı, Y. (1976), *Günümüzde Okunan Mevlid-i Şerif* (Istanbul, Irfan Matbaası).

Touma, H. H. (1971), 'The Maqam Phenomenon: An Improvisation Technique in the Music of the Middle East', *Ethnomusicology*, 15/1: 38–48.

Türk Dil Kurumu (1951), *Türkiye'de Dil Devrimi (Language Reform in Turkey)* (Ankara, Türk Tarih Kurumu Basımevi).

Turner, V. (1967), *The Forest of Symbols: Aspects of Ndembu Ritual* (Ithaca, NY, Cornell UP).

Ufki, A. (1976), Fac. of 1659 British Library MS, Sloane 3114 9b-181b, *Mecmûa-i Sâz ü Söz*, ed. S. Elçin (Istanbul, Milli Eğitim Basımevi).

Ullin, R. (1991), 'Critical Anthropology Twenty Years Later: Modernism and Postmodernism in Anthropology', *Critique of Anthropology*, 11/1: 63–89.

Uludağ, S. (1976), *İslâm Açısından Mûsikî ve Sema* (Istanbul, İrfan Yayınevi).

Wallis, R., and Malm, K. (1984), *Big Sounds from Small Peoples: The Music Industry in Small Countries* (New York, Pendragon Press).

Waterman, C. A. (1990), *Jùjú: A Social History and Ethnography of an African Popular Music* (Chicago, Univ. of Chicago Press).

Wright, O. (1990), 'Çargâh in Turkish Classical Music: History versus Theory', *Bulletin of the School of Oriental and African Studies*, 53/2: 224–44.

Yekta, R. (1922), 'La Musique Turque', *Lavignac Encyclopédie de la Musique et Dictionnaire du Conservatoire* (Paris, Librairie Delagrave).

Yener, S. (1987), *Bağlama Öğretim Metodu* (Trabzon, Kuzey Gazetecilik Matbaacılık).

Yılmaz, Z. (1977), *Türk Musikisi Dersleri* (Istanbul, İsmet Şedele Matbaacılık).

Yönetken, H. B. (1961), 'Türk Halk Müziği Dizilerin Tarafı Meselesi', *Türk Folklor Araştırmaları*, 6: 2362, 2387, 2418, 2521.

—— (1962), 'Arap Makamlarının Yunan Modlarının Acem Makamlarının da Majör-Minörle izahı', *Türk Folklor Araştırmaları*, 6: 2609.

Yücel, T. (1982), *Dil Devrimi ve Sonuçları* (Ankara, Ankara UP).

GLOSSARY OF MUSICAL TERMS

aksak 'limping', the generic term for irregular rhythms in Turkish music
aranağme/arasaz instrumental section in a vocal piece
ayak modal structure in folk music
bağlama long-necked fretted lute
bateriya Western drum and percussion set
beste composition
cemiyet club, society
chromatic making use of smaller intervals falling in the gaps between the notes of a diatonic scale
comma *see* **koma**
counterpoint the simultaneous and systematic combination of two or more melodic lines
darbuka goblet drum, of which the **çömlek** is a slightly larger and more elaborate version
davul large frame drum, usually played with two sticks and suspended from the neck of a standing player
def frame drum (also *tef*)
dershane, dernek private school, or club or conservatory
diatonic the most elementary type of seven-note scale, employing two kinds of intervals, tones and semitones
elektrosaz **bağlama** with built-in electrical pickup
finalis final note of a mode
gazel an improvised vocal piece in the art-music repertory
gazino a kind of restaurant usually offering musical entertainment
halk the people, 'folk'
heterophony the polyphony that results in the performance of one melodic line by an ensemble of different musical instruments
kanun plucked trapezoidal zither, played horizontally, usually resting across the knees of the seated performer
kaval end-blown ductless flute
kayde a fixed melodic pattern used for vocal improvisation in the Eastern Black Sea area
kemençe Black Sea fiddle, or the small pear-shaped, round-backed fiddle used in art-music ensembles (**fasıl kemençesi**)
kıraat Koranic cantillation
koma interval between a limma and an apotome, represented as 24 cents or the fraction 524288/531441, being the smallest interval in Ancient Greek music theory; in modern Turkish theory there are nine commas in a tone

ligature notational convention in which a line groups quavers and smaller rhythmic units
makam modal structures in art music
mode a pattern of fixed pitches regulated by rules governing melodic progression
monophony *see* polyphony
ney end-blown ductless flute
organology branch of ethnomusicology dealing with the history, distribution, construction, and classification of musical instruments
pavyon place of entertainment resembling a *gazino* but offering cheaper entertainment and generally catering for men only
polyphony the simultaneous combination of more than one sound at any one moment; opposed principally to 'monophony', a single line of unaccompanied melody
şan vocal section of a song
sanat (musikisi) art (art/classical music)
şarkı song
saz generic term for instrument, or more specifically, the **bağlama**
sema religious music and dance associated with Turkish Sufism (*tasavvuf*)
sequence musical pattern repeated on consecutively ascending or descending degrees of the scale
tambur long-necked fretted lute
tarz genre
tavır style, manner
tessitura vocal or instrumental range
tetrachord unit of four consecutive notes in a scale
tone a unit of fixed, named pitch
tulum bagpipe
ud short-necked fretless lute
usul rhythm, measure
yay string/string section in an arabesk song
yorum commentary, interpretation
zikr ritual act of reciting the names of God
zurna a keyless shawm

INDEX